SUNSHINE/NOIR II

SUNSHINE / NOIR II

Writing From San Diego & Tijuana

edited by **Kelly Mayhew & Jim Miller**

SD CWP

SAN DIEGO CITY WORKS PRESS

ISBN 978-0-9765801-4-0
Library of Congress Control Number: 2005901269

San Diego City Works Press is a non-profit press, funded by local writers and friends of the arts, committed to the publication of fiction, poetry, creative nonfiction, and art by members of the San Diego City College community and the community at large. For more about San Diego City Works Press please visit our website at www.cityworkspress.org.

San Diego City Works Press is extremely indebted to the American Federation of Teachers, Local 1931, without whose generous contribution and commitment to the arts this book would not be possible.

Cover Design: Rondi Vasquez
Front Cover: *Some Like It Hot* by Perry Vasquez
Back Cover: *Palm Fire* by Perry Vasquez
Production Editor: Will Dalrymple | Layout & Editing | http://www.willdalrymple.com

Published in the United States by San Diego City Works Press, California
Printed in the United States of America

To our friend, mentor, fellow traveler, teacher, and poet

Steve Kowit

Rest in Peace

everything shimmering
everything just as it is

CONTENTS

introduction

i. the border is a fight

ii. beneath the postcard

iii. memory and loss

iv. through a lens darkly

IMAGES

Still Searching for Literary San Diego

Historically, it seems, San Diego cannot represent itself, and is barely represented by others.
—David Reid on literary San Diego

It's been ten years since San Diego City Works Press published its first book, *Sunshine/Noir: Writing from San Diego and Tijuana*, and, much to our surprise, in many ways, we are still here. Despite the trials and tribulations of running a very small, entirely volunteer, non-profit press, the members of the San Diego Writers Collective and other supporters of San Diego City Works Press have kept our beautifully useless endeavor afloat because, unfortunately, we still occupy a unique space in San Diego's cultural landscape as the only local press primarily dedicated to publishing books by San Diego writers. And while many people may still feel that, as a disinterested literary agent once told one of our writers, "Nobody cares about San Diego outside of San Diego except as a place to come and get a tan," there are still a good number of us here beneath the postcard laboring away, trying to write in and/or about what artists David Avalos, Louis Hock, and Elizabeth Sisco once called "America's Finest Tourist Plantation."

Because San Diego is a place where so many people are from someplace else and/or want to believe our city's self-marketing as the locale where only "happy happens," it's easy to forget there is a history here. As I noted in the introduction to the first edition of *Sunshine/Noir*, in 1896, Theosophist Katherine Tingley had a dream of "a white city in a golden land by the sundown sea," which she came to associate with the gleaming coast of San Diego, California. Tingley's visionary imagination was a nice complement to the inflated mythology penned by the city's boosters, but not all observers fell in line with the sun-drenched utopianism of the Anglo elite. Indeed, in the thirties, Edmund Wilson derided San Diego as a dead-end of false hope in "The Jumping-Off Place," and Max Miller's *The Man on the Barge* spoke of alienation and unease underneath our perfect sun.

In the decades following the thirties, San Diego was virtually absent from the world of serious literature, seemingly existing only as a unique setting for the occasional mystery or pulp novel, with the significant exceptions of the work of Jim Thompson and Oakley Hall who I discuss in "Excavating San Diego Noir: A Jumping Off Place" later in this volume. Even though the city is now home to a number of prominent writers, the idea of a literary culture still seems like an alien and improbable notion to many San Diegans. Perhaps the suffocating banality of official San Diego's pious "America's Finest City" mantra has led even those who know better to think that nothing is possible here other than the affectless pleasure that comes from drifting back and forth between the beach and the mall. Nonetheless, underneath San Diego's superficial postcard sunshine, writers have found both grit and genuine transcendence. Perhaps the city is best captured by the incongruous juxtaposition of the evanescent beauty of the gleaming coast with the muted gray façade of America's multi-billion dollar killing machine. San Diego is also the sex oozing from the teeming Pacific Beach boardwalk in mid-summer and the lonely deaths of migrants in the unforgiving winter desert. It is a city of lurid scandal and right-wing vigilantism as well as a home for increasingly creative, diverse and progressive communities. San Diego is neither beyond alienation, nor devoid of ecstasy. It is both Sunshine and Noir.

San Diego is the Anglo Mission fantasy that evolved from the days of Helen Hunt Jackson's *Ramona* and the place where Henry James wrote, "[T]he sense of the shining social and human inane is utter." San Diego is where Henry Miller was converted to free love and radicalism by famous anarchist Emma Goldman on the way to a Tijuana brothel, and the place where right-wing vigilantes tortured and murdered Wobblies for speaking on soapboxes at the corner of 5th and E. America's eighth-largest city has produced a minor noir tradition and a sizable canon of gay sailor pulp novels. Thomas and Anna Fitch blew San Diego up in *Better Days: Or, A Millionaire of To-morrow* in the nineteenth century, and Raymond Chandler drank himself to death here in the twentieth.

Carey McWilliams chronicled the free speech fight in the first part of the twentieth century, and, from the 1960s to the 1980s, journalist Harold Keen was the most insightful observer of San Diego, deftly portraying the racial turmoil, political corruption, and labor unrest that simmered underneath the glossy "America's Finest City" veneer. Jack Kerouac bemoaned, "San Diego rich, dull, full of old men, traffic, the sea-smell—Up the bus goes thru gorgeous seaside wealthy homes of all colors of the rainbow on the blue sea—cream clouds—red flower—dry sweet atmosphere—very rich, new cars, 50 miles of it incredibly, an American Monte Carlo," but as David Reid unearthed in the first edition of *Sunshine/Noir*, loved Jacumba, "the sleepy border street of shacks and trees and backyard dumps." Even Bruce Springsteen got in the act in the nineties, adding "Balboa Park," his Guthrie-esque story of the lives of homeless child prostitutes, to his album *The Ghost of Tom Joad*.

In the 1960s, an aging Herbert Marcuse was strolling the local beaches and musing about *One Dimensional Man* while the youthful Cameron Crowe was cranking out rock journalism for *Rolling Stone*. The local countercultural papers during that period, *The Door*, *The OB Rag*, and *The San Diego Free Press*, were busy afflicting the city's power elite and some of the same folks still are, as Doug Porter's and Frank Gormlie's pieces in this anthology amply illustrate. San Diego is described in Thomas Pynchon's *Vineland* (1990) as the home of the mythical "College of the Surf" and its neighboring countercultural enclave:

> Against the somber military blankness at its back, here was a lively beachhead of drugs, sex, and rock n' roll, the strains of subversive music day and night, accompanied by tambourines and harmonicas, reaching like fog through the fence, up the dry gulches and past the sentinel antennas, the white dishes and masts, the steel equipment sheds, finding the ears of sentries attenuated but ominous, like hostile-native sounds in movies about white men fighting savage tribes.

While the halcyon days of the late-sixties counterculture may be long gone, those who yearn for a home-grown culture not dominated by a narrative written by real estate developers and public relations specialists might still feel a bit like the savages on the outside of the military industrial complex/theme park that the city's old guard insists defines San Diego. That and the highly trumpeted virtue of "not being Los Angeles" have sufficed for so many years as the city's primary markers of identity that the cultural imagination of San Diego sometimes seems ossified. San Diego has produced everything from *The Wizard of Oz* to cyberpunk novels about biotechnology, but it still has a hard time imagining itself as the diverse, complex, and, at times, absurd comedy and tragedy that it is. We insist upon the sunshine while ignoring the noir, like a politician sticking to his talking points.

Nonetheless there have still been a good number of contemporary efforts to represent San Diego's rough edges such as *The Gangster We Are All Looking For* by Thi Diem Thuy Le (2003), Matt De La Peña's portrait of National City in *Mexican WhiteBoy* (2010), Marisa Silver's compelling story of underclass life by the Salton Sea in *God of War* (2009), William Vollmann's sprawling *Imperial* (2009), as well as my own humble efforts to represent San Diego life, city space, and history in my novels *Drift* (2007) and *Flash* (2010) and my muckraking enterprise with Mike Davis and Kelly Mayhew, *Under the Perfect Sun: The San Diego Tourists Never See* (2003). More recently, *The Far East Project: Everything Just As It Is* (2012) did a fine job of representing the unrepresented in San Diego's east county, but was met by a hostile, defensive response in some quarters of the local booster media. Another anthology, *San Diego Noir* (2011), drew less vitriol precisely because it mostly failed to move beyond tourist stereotypes.

Contemporary San Diego maintains its paradoxical sunshine and noir identity, but as the city has grown, it has become increasingly difficult for the boosters to conceal its ugly corners. An old bumper sticker used to express beach chauvinism by proclaiming: "There is no life east of I-5." In 2015, however, the life east of Interstate 5 (the highway that cordons off the beach communities and downtown from the rest of the inland areas) has made itself known and is changing the face of the city, even more so today than when the first volume of *Sunshine/Noir* was published. San Diego is one of the most ethnically diverse cities in the United States. It also has one of the largest gaps between the rich and poor in California and juxtaposes a carefree postcard reality with a massive military industrial complex and a heavily fortified international border. San Diego County goes from the desert to the sea, contains mountains, wild spaces, and the sprawling suburbs which threaten them. In many ways, it is a region on the cutting edge of the Pacific Rim.

Still, no major literary culture has evolved despite the large numbers of novelists, poets, and nonfiction writers who live and work in the area. Works such as those listed above appear, but almost never seem to do more than ripple our placid waters. It feels at times that we are trapped in our own hall of mirrors. In sum, despite a few noble efforts, San Diego is still a city in need of a literary voice, a cultural identity that goes beyond the Zoo, Sea World, Legoland, and the beach. With *Sunshine/Noir II* we persist in our romantic, perhaps Sisyphean, effort to address this need and expose the true face of "the other San Diego."

Like the first edition of *Sunshine/Noir* this anthology presents the reader with a wide range of contemporary San Diego writers of fiction and nonfiction alike as well as poets, artists and photographers. It explores San Diego and Tijuana's border culture; San Diego's multiple identities and lost history; the city's natural beauty and endangered ecologies; its role as a center of the culture of war; and San Diego writers' attempts to investigate the meaning of place. By using a multicultural, multidisciplinary, pan-artistic approach, this anthology offers the reader a fresh look at a city yet to be explored in such a fashion. *Sunshine/ Noir II* is not comprehensive, but rather stands only as a place marker in the continuing exploration of literary San Diego that leaves many borders yet to be crossed. This anthology includes many acclaimed and award-winning poets and writers as well as emerging authors. While most of the authors anthologized here are from San Diego, a few are not, though we welcome them as good hosts. All in all, we think we have assembled a gorgeous hybrid monster. Enter at your own risk.

Sunshine/Noir II marks the ten-year anniversary of San Diego City Works Press, a project of the San Diego Writers Collective. The San Diego Writers Collective is a group of San Diego writers, poets, artists, and patrons dedicated to the publication and promotion of the work of San Diego–area artists of all sorts. Our specific interests include local, ethnic, and border writing as well as formal innovation and progressive politics. The Collective's main focus is local, but we have engaged in occasional collaborations with writers from around the world. City Works Press is a non-profit press, funded by local writers and friends of the arts, committed to the publication of fiction, poetry, creative nonfiction, and art by members of the San Diego City College community and the community at large.

Over the last ten years, San Diego City Works Press has published novels, collections of poetry, creative nonfiction, and anthologies by a wide range of authors, including: *Sunshine/Noir: Writing From San Diego and Tijuana* edited by Jim Miller; *The Commuters* by Cheryl Klein; *Gods of Rapture: Poems in the Erotic Mood* by Steve Kowit; *The Unmaking of Americans: 7 Lives* and *The Encyclopedia of Rebels* by Mel Freilicher; *Atacama Poems* by Adrián Arancibia; *Rita and Julia* by Jimmy Santiago Baca; *Peeping Tom Tom Girl* by Marisela Norte; *Hunger and Thirst: Food Literature* edited by Nancy Cary, Alys Masek, Ella deCastro Baron, Trissy McGhee, and June Cressy; *Dynamite and Dreams* by Robert V. Hine; *Lavanderia: A Mixed Load of Women, Wash, and Words* edited by Donna J. Watson, Michelle Sierra, and Lucia Gbaya-Kanga; *Itchy Brown Girl Seeks Employment* by Ella deCastro Baron; *Mamas and Papas: On the Sublime and Heartbreaking Art of Parenting* edited by Alys Masek and Kelly Mayhew; *Vanishing Acts* by Forrest Hylton; *Wounded Border/Frontera Herida* edited by Justin Akers Chacón and Enrique Davalos; *Lantern Tree: Four Books of Poems* by Chris Baron, Heather Eudy, Cali Linfor, and Sabrina Youmans; and *Not Far From Normal* by Tamara Johnson. It's been a good ten years. Time to write the future.

Jim Miller
San Diego Writers Collective
San Diego City Works Press
www.cityworkspress.org.

The Northern Prison | *Juanita Lopez*

I. THE BORDER IS A FIGHT

Michael Cheno Wickert

The Border Is a Fight

The border is a fight
una lucha constante
It is antagonistic and suspicious
It is smoggy everyday crossings
The rat-tat tattle of cuantas garita abiertas
Cuantas almas en cada fila seeming to bowing in deft reverence toward the
almighty dollar
lurching forward
sucking in smog for survival
and Esperanza
a daughter in the back seat on her way to school huddled in books and dreams
nibbling on burritos de chorizo con papas
sipping chocolate
her head resting on the window
ventana fría
ventana cerrada
ventana quebrada
         de América
It is ignorant American tourists crossing bridges
Passing taco stands
browsing Avenida Revolución borracho on cheap tequila
And two for one beers
fearful of Mexican thieves.
It is fourteen year old girls en La Coahuila bars serving themselves alongside
Sex on the beach shooters, piña coladas, and Wild Turkey
Un amor imposible que atraiga los norteamericanos noche tras noche
Saying, "Hey sailor. Hey Huero. Hey Mr. Businessman. I got something for you."
It is hunger for the other
A thirst pa'l otro
Al lado de ella

acostada
Gitana
Mestiza
Mexica
Mujer con ojos obsidianos
El aroma de su aliento, perfume de su ser
Haciendo caras
Señalando con sus labios temblando
Parada en la oscuridad
Escondida
Llena de miedo
Feroz
Continuous
Tijuana is urban over-growth wind-swept with dust and salt where stray dogs
hustle through the continuous chop and sizzle of day-long taqueros
San Diego is grandma's garden, all laid out in straight rows and divided,
beckoning with its high-rise temples
The border is a pointing of fingers
a sideways scowl
a series of questions
a reason for waving flags
Check-point Carlitos
a wall
una casa de cambio
raíces enramados
murals through one-way mirrors
it is an archeological find waiting to happen
The border is an accusation
It is rusty metal sculptures standing in formation
futility disregarding the soul
eyes peering out car windows up and down La Internacional
it is early morning laborers drinking coffee on the corner of 25th and Market
watching lights blink messages above el Cerro de las torres
The border is a collision of flesh
    words
    blood
    sweat
    and breath banging against a wall until the bed breaks in ecstasy
        panting
        eyes rolled

head back
mouth open
   twitching
gasping
ready to pay the price for one more day defying the line

Marilyn Chin
Brown Girl Manifesto

I. A performative utterance: each utterance of the first-person "I" as the speaking subject combats the history of oppression which extends to me. Through the spoken word, the "I" critiques, questions, corrects, annotates, examines, mocks, derides, offends, and talks back at the prevailing culture.

When I perform my poetry, the "I" speaks not only as the "poet" but also through enacted "difference"—through a body inscribed by historical determinations: brown (dirty), immigrant (illegal alien), girl (unwanted, illegitimate). An "I" as the brown-girl body who faces her audience stands there vulnerable to the perennial history of pre/mis-conceptions, racism, and hatred. (If we think the brown-girl figure is no longer viewed by historical determinations, then we are in denial of our role in her existence in the global situation.)

II. Who is this "I" that is not "I"? The sex that is not one. She who is not allowed to speak. Like the old world feminist that I am (who represents something larger than myself—why should I not have ambitions for an art that is political?), should I not want to speak on behalf of the marked brown-girl:

the veiled "subaltern" from the (un) "Holy Lands"? the girl who is burned for a better dowry? the 24-year-old undocumented worker whom you both need and despise who died in the desert south of Dateland, Arizona traveling across the border? the nameless girl amongst thousands toiling in the factories in Gwangdong? a nameless girl murdered near the maquiladoras in Juarez? The perennial girl orphan, starving, crying, pushed from refugee camp to refugee camp? The most annoying of all, she is also your immigrant neighbor, the one with the screaming baby on her hip; the one you despise most of all, because her very existence, her moving into the neighborhood, has brought down the value of the real estate.

III. The speaking subject is always an oppositional voice. If the majority says, "no dogs allowed," she says "grrr" and wags her tail and bites the man in the ass and won't let go. If the majority says, "we don't want you, immigrant, we'll send you back," the speaking subject writes on the walls of Angel Island, "I shall stay firm, I shall endure; I shall not be erased."

IV. Artistic subjectivity: the "I" authorizes first-person subjectivity and enables artistic expression, which differs from autobiography. A brown-girl subject is not necessarily for sociological or ethnographical inquiry.

My grandmother is in the kitchen making dumplings. Yum, you say, what are the ancient ingredients—better yet, what ancient rites are you conducting? Don't you perform ancient rites in the kitchen?—let me bring my notepad, and my camcorder—this is important research (I'll get tenure).
But wait a minute, this is poetry. My grandmother is in the kitchen making dumplings out of General Iwane Matsui's liver, and we have entered the realm of magical realism.

Perhaps you better not stay in that kitchen and get the hell outta there!
Why should Maxine's "cutting the frenum" be forever subjected to the litmus test of an "authentic" autobiographical (ethnographical) experience when even Gregor Samsa gets to speak? Why is a cockroach a speaking subject (laconic, nonetheless, decrying "mother, mother")? The ethnographers never question whether or not he is a descendent of other cockroaches. But seriously, why should you get to imagine yourself as Luke Skywalker and I can't imagine myself as the Woman Warrior? Aren't Chinese girls allowed to have a surreal imagination?

V. The speaking subject is also the lyric poet: am I making art or am I only producing material for your ethnographical interest? Am I not also spewing out sonnets, palindromes, epigrams, rondeaus, haiku, renku, ballades, jueju, fu, ghazals, prophetic hallucinations and all the sweet and wild brilliant variations of the above? Am I not the poet of witness? Do I not take after Nellie Sachs and Paul Celan trying to describe the horrors of the Holocaust, meanwhile inventing a new lyric, which questions the possibility/impossibility of poetry after the most heinous episodes of history. Am I not a descendent of Qu Yuan, whose lyric intensity caused him to drown himself in the Mi Lo River in protest? And the descendent of the courageous Feminist poet Qiu Jin, who recited a poem on the path to her own beheading?

VI. A Call for Unity. Brothers and sisters of the revolution: contemplate for a moment, are we really now in a "post-identity, post-racial, post-feminist era—and all is groovy and color-blind—equal work equal pay, equal justice for all? We are in the second term of the first black presidency in the U.S.A. Are we therefore all emancipated and free? Do we all have a stake in the American dream? Do we all have a place at the table (or do we still have to cook it for you, serve it and wipe the floor after you too, and sit quietly in the dark kitchen while you delight in that lush banquet)?

Why am I still standing here trying to answer to you:
hegemonic economy, mordant philosophers! poebiz mongers! treacherous cognoscenti! cultural flesh-traders, fascist (es)states! trickster patriarchs! pallid leaseholders, cleaver-wielding grandmothers! erst-while dreamers, readers, over-lords: yeah you, you are never fucking satisfied!

Keep On Crossin' Billboard | *Xavier Vasquez*

Perry Vasquez
The Future of Post-Bordernity

> *The wall is the materialized representation of this idea of a border. In English people call it a "fence" and in the U.S. that fence means "defense"; something that in American minds brings protection. Interestingly enough you would have to ask them, "Protection from who or what?" And this same wall or barrier or fence means an "offense" to Mexicans.*
> —Norma Iglesias Prieto

The U.S./Mexico border is falling apart. Like Chipotle Swiss cheese, it is shot through with gaps, holes, *lacunae*, erasures, and stretches of emptiness. The border exists—but at times its existence seems to collapse beneath the weight of its own sovereignty. How does the border both exist and not exist at the same time? How does it manage to appear in strategic locations and disappear in non-strategic ones? Why do we think of the border as having a fixed and permanent national identity instead of a contingent and temporary one? Like every national myth, the U.S./Mexico border began life as a collective act of imagination. Established by the Treaty of Guadalupe Hidalgo in 1848, the border between the two countries was born as an implied line in the sand, a mere projection on paper inspired by the territorial aspirations of the United States government, legitimized by its military victory, negotiated by diplomats and mapped by cartographers and surveyors. In its infancy, the border consisted of a scattered series of perishable markers set miles apart in the desert. As a slight trace on the surface of the earth, its claim to reality was tenuous at best. But a confluence of historical events helped harden the border over the late 19th and early 20th centuries, including early crises like the genocidal war against the Native population, the rise of border violence during the Mexican revolution and the racial fear of the other that resulted. Capitalists and capitalism seeped into the area and economic interest began to grow. To control the flow of goods and property became the state's highest priority. It wasn't until the 1920s that the border began to evolve into a militarized defense meant to hold the line against illegal immigration. Today, the 1,989-mile-long border between Mexico and the United States exists in the guise of border agents, fences, boundary markers, walls, narrow strips of raked soil, sensors, drones, camera traps, customs houses, laws and statutes whose primary purpose is to control the flow of illegal immigrants, drugs and to prevent terrorist invasion. Advances in technology and new legal sanctions have made control of the border more efficient than ever before but have not yet succeeded in permanently eliminating the gaps and cementing the myth of inviolability so important to our sense of national security in a post 9-11 world. In her history of the U.S./Mexico border, Rachel St. John writes this about ongoing binational efforts to settle and maintain the border, "Neither government set out to close the border, but rather to improve its ability to manipulate spatial controls to reflect state priorities."[1] Historically and geographically speaking, the border's identity is only as meaningful as the degree to which each state controls it. In the absence of that control the border vanishes like a ghost.[2]

2.

In 1987, Mexican-born performance artist Guillermo Gómez-Peña wrote "Documented/Undocumented," an essay in which he defines a theoretical approach to the binational border region with an emphasis on the border as an ecosystem or an interzone of commingling cultural influences and continuously shifting identities. To describe his generation's experiences of the border he writes, "We witness the borderization of the world, by-product of the 'deterritorialization' of vast human sectors. The borders either expand or are shot full of holes. Cultures

---

1 Rachel St. John, *Line in the Sand* (Princeton University Press, 2011), p. 6.

2 Jamex and Einar de la Torre, two binational artists from Ensenada, Mexico, have gained extensive experience over the years dealing with customs agents as they crossed their art over the border for gallery shows in the U.S. The first time a customs agent asked them to describe the contents inside the shipping crates. In response, Einar attempted to give an objective description of the formal and aesthetic qualities of their work. "After a few minutes the agents eyes rolled back in his head," said Einar. The discourse of contemporary art was a foreign one to the agent and perhaps even represented a challenge to his authority. After significant delay, the artwork was finally allowed to pass through. This experience taught the brothers an important lesson. In future interviews they described their work as "children's art" and were promptly waived through.

and languages mutually invade one another."[3] Gómez-Peña's definition, linked to post-modernity's emphasis on terms and conditions such as deterritorialization, alterity, the fiction of the unified self and the global impact of late capitalist development on diasporic populations, emphatically throws down a rhetorical challenge to the definition of the border as the focality of state spacial control. Elsewhere he writes:

> We share certain thematic interests like the continual clash with cultural otherness, the crisis of identity, or, better said, access to trans- or multiculturalism, and the destruction of borders therefrom; the creation of alternative cartographies; a ferocious critique of the dominant culture of both countries; and lastly, a proposal for new creative languages.[4]

Such a view opens up a way of thinking about the border as a messy, permeable zone of mutual influence rather than a hardened barrier standing between two monolithic, diametrically opposed bodies politic. Gómez-Peña's alternative border is not the focality of classic Cartesian space drawn with receding lines of perspective and mechanical explanations of colliding physical bodies. Rather, it is a blurry aerosol mist hovering without definitive references or a corresponding sense of depth; not as a structure built onto the landscape but as a wound carved out of the earth. Gómez-Peña's "new world border" is a cracked mirror reflecting our own *noir* images back at us in a disturbing kaleidoscope of self and other; a bathymetric map projected onto dry land, familiar yet richly strange, proportionally correct but upside down and inside out. Through the production of his multiple hybrid border identities, shamanistic performances and poetic and non-academic writings Gómez-Peña has de-constructed the border and successfully detached it from the idea of a space defined by state control where nationalistic forces must always override local influence.

3.

Peter Schneider's 1983 novella, *The Wall Jumper*, tells the story of Kabe, a West German whose fixation with the Berlin Wall turns him into a serial border

---

3   Guillermo Gómez-Peña, "Documented/Undocumented." *Warrior for Gringostroika* (Graywolf Press, 1993), p. 39.
4   Ibid., p. 38.

jumper. Fifteen times, Kabe successfully jumps the Wall from West to East Berlin even as East German jumpers risk being shot. To outside observers his provocations seem void of ideological motivation and without political meaning. In fact, Kabe's unprecedented jumps are so far off the ideological, political and legal maps that neither West nor East know what to do with him. After each jump the East Germans return him safely to the West. West Berlin authorities consider bringing charges against Kabe, but by the logic of Cold War politics the West never recognized the existence of the Berlin Wall as a sovereign state border. Therefore, Kabe had "illegally" crossed a state border, which didn't exist. A final solution to the conundrum of Kabe is to have him declared incompetent.

> The doctor in charge found nothing wrong with Kabe other than an irresistible urge to overcome the Wall. Rather than a straight-jacket, he recommended that the authorities recognize the Wall as a border. They replied that the Federal Republic of Germany couldn't recognize the Wall of Shame as a state boundary just for Kabe's sake. This didn't prevent the doctor from declaring Kabe competent.[5]

Nonetheless, with each jump, Kabe realizes a stronger sense of the perfection of his own gestures until they gradually take on the contours of an unintentional border crusade. But what does it mean to deport oneself in the name of an ambiguous protest against reality? What does it mean to launch yourself over sovereignty's threshold into the belly of a state that bureaucratically vomits you back each time? Is there a larger meaning behind Kabe's actions? Like Joshua at the Battle of Jericho, does Kabe the Wall Jumper think of himself as a shaman whose wall jumping performances aim at collapsing the Wall under the weight of its own political, legal and moral contradictions? Or was he simply ahead of his time? Twenty-five years after its fall the Berlin Wall has become a lucrative tourist attraction. Berliners cross freely where it once stood, a victim of its own temporal limitations. The Wall no longer exists except as an historical artifact worthy of preservation in museums. For young Berliners the Wall is neither controversial nor urgent. History has taught them that borders, like everything that exists in time and space, are merely temporary.

---

5   Peter Schneider, *The Wall Jumper* (Pantheon Press, 1983), p. 33.

4.

Running to its western-most limit the U.S./Mexico border fence plunges into the Pacific surf west of Tijuana. Here is the location of Friendship Park, located atop Monument Mesa, inside California's Border Field State Park to the north and Playas de Tijuana to the south. The park is a meeting place where friends, strangers and loved ones can speak to each other through the vertical bars and mitigate the pain of separation and loss. Over the years, the Park has been the scene of many art performances and media events designed to highlight the border's history and complex identity as something that both divides and brings people together. In 2012, Mexican artist Ana Teresa Fernandez created a video performance on the Mexican side titled *Borrando la Frontera (Erasing the Border)*. Dressed in a black skirt and black high heel shoes, she climbs up a 30-foot tall ladder and paints the individual metal pickets of the border fence light blue. Little by little, the fence seems to disappear until by the end all that's left is the image of her hovering in the air as she paints over an empty blue sky where once there was a fence. Fernandez' black clothing helps to make her visible against the light background but also serves to add a melancholy note as she links it to the funerary symbol of *luto*, a year-long period of mourning observed in Mexico, in honor of those who have died attempting to cross the border. *Borrando la Frontera* recalls the surrealist paintings of René Magritte who also used erasure and displacement to express the illusion of reality. "To make of the absurd a metaphysics brought to the simplest acts."[6] The words of Mexican writer Juan Manuel Di Bella seem to hint at the oblique purpose behind Fernandez's poetically iconoclastic performance. Without physically overcoming the border fence she paints it with the visual marker of its own non-existence and in the process throws into relief the arbitrary and indiscriminate pattern of pain and anguish that grafts it to the earth like a scar.

5.

Cyber space has haunted the idea of the border since the early days of the Internet. The development of digital technology into drones, remote cameras and sensors has contributed to more efficient ways of controlling the line. Seen from

---

6 Juan Manuel Di Bella, "The Card." *Nailed to the Wound* (San Diego State University Press, 1993), p. 23.

the other side, these developments have played a distinctly antagonistic role by opening the border to better surveillance while making crossing more difficult. Not surprisingly, homegrown Mexican sci-fi themes have deviated from Hollywood's brand of spaceships, rockets and invasion plots in favor of those focused on the interplay of labor, economics, religion, politics and human interactions. Following the short-lived boom in science fiction writing in Mexico during the 80s and 90s, moviemakers have recently embraced the genre as a way to explore the border. Peruvian director Alex Rivera's *Sleep Dealer* (2009), is the story of Memo Cruz, a young hacker from the Mexican interior, who has his body implanted with nodes that enable him to control robots at remote locations. The film projects the historical experience of the *braceros* of the 1950s and 1960s into the near future and recasts them as *cyber braceros*.

At the beginning of *Sleep Dealer*, Memo's innocent eavesdropping on the drones that protect the privatized dam near his home draws the attention of undisclosed security forces operating out of San Diego. Profiling him as a terrorist threat, they retaliate by launching a missile strike on his ramshackle house, killing his father and forcing him to flee to the border to make money to support his family. In one of the film's definitive scenes, Memo arrives in Tijuana ready to cross into the U.S. only to be informed the "Border is closed but the network is open." With the help of Luz, he is introduced into the shady world of the node-enhanced *cyber braceros* who work 24-hour shifts operating robots that do everything from pick fruit on a California farm to weld I-beams in a Chicago high rise. The film deftly elaborates on borders of technological, biological, economic and political construction. Scenes of Memo receiving his implanted nodes give way to textural and abstract images of liquid flowing across the screen in warm and cool colors. Is it data uploading to the network, the blood moving through his veins or the memory of the river water that once rolled freely by his family's ranch in the days before multinational interests diverted it? Through this repeated sequence, Rivera hints at the hidden fabric of reality and successfully captures the state of flux and movement, which is at the core of *Sleep Dealer*.

The technological forces aligned against Memo are represented as ever-present and all-powerful. The principle resolution at the end of the film comes when

Memo and Rudy, the Chicano drone pilot who assassinated his father, reconcile and seize the apparatus of control. In an act of binational retribution, they strike back at the powers that set them against each other. *Sleep Dealer* portrays the border zone fence in future tense as a hawkish utopia where technology not only shuts down opportunities to cross the border it also removes the need to cross thereby. This dream of a technologically superior border complemented with the freedom of movement in cyberspace allows labor to be extracted from alien bodies without ever having to bring those bodies across sovereign state lines. By the end of the film the hardened relations at the border begin to unravel. In an interview on the Crossed Genres website, Rivera said, "The technologies that in the beginning were forces of alienation become converted into tools that serve the characters in a deep and hopeful way, even if it's just for a few moments."[7]

6.

Amy Sanchez and Misael Diaz are the founding members of Cog•nate Collective, a binational art collective whose interventions into the social, cultural and economic exchanges across the Southern California border region are meant to analyze and open up dialogue around these complex relations. For *Dialogue in Transit—Evolution of a Line*, they organized a mobile conference over pirate-radio frequency 87.9 FM. The conference took place at the Tijuana Port of Entry on Saturday, March 15, 2014, at 12 p.m. from inside a caravan of moving cars. The panelists included Professor and Director of the Chicana/o Studies Department at SDSU, Norma Iglesias Prieto; Professor and Director of the Bi-National Human Rights Center in Tijuana, Victor Clark Alfaro; and Tijuana visual artist and poet Omar Pimienta with Sanchez and Diaz moderating. For the duration of the three-hour border crossing, the group reflected on the changes that have had an impact on the economic and social life of the border since the 1994 North American Free Trade Agreement.

During the first part of *Dialogue in Transit*, the panelists construct a discursive series of snapshots of the border as it has contracted and expanded over the last twenty years in response to changing events, influences and conditions.

7   Alex Rivera as quoted in "Alex Rivera Interview" (2011). http://crossedgenres.com/archives/024-charactersofcolor/interview-alex-rivera/.

Like road kill, received ideas about the border quickly start to fall. In the opening exchange between Diaz and Prieto the word "fence" is placed in tension
between the words "defense" and "offense," in the process revealing fundamen-
tally different ways in which the border is perceived in Mexico and the United
States. Prieto says:

> The wall is the materialized representation of this idea of a border.
> In English people call it a "fence" and in the U.S. that fence means
> "defense"; something that in American minds brings protection.
> Interestingly enough you would have to ask them, "Protection
> from who or what?" And this same wall or barrier or fence means
> an "offense" to Mexicans.[8]

Unlike typical conferences, which are spatially static, *Dialogue in Transit* moves
forward in time *and* space, migrating through the line in unison with the general
population of border crossers. Listening to the audio archive of the conference
it becomes clear that the life of the city, pouring in from outside, is as much a
part of the dialogue as the panelists are themselves. Rolling jauntily along on its
pedagogical border trip, the broadcast booth, dubbed the Cog•nate Cruiser, a
battered Chevy wagon covered in black and white murals that include cartoons
of Zapatista rebels, blasted out its program, looking every bit the rasquache
pirate ride. During Part II of *Dialogue in Transit*, Diaz steers the car off of the
line and parks beside an artisan market where the panelists carry on their dialogue with local merchants. Moving towards the "temporal plane of the future,"
Part III engages pedestrians to predict the future of the border. Their responses
run the gamut from hopes that the border will fall, to doubts that it will ever be
brought down.

> To me the border—whether twenty years ago, or today, or twenty
> years in the future—I believe, and it is also my hope, that we can
> always see it as an opportunity for encounter. Whether there's a line,
> no line, a wall, no wall, I think that the opportunity for encounter
> continues and as things become more difficult on the border, or
> maybe easier for some people, the point stands that we will con-
> tinue to get more opportunities for that and those opportunities

---

8 Norma Iglesias Prieto, as quoted in Amy Sanchez and Misael Diaz, *Dialogue in Transit* (2014),
p.11. http://www.dialogintransit.com/Translation-1.pdf.

are going to grow and become more multidimensional, ever more complex. Hopefully we can infiltrate those spaces of opportunity as individual subjects. I would like to see the border go more in that direction with regards to how it's lived and practiced.[9]

Dialogue in Transit—Evolution of a Line successfully embeds the format of a radio talk show into the experience of driving through the U.S./Mexico port of entry. Its slow-rolling perspective allows it to capture the carnival-like atmosphere of the borderline with its perambulating vendors, strolling musicians and gaping tourists. The static flow of border traffic becomes the perfect opportunity to introduce the free play of a pirate radio broadcast.

7.

Even since the 1848 Treaty of Guadalupe Hidalgo decreed the present day border between Mexico and the U.S. as a geo-political reality, the border's identity has evolved and its legitimacy has often been contested. Social, political and economic forces from both sides manipulated it to fit their own interests. State control over the border has been crucial to maintain claims of national sovereignty and preserve territorial integrity, but the balance of control has always deviated preferentially towards the United States. Nationalized images of the border as sovereign, transcendent and inviolable stand in contrast to its humble origins as a collective work of the imagination—as a line in the sand. Closing the border completely has never been a state priority since it must ultimately allow passage for those who fit within privileged national identities. Yet, in an age where global economic crises continually shock the relations between rich and poor nations, old definitions of the border continue to come under pressure from a variety of sources. Border artists have been instrumental in developing innovative strategies for contesting official notions of the border as a divider that separates along lines of racial purity, economic privilege, and national identity. The future of post-bordernity can be read in their creative and humane responses and their alternative visions will continue to give way to dialogue, openness, fairness and compassion as long as there are borders to contest.

---

9   Ibid., p. 59.

Dialogue in Transit | *Cog•nate Collective*

Perry Vasquez
Emancipation Song

If only I could cast my song into a mold at once so bold and free as to seem unwittingly to be unique and wondrous to behold that every tyrant who dares enslave me would be cast out unmercifully and with impunity as wood is cast on fire and soon reduced to ashy flower liberated castigated caste and fated repeatedly ululated eventually to be reborn as emancipating dance or as ripening fruit on branches hanging from a tree.

As freedom-formed we are but songs that wind and storm cast up and turn to sounds then stored magnetically to be broadcast thunderously but somehow still entombed when cast onto an ocean blue like clues that float along eternally on surging swells and overwhelm the crashing rocks until they cede their drowned and solemn histories.

Borrando la Frontera | *Maria Teresa Fernandez*

Francisco J. Bustos

Así no: not like this
—*Deportado el 24 de Diciembre del 2014*

Así no
not like this,
no quiero regresar a casa de esta manera.
Me esposaron las muñecas, *by force*
me metieron a una van, me metieron a un cuarto
Me apagaron por completo y lloré como un bebé, solo, en la oscuridad.
Perdí la vista de los pájaros y perdí la vista del cielo.
Perdí mis sueños, todos.

Así no
not like this,
no quiero regresar a casa de esta manera.
Yo vine a trabajar, a comer, y a sobrevivir
Yo vine a trabajar, a comer, y a sobrevivir
Yo soy un buen hombre, sabes.

Nada now
que me corren y me sacan,
Nada now, que detienen mis sueños y detienen nuestra comida.

Nada now
que me sacan y me corren, nada nada nada nada now,
Yo soy un buen hombre, sabes.

Voy a tener que regresar a como de lugar.
Encontrar la manera de plantar mis sueños de nuevo, *aquí*.

Sin duda,
y-crean-me-cuando-lo-digo: *sin duda*

así no,
not like this,
no quiero regresar a casa de esta manera.

Así es que tendré que regresar a como de lugar.

Ya lo verás. Ya lo verás.

Así no: not like this

—Deported on December 24, 2014

Así no
not like this,
don't want to go home this way.
They put cuffs on my wrists, *a la fuerza*
they put me in a van, they put me in a room
They shut me down and I cried like a baby, alone, in the dark.
I lost sight of the birds and I lost sight of the sky.
I lost my dreams, all of them.

Así no,
not like this,
don't want to go home this way.
I came to work, to eat, and to survive
I came to work, to eat, and to survive
I'm a good man, you know.

Nada now
that they kick me out,
Nada now, that they stop my dreams and stop our food.

Nada now
that they kick me out, nada nada nada nada now,
I'm a good man, you know.

I'm just going to have to find a way to get back.
Find a way to plant my dreams again, *aquí.*

Sin duda,
and-be-lieve-me-when-I-say: *sin duda*

así no,
not like this,
don't want to go home this way.

So I'm just going to have to find a way to get back.

You'll see. You'll see.

Elizabeth Cazessús
Mimetismo

La falta de deseo en la piedra: reseca cantera
se mimetiza en la mirada del camaleón
Nada pasa por su iris y todo pasa por su iris
Incólume como la piedra
Inamovible
     Gárgola viviente
         Petrificado perfil
desborda por sus ojos su alucinante microhistoria.

Desierto de Vizcaíno, B.C.S. 1992.

Mimicry

The lack of desire on the stone: dried up quarry
camouflages itself in the chameleon's gaze
Nothing passes through its iris and everything passes through its iris
Unharmed like the stone
Immovable
     Living gargoyle
         Petrified profile
overflows through its eyes, its hallucinatory microhistory.

Biscay's Desert, B.C.S. 1992.
Translated by Francisco J. Bustos

Jhonnatan Curiel

Narcocold

The narcopolicemen arrives to his narcohouse
Gets welcomed by his impatient narcospouse
while his narcoboys run towards him
and ask for narcodollars to rapidly spend
in the narcomarket on the corner

He orders them not to leave the narcoyard
Because that night will occur narcoabductions
Narcotortures
Narcoshootings

They understand the narcomessage
and the uneasy narcofamily
will try to sleep under the narcoblankets of the bed
that despite being heavy narcoprotectors
they will not be able get rid of
the narcocold.

Split Dreams | *Juanita Lopez*

Juanita Lopez

From the Border to the Fields

It is the year of 2014 and both of my grandparents are very old but alive, though suffering from dementia. I decided to pay them a visit to interview them. Believe it or not, they still live in the same one-bedroom apartment in San Ysidro where they established their U.S. residency in the late 1970s. From their yard, I am able to look at the thousands of tiny houses in Tijuana, where they once lived, dreaming of crossing over for a better opportunity. I look at my dark-skinned grandmother and admire her toothless smile. Her eyes light up every time she sees me. She normally asks me how my brother is doing, and I tell her he's okay, working like always since he has a baby to take care of now. She smiles and two minutes later asks me the same question. I go over to her kitchen and wash some strawberries that were in her refrigerator. I offer her some after I cut them and sprinkle some sugar on top—my grandmother smiles again and starts telling me about her life, a not-so-sweet story about the times she labored as a farm worker picking strawberries and cutting flowers.

Carolina is my grandmother and Alfredo is my grandfather, who's in his hospital bed in the room watching a baseball game. He can hardly get out of bed these days. They had a total of four children in the state of Michoacán, Mexico. Looking for a better opportunity, my grandparents decided to travel north and landed in La Colonia Francisco Villa, Tijuana to be exact, in the early 1960s. Here, they had six more children—some died as infants, and others were born dead. I ask my grandmother for the specific location of where she buried my uncles, but she doesn't remember the location.

My grandmother began telling me that in the 1950s my grandfather became a bracero. "Braceros were given permits to work in the U.S. for cheap labor. Your grandfather and many other Mexican men didn't care about that, they just wanted to work," said my grandmother. The horrible things that they had to do to come across were shocking to me as soon as my grandmother began to describe them. She said, "Your grandfather would get on the train that would last several days. A few of his friends lost their lives because of asphyxiation and were just thrown off from the train. They were stripped naked and were sprayed on their genitals to get rid of any lice or any disease." I couldn't help but compare those images to the Holocaust. "But there he was, ready to come to work on this side of the border. He worked in Blythe, Delano, and Fresno, eventually sending his money back home so that your dad and uncles could go to school and have something to eat, but they only went up to the 3rd grade." Soon after, unhappy that my grandfather wasn't spending time with his family, my grandparents decided to move.

By the time they got to Tijuana, my grandmother discovered that she was a U.S. citizen. "I wasn't aware where Manteca would be in in the U.S. I thought it would be in Mexico. I discovered that in fact Manteca was located in northern California," said my grandmother in a high-pitched voice. You see, she never learned how to read or write, because she had to serve others after she became an orphan at the age of five.

I decided to change the subject, so I asked my grandmother to describe her city back then. She said, "Tijuana wasn't the Tijuana that it is now. Tijuana back then was the place to go and have fun. If I needed a bar of soap, which most of the times I did because we didn't have washing machines, I had to wash by hand, or if I needed some rice or beans, anything, there were small stores near each corner called *tiendas de abarrotes*, that had all of that." Wow, I thought. Nowadays, we use liquid soap and have washing machines at home and normally you go to the grocery store to buy food of that sort. "If you wanted to go and have a good time with the family, you would go to La Avenida Revolución. Here is where thousands of tourists, a lot of Americans mainly, or artists came to have a good time. Many even took the famous picture on the zebra which was actually a donkey painted as a zebra. The whole avenue was full of restaurants, discothèques, *tiendas de artesania*, bars…you name it. Oftentimes your uncles would go and listen to the popular Tijuana bands of the time like Los Moonlights or Los Old Friends." I told her, "The last time I went to La Revolución, I tried looking for a taco stand around 6 p.m. and there was only like one or two people selling tacos and the stores were closing down." I guess times have changed.

Eventually my grandmother began crossing the border every day to work in Encinitas, a city in San Diego's north county. Many people aren't aware that Encinitas is an agricultural city, a very wealthy city too, but the reality is that many migrant workers work there. She was a farm worker, picking strawberries and also laboring in the flower fields. Both jobs required my grandmother to wake up early, around 4 a.m., so she could cook breakfast and then cross the border. She would meet up with friends so she could carpool to her job, because she never learned how to drive either. My grandmother closed her eyes as she recalled:

> I would be knelt down on my knees from the crack of dawn till the sun came down. I would ache from my body, for days. Often I would walk with a limp. I would start getting deep cuts in my hands from cutting the flowers. I would sweat heavily from my dripping head down to my feet because the strong sunrays would beam at me all day long, although sometimes I would be under the white plastic houses. Oftentimes I would also get blisters on my toes because of my poor shoes and being on my feet for too long. I would be so dehydrated, with a parched mouth, and so hungry with a growling stomach.

This was the sacrifice that she had to endure for many years until she was able to make my uncles and grandfather U.S. residents. Since my grandfather's bracero visa had expired, he would work in Tijuana, and my uncles would work there too. Soon after, some of my uncles, including my dad, got married.

After saving up for some time, in the late 1970s my family moved to San Ysidro. My grandparents' choice of moving to San Ysidro was so clever—they wanted to be closer to Mexico, and Tijuana was the closest they got to their roots. They wanted to be able to cross to Tijuana, whenever they wanted. They would go and see the dentist over there, or go there for their weekly groceries because it was cheaper to buy more there than over here. My grandmother laughed as she said, "The meat was much fresher over there, and I sure loved cooking." She remembers the border with fewer doors and officers, shorter lines—all you had to say was that you were a U.S. citizen and, well, she was. I told her, "Yeah, let me try saying that phrase now. I need to show proof of that, and even with proof, I am asked a million questions such as, where do I work or go to school, and why did I cross to Mexico?" Can't I just cross to eat or visit family without being bombarded with all of these questions?

At first, only my youngest uncle came to live in San Ysidro with my grandparents. In fact, he even went to high school here, adopting the Chicano *calo* slang and style. My older uncles and dad decided to have their children in Tijuana because the hospital bills were cheaper there. They didn't know that it would've been easier for their children's future to have been born in the U.S., since later on those children would get deported. Once those children were a bit older, my uncles and dad decided to move to San Diego, and landed in Logan Heights. My two uncles and dad also worked in Encinitas in a nursery, mainly, cutting flowers, from gerbera daisies to chrysanthemums, you name it. But my dad's favorite were the sunflowers, those big yellow flowers which often were on my kitchen table. My uncles and dad were very proud of that agricultural work—it was hard but at least their children were getting a better education than them, and they had dignity.

I smiled at my grandmother and I couldn't believe that I was able to have this long conversation with her. Given her condition, I was shocked that she could remember the past so clearly, but not the present. I've heard these stories many times before—they are not foreign to my ears. I can't help but weep sometimes because it's difficult to picture my old wrinkly grandparents going through all of that hard work so that I can have a better life. So I am grateful for what I eat—something as sweet as these red strawberries that my grandmother once picked, that once made her body throb in pain. Or admire the beauty and the beautiful smell that my flowers have in my living room—flowers that she once planted, or cut, which left blisters on her hands for days. I can't help but think of Tijuana today, a city that was once the loudest, most festive, and commercialized place. Now it's more like a ghost town that creates fear, and one becomes hostile to it. The border that was once more open has become so militarized, and has made it harder for people to reunite with their roots, their people, my people. At least my grandmother doesn't have this new image of it since she hasn't crossed the border in over ten years or so. One of her sons had to stop working and had to get knee surgery because of the agricultural work in the flower fields, and her other son, my dad, died. The only son that still works in Encinitas is my uncle; he now is owner of his own flower shop and also his son has a shop of his own.

Something that started as a very necessary job became a family job, and an honorable one at that.

My grandmother still has this vision that one day she will cross back to Tijuana and visit her "terre" as she calls it, short for *terreno:* land. She wishes to find those lost graves of her children and be reunited with her grandchildren and great-grandchildren who she has never met but who now live there. Unfortunately that is not going to happen because of her health.

There's only one strawberry left on my plate, and as I look at my grandmother she smiles and says, "Ooh, I remember when I used to work picking them, here in Encinitas, the city of the poinsettias!" I smile and say, "*Ay abuelita*, do tell me about it." Once more, over and over, I hear the story that each time leaves me speechless.

Jimmy Santiago Baca

Coming Into San Diego

1.

How stunning the morning desert was to Vito. His heart burst with pleasure and a desire for his childhood days when the sun radiated one tiny ray of faith on his life, a ray that had weight, one he could toss from hand to hand and hold up and carry in his pocket and embrace before sleep and kiss at daybreak.

Fields steamed dew as the pickers arrived. Men, women, and children humped in the furrows, picking. Carmen slept the whole way. He was thinking bad thoughts as her chest rose and fell. He looked away, told himself to stop thinking of touching her. He told himself to shake it out of his head, he could control his mind, he was a trained boxer, he could discipline his body and mind, he could fuck any chick he wanted, but something else was pulling him.

In the miles that stretched out before them he wished Carmen wasn't engaged to his brother, that she was like so many he'd had—a free-loving chick who just wanted to fuck all night. But no, he was on a mission, and he would never betray his brother.

Still, he reached out and his fingers grazed her cheek and the sweetness of her sleeping face and her breath made something in his chest tighten.

He forced his mind to obey his will and pulled it back to what he was going to do—the upcoming fight—but her jeans were tighter at her crotch and the fine black hair on her arms and upper lip and between her eyebrows made his dick hard. He quit looking at her, determined to be strong and allow no thought of her body to fill his mind. He turned up the radio, shifted in his seat, and started thinking about the fight.

A few miles down the road he slowed for a roadblock. The solemn radiance of the desert morning convulsed suddenly into a military camp as armed National Guardsmen approached. They eyed him quickly, squinting into the passenger-side window at Carmen still asleep, waved him through, their eyes following him with suspicion.

Thirty minutes later, he saw a concrete building a few hundred yards from the freeway and he guessed there were at least four hundred people standing behind the barbed-wire fence that encircled a big, dirt yard. A gun tower stood at each of the corners. A large sign facing the freeway read HUTTO PRISON.

He felt queasy. The prisoners stared at him as he drove slowly past tanks and soldiers and laser-beam monitoring machines and sound and motion sensors. Some of the women, children, and men were confined in chicken-wire cages. Others were milling around in a larger cyclone-fence enclosure. A few more, a dozen or so, had their backs turned to him and were lined up against a wood fence.

He guessed it was some kind of temporary holding facility for Mexicans caught crossing the border illegally but it looked too much like a military war encampment with the jeeps, armed guards, military personnel, and white trailer offices. It scared him.

He watched as a canvas-covered Army jeep pulled into the encampment and was inspected by the guards at the gate, which was swung open by guard-tower sentries and allowed to enter and park. He watched as inmates of all ages—the men all handcuffed—were led out of the back of the truck and escorted into a fenced yard.

What the hell is going on, he wondered as an ICE helicopter shattered his thoughts, patrolling overhead. Then it flew off, trailing armed guards in a machine-gun jeep that drove out to the desert.

Once he passed the Army operations base, he locked cruise control at eighty, lowered his window, and relaxed. Twenty minutes later a group of Mexicans rose like roadside ghosts in the shimmering heat. Beyond the road shoulder, dehydrated and clearly in need of medical attention, they pled for him to stop. He kept driving, not daring to look back in the rearview mirror. He was afraid.

2.

They arrived in San Diego on Thursday night, eight hours after they had left Las Cruces. Carmen was delighted to be there, energetic and revived. She directed him through middle-class Mexican neighborhoods for a half hour until they pulled up to a rundown bungalow rental in the university area.

She invited Vito in, adding that her friends were throwing a big party and he better come, but he needed to get a motel room and rest, take a nap, then go to the storage facility nearby and load up all the belongings she wanted to take with her. He'd be back later.

When he returned hours later, the party was well underway. College kids came and went and girls danced on the porch and lawn to blaring music.

Carmen was already high on life and giggly on pot when he arrived. She had a lot of friends and the house was packed shoulder to shoulder, everyone hip bumping to the music and talking loud. He gulped down the first mixed drink offered and lost count after that. He was having a lot of fun telling stories of his life on the road as a boxer and the women surrounded him three deep.

They were party girls, carefree and smiling with no idea how the night was going to turn out, smiling with the expectation that it was going to be a lovely evening. And it was. People gathered around the barbecue laughing and eating, girls ran from guys, couples jumped in the pool and wrestled. The music was oldies but goodies, the weather was perfect and balmy.

Late at night the party started to dwindle, and after a while there were only six or seven people left, smoking weed and philosophizing.

He didn't remember how he and Carmen were left alone. They said good night to everyone leaving and the hostess went to her bedroom with some guy. He and Carmen were sitting on the couch—the room and the house were mellow, the lights amber and shaded low, Van Morrison on the stereo.

One of Carmen's girlfriends saw them fucking on the rug but Carmen was oblivious to the world. She was in a totally different zone and her mind was not fully conscious of what she was doing or the consequences of it, her body was feeling such intense pleasure, such sheer joy and lust in fucking.

Her friend's house with the windows illuminated by street lights, the bawdy voice of Morrison, the sultry moist ocean air, the wine and the weed and Vito's strong hands and firm body, all combined to create an erotic weight that pressed in on her from all sides and kept her down on her back with Vito on top of her as she whirled into an oblivious meltdown of dizzying joy.

For that twenty minutes she had him.

Then something blew inside of her, crossed from outside to inside and swept through her with a cold embracing chill, telling her she knew what she was doing, telling her she was lapping the kill's warm blood, filling her with the knowledge that she'd never give up those twenty minutes of her life and that she'd sacrifice everything for those minutes with him, and she grieved that she did.

That twenty minutes was her twenty and she had control of everything.

3.

They left San Diego at dawn, her belongings in the back of the truck and covered with a tarp, and they hit open prairie after an hour, her eyes closed in self-disgust. Everything she looked at reflected her self-loathing. Behind her eyelids she smelled her unwashed hair. She scratched one bare foot with the other, wiping dirt off her soles with her toenails. Some things you could wipe off; others leave an indelible stain.

Her silence made him anxious so he told her he had seen the National Guard erecting electric fences, laying sensor-detection cable, that there were aerial drones following above.

He mentioned seeing the prisoners waving at him on the drive to San Diego, that he had kept on driving. He threw in that he didn't think it was right to cross without a legal permit. People crossing over in the thousands created chaos.

He should have woken her, he should have stopped for them, she grumbled.

What about his parents? she asked accusingly.

It was a different time and circumstance, he countered sharply.

She was pissed off and there wasn't much to say—he sensed her temper had deeper levels, a long white trail of fiery debris.

Her big brown eyes settled on him, studying his face.

He shuddered under the heaviness of his betrayals—Lorenzo, still awaiting his bail hearing in jail, and the Mexicans he just drove by.

She swallowed hard. She felt like she might burst out weeping. She looked away, drowning in her own confusion and the guilt that filled hundreds of prairie miles, extending all the way to the horizon.

Vito was lost in his own thoughts as they drew ever closer, with every mile, to his brother's eyes.

He wanted to blurt out, scream and slam the dashboard with his fist, that it hadn't happened, that someone put some kind of drug in his drink, that it was her fault, that something evil had possessed them, someone had slipped them a poison and that was, that was, that was…but it wasn't why.

He saw the outline of the mountains behind the town and knew that within an hour he'd be standing in front of his brother. Lorenzo had said he would make bail and meet them at the camp. Vito was afraid to call and confirm that he was already there. Lorenzo was certain to notice the tremor in his voice. Numbed with fear and grief over doing this to his brother, Vito gripped the wheel and stared ahead, seeing nothing but what he had done.

Would he shoot him, beat her, move away, never come back, never see him again? He drove on with an urge to yank the wheel hard, right into one of the oncoming tractor trailers roaring past, one behind another, from the opposite direction. His eyes locked on Carmen's, asking for help, for reasons, for anything that would alleviate his regret.

It could have been five minutes or five hours. The sky was darkening, sunlight spreading across the familiar landscape of the workers' trucks and cars parked alongside the fields while the workers were huddled together in the rows.

He pulled off the highway and turned west, down a long slope toward the river and the camp. Then he turned right, down a long row with trees on the left, thick and green running parallel to the road. Kids fished, women visited on porches, dogs chased his bumper. Normal images, and yet the world as he knew it had shattered into a million pieces.

He turned right, then left, into an open clearing, going past the boxcar and their house and other one-room homes, and bearing off to the left, scattering chickens, goats, and dogs, finally parking in front of the barn where he could see women boxing chili.

Lorenzo appeared framed in the doorway like a hero in a cowboy movie, shining and compassionate, smiling with extended arms wide in a mock embrace, elated.

He dashed out, slammed the hood of the truck with the palm of his hand, woke Carmen up, and swung her door open. She leaped out of the cab, rushed him and kissed him, weeping.

And as Lorenzo hugged her, laughing and asking why she was crying, he looked over her shoulder at Vito, sitting, unable to move or smile.

Reprinted from A Glass of Water *with permission of the author*

Steve Kowit

Refugees, Late Summer Night

Woke with a start, the dogs barking out by the fence,
yard flooded with light. Groped my way to the window.
Out on the road a dozen quick figures
hugging the shadows: bundles slung at their shoulders
& water jugs at their hips. You could hear,
under the rattle of wind, as they passed,
the crunch of sneakers on gravel. *Pollos.* Illegals
who'd managed to slip past the Border Patrol,
its Broncos & choppers endlessly circling
the canyons & hills between here & Tecate.
Out there, in the dark, they could have been
anyone: refugees from Rwanda, slaves pushing north.
Palestinians, Gypsies, Armenians, Jews....
The lights of Tijuana, that yellow haze to the west,
could have been Melos, Cracow, Quang Ngai....
I watched from the window till they were lost
in the shadows. Our motion light turned itself off.
The dogs gave a last, perfunctory bark
& loped back to the house: those dry, rocky hills
& the wild sage at the edge of the canyon
vanishing too. Then stared out at nothing.
No sound anymore but my own breath,
& the papery click of the wind in the leaves
of that parched eucalyptus: a rattle of bones;
chimes in a doorway; history riffling its pages.

Steve Kowit
Romero

By early December the dirt road will be nicely macadamed,
& the backcountry dust will no longer blow through the window
into my hair. In the chill of the oncoming winter
I'll rise from my chair & throw pitch-pine & oak on the fire—look,
it is nearly winter already! By now Romero
should either be up around Fresno, working construction,
or back in Tuxtla Gutierrez, yoked to a cart of *paletas*,
& mending his socks—& plotting another go at the States.
When he stepped from the canyon I pulled to the shoulder
& opened the door. We were north of Tecate: the border patrol
swarming over the highway. Did I have any neighbor,
he wanted to know, who needed a worker?
So all morning, at my place, we cut back the wild chamise
by the shed, though we ended up arguing over money:
he wouldn't take a cent—that was to pay me for picking him up
in the first place. "Romero, for god's sakes
you can't work for nothing!"—& kept at him until he relented.
Mary, what fine enchiladas! what heavenly pears!
How exhausted he was, & dusty & hungry & hopeful!
Late in the evening, we wove our way out of the mountains:
the Barrett grade thru Dulzura down to Spring Valley
& north to Santee. It was August. The night sky a bucket
of coins spilling over the hills. Now & then meteors
flared thru the darkness & vanished. "Right here
is good," he said on a back street, at a grove of black
eucalyptus. I pulled to the curb. It was where he would sleep.
In the morning, a truck cruising Magnolia
would take him to Fresno,
where *la migra* was scarce & plenty of guys like himself,
without papers, were working construction. He slung his blanket
over his shoulder, picked up his bag, & asked me again

in his broken, measured, tentative English, please
to thank my *Maria bonita* for all of her kindness. I said that I would.
"Romero, take care…" & under those fugitive stars
we gave each other a long, final *abrazo.* Country
of endless abundance & workers with nowhere to sleep.
"Esteban, I…" —& he nodded, & turned,
& walked off into that tunnel of trees & was gone.

Jim Moreno

huellas en la arena
(footprints in the sand)

—for enrique morones & the border angels

we carry the water down   we carry the water down   llevamos el agua abajo
to the floor of the canyon   carpeted with sand   we carry hope down   we carry hope down
        llevamos esperanza abajo   we carry compassion down   we carry inoculation for hate
intoxication   racist hate that sliced full life water bottles   bigoted blades draining liquid life into the sand

we replace the empty with the full   we replace the empty with the full   reponemos el vacio con
el lleno we replace the senseless with the sane,   we transform the greed with the sage   change fascism to
freedom   reverse hot hate consternation with cool water of life   singing Indian songs recalling simpler
times   when sand was not symbol   of desperate human rivers   when human beings were not for sale
        when a wind called justice   danced to one land sans borders
                        to border angels' smiles

but we are symbols too we are symbols too   somos simbolos tambien   we are reminders that in
a sea of hatred insanity in an ocean of fascist freedom thieves   we embrace strong raza care   over the glacier
carried stones   over cactus and scurrying critters   among a dozen hundred rivers of footprints painting
sand   bringing liquid peace among briars and burrs   among snakes and scorpions   with a dearth of
clouds in the burning desert sky and almost never never life saving shade   in the desert what don't sting or
stick   cuts scrapes burns bruises or bites   and when the sunshine state wildcat
        succumbed to the boil the brain heat   vomiting the unbelievable manipulation puking the unbearable
exploitation   of the poor and the marginalized to the ad nauseam   a great reprieve was spoken by the elder
        the ancient admonition that was handed down from generation to generation somos todos rayos de la
misma rueda   that we are all spokes on the same wheel
                        connected in the center unidos en el mismo centro

and the 700 buried not too far from here los sietecientos enterrado cerca de aqui forced by brutal bigot
bersin to die in brutal bigot heat the 700 murdered by state violent paper writ,   by the new bottle old poison
eurocentric hegemony hate,   the 700 buried so far from home   might have left this river of injustice
tracks   to remind us that this desert death is unjust   this desert dying is as unamerican as corporate kings and
queens plundering broken lives from impunity from let them eat cake arrogance, from fascist foreign policy—
their crimes only exceeded by their contempt for us.

so we carry the water down we carry the water down llevamos el agua abajo we move—dousing
hatred's fire of those who have never been hungry   those who have never been thirsty   those
who hold the gold, making racist rules   sponsoring vigilantes breaking hearts and breaking lives,
        descendants of immigrants crucifying immigrants   deputies of injustice slaughtering 10,000
innocents   pale writers of so many unnecessary epitaphs

but we are writers too we are writers too   somos escritores tambien somos somos escritores
and there are more of us than there are of them   so for this panegyric for *this* panegyric we all carry the

water down   entonces llevamos todas el agua abajo   until there are no more footprints in the sand   all of us carry the water down   through the prickly cactus in the suffocating heat   we all carry the water down to raise the hopes of desperate desert walkers   we all carry the water down   all of us carry the water down   singing songs of justice   singing songs of peace   singing Indian songs of freedom until one glorious day   there are no more desert deaths see that beautiful day when there are no more no more no more footprints in the sand   No Mas!   no mas huellas en la arena

Adrián Arancibia
what you gave away

no one will ever forgive you
no one will ever give you the years back
no one will ask you what your parents' life was like
when they grew up in the homeland
you'll only have words
to explain the shacks
the dirt or wood floors
and maybe the
smell of the houses.
yes, the places they called houses.

and what you give away
will be a set of words.
like the story you wrote
explaining
what it meant to be
a political prisoner
to children.

this, while you only
have the smallest understanding
of protest. but you want
to be forgiven for leaving.
for wanting more.
por entregarte to another
battle. in another country.
in another time. and this distance
you carry in your heart.
always made the past
difficult to negotiate.
even after you learned

your color. your place.
space. time.

and the songs
from the homeland
you've sewed to your heart,
they are songs you'll
never share with your primos
because they will never understand
the distance.
of home.

the way words pick.
and chop. like a memory
of your abuela chopping
cilantro.

do you remember
the christmas you were there?
you asked your tíos
what she needed. another knife.
another tool for the kitchen?
and your tío fernando pointing
to a row of knives,
says throwing one down
on the counter,
"creí que ella necesita
más?"
and so, you buy a hand
carved box that she can
keep the precious things inside.
perhaps, keep the memory of you.
inside.

what we leave
behind is this.
this visceral
memory of what it
was to be.
home.

Murrieta: land of the ugly, home of the bigots.

Adrián Arancibia
there are no winners tonight

our last hope of america,
the united states lost today.
it lost in more than one way.
it lost by points
but also, by way of a lost
love of america. it lost.
it lost its head, it lost its heart
it lost its word.
it lost its hope.

during the match,
the post from the child
says, "lo que me gusta
de la selección estadounidense
es que nunca se da por vencido"
the u.s. team never, ever
gives up. this, while i look
on and see the failure
of soccer moms. the failure
of status quo. the failure of
signs and of protest.
and truth be told,
there weren't enough
brown and black faces.
there were not enough
poor faces. faces with legs
willing to run to another
country to win.

such are the days
we live in. we have

never seen war. we've
never seen drugs or la bestia.
we don't know survival.
and we've pushed
the border so far south
that central america
is now the beginnings
of the fence.

when i was
thirteen, i recall seeing
a man at plaza bonita
one day. he asked me what direction
and how far los angeles was. see,
he'd just crossed. and i pointed.
north. he'd told me
he'd walked from
guerrero. guerrero.
to los angeles.
from san diego.
from my home.
didn't seem like
a distance too far
if you've traveled.

and two weeks ago,
i didn't even want
to ponder the depth
of the rabbit hole
children might have traveled.
such are the days
when i try my hardest
to understand a broken
system. it hurt just
to think of children
that have walked
from honduras,
from guatemala,
from el salvador.
and as a parent,

i couldn't bear it.
the weight of so many
paces. alone.

today, we lost a match
we lost a game.
but life continues on.
the cruel cynicism
slaps me straight in the face.
it slaps me and tells me
i may not be "american"
enough. and yes, i feel anger.
i feel anger for the young
lives turned away.
i feel anger for having protested
and being treated like a criminal
while the rights of others
are respected.

today, we lost a match.
there was no fire.
there was no next time.
there were only children.
children held in prisons.
children left alone.
children wondering
when they will see
their mothers again.
children with lives
like my children and
we couldn't do so much
as offer shelter
or food.

what would've jesus
said? i can tell you jesús
believes in america.
in his posts. during the game,
he believes, we should love.
believes that we can

be both mexican and american
and american and mexican.
but he wonders if these are the values
we've shared?

the match was too long.
and we lost. we lost our perspective.
we called them wetbacks
we told them that they carry
diseases
gangs
dirtiness
has the story ever changed?

this, this is the jimi hendrix
star spangled banner
crashing. this is the
bald eagle that has died
from DDT. this, this is the
home for refugees
following an armed conflict.
but not one from a conflict
caused by our consumption.
policies. police. drugs.

this is the day that we lost.
we lost our heads.
we lost our hearts.
we lost the game.
we lost the love.
of what it means
to be
american.

Sonia Gutièrrez

In the Time of Memories and Dreams

It was November—in the time of memories and dreams. She wore her hair down over her shoulders and her favorite white gown touching her calves. Her bare feet were dry like the desert dust, craving for a drop of water. Under the cherimoya tree, she sat on a bench taking in her surroundings and then continued on her journey.

She saw the rabbit on the moon peer through the tall almond tree heavy with flowers; its leaves glistened and danced feverishly as she passed by. Even though the smell of eucalyptus trees permeated the back yard, she could not smell it as much as she tried. Something else called her—a smell more powerful—the smell of cempazuchitl flowers.

As she got closer to the backside of the house, she recognized the geranium clay pots lining alongside the house. For a second, she thought they were hers. She approached a window and saw her face reflected. She didn't know if she was La Llorona or a bruja or the two of them in one. Through her eyes, she didn't look terrifying—not to herself. Looking at her face did startle her a bit, but what startled the most was that her feet weren't touching the ground. Her body moved slowly, heavy with time on her shoulders, to her altar, where she found her picture in a wooden frame, the only picture of her, the one with her hair tight in a long braid. She remembered who she was—she was Aurora. And her granddaughter, Sofía, had guided her to the place of the living.

After visiting loved ones placed next to her, Aurora then visited Elena, sleeping next to her husband. She found her in the same position she slept as a child. Staring at her daughter's grown woman's face, Aurora leaned over and kissed her daughter on the forehead. Elena woke up, stayed still and asked, "*¿Mother, is that you?*" With no answer and heavy with sleep, she went back to sleep.

When I woke up, I was confident my grandmother had visited her altar I had helped Mother adorn the night before. I sat on my bed recollecting my dream then rose to my feet and stared out the window. I had dreamt that I was La Llorona but wasn't sure if the woman in my dream was my grandmother—Aurora.

Restoring Our Cultura | *Juanita Lopez*

II. BENEATH THE POSTCARD

Anna Daniels

Samsay on the Porch

The sudden attentiveness of the cats alerted me to the faint sounds coming from the front porch. Moments before they were curled like fur commas around the suitcase that was splayed open on the bed. I straightened up from the suitcase that I had just finished packing and turned toward the window and the darkness beyond.

The sounds were faint and intermittent. It was probably just one of the opossums that routinely visited the porch at night cleaning up the last bits of cat kibble in the bowls. After zipping up the suitcase and setting it on the floor, I patted my pocket yet again to make sure that the little pill case with the valium was still there.

I was as ready as I possibly could be for the dreaded red eye flight to Pittsburgh. My brother and sister had convinced me that our mother was dying and that I had to go back—now. George W. Bush had recently begun playing Cheerleader in Chief for Dick Cheney's plan to invade Iraq. Both the imminent war and my mother's imminent death were equally incomprehensible and alarming.

After blowing kisses to the cats and intently gazing at the art work on the walls as if for the last time, I stood at the front door.

"Rich! Come here!" I hissed to my husband. "There's someone on the porch." I quickly threw open the door, trying to adjust my eyes to the dark edges of the porch where I could barely make out a figure crouching there.

"What do you want? Who are you?" The forcefulness of my voice belied my racing heart.

"I am Samsay. The bamboo. I come here to pray." The disembodied voice was quiet and unhurried.

I could now make out a slender figure kneeling on the porch, facing the black bamboo forest that overran half of the front yard.

"Go pray somewhere else. Get out of here right now!" I could hear the click of the gate behind the departing figure as it dissolved into the night.

"Drive around the block, Rich. He may come back to break into the house." And so began the succession of weeks and months in which death and danger and loss never seemed far away.

◆ ◆ ◆

The suburbs and rural areas around Pittsburgh that March were a gloomy reminder of the long winter. Dirt stained piles of snow had been bulldozed from the streets into enormous mounds on shopping center parking lots. They would not disappear completely until that April. The hillsides wept snow melt in long glistening streams down their craggy faces.

My mother, the color of ashes, spent her days alone since my father's death curled up in her orange television-watching chair, subsisting on Hershey Kisses and little else. She left a trail of little foil balls and strips of paper in the ashtrays scattered throughout the house.

I watched the made-for-TV version of the invasion of Iraq far from the sunlit and comforting ordinariness of life in San Diego. My mother would have preferred to watch her game shows and soap operas and didn't seem to understand what I found so riveting.

The daily phone calls between Rich and me always included my anxious question, "Has that guy come back to the house again?" My relief to hear that he hadn't would only last momentarily and I'd ask again the following day.

On May first of that year, President Bush declared mission accomplished in Iraq, a monstrous lie that began to unravel immediately. A few weeks earlier,

I was a pallbearer for the woman who had once carried me for nine months within her own body.

The routine of work and my husband's quiet constancy enabled me to get out of bed every morning and blindly push through another day, oblivious to almost everything except a searing emptiness.

I returned home from work one afternoon and saw someone rocking rhythmically on his knees on the front porch. The figure was turned toward the bamboo and chanting something.

I was more bemused than afraid as I walked up to the porch. "Hey! Who are you? What are you doing here?"

"I am Samsay. The bamboo. I come to pray." He had turned toward me but remained kneeling.

With that reprise of the interchange that had occurred two months before, a peculiar relationship was struck up between the two of us. It unfolded over that whole summer on the front porch, its exclusive setting.

While that relationship was an odd one, it was hardly the first time that a stranger had shown up in the yard or on the porch. The neighborhood where I live in the old inner city community of City Heights is largely poor, overwhelmingly immigrant and filled with unlovely apartment houses surrounded by concrete and cars.

The shaggy bamboo forest and the tree that shades the gate of our house form a diminutive oasis, a reprieve from the scorching summer heat and ubiquitous cement. Strangers routinely stop there to rest or talk to me if I'm around and, from time to time, walk inside if I'm not.

At first it was crack heads and tweakers banging on the door at night, asking for money to get Similac for their baby or gas money to get to work or simply stealing what wasn't nailed or chained down. Over time, the bamboo grew taller and took over more of the yard while the neighborhood began to change. The visitors changed too.

Neighborhood men and boys would come by, desperate for work, any work. They assured me that they could limpiar el jardín for a good price. One day I arrived home and found a woman waiting at the gate. Her face was swollen, her eyes red. She pointed to a station wagon parked on the corner where she said her family was waiting.

Would I please buy a flan, hecho en casa? Her son had died suddenly and there was no money to bury him properly. We ate flan for days and so did our neighbors.

A little girl scared me half to death when I unexpectedly came upon her wandering around in the bamboo next to the door. Her face turned upward, she kept repeating, "This is a jungle. This is a jungle," in an odd combination of childish amazement and disbelief.

I have come to realize that City Heights is a shape-shifting Scheherazade. The bamboo grove and front porch have been an unexpected setting for listening to her stories.

Now it was Samsay, kneeling on the porch.

◆ ◆ ◆

"My name is Anna." "Ah-nah," he repeated back to me. Samsay had stood up and I offered him my outstretched hand.

"Ah-nah, do you pray to mother ancestor and father ancestor?" I wasn't expecting this follow up to our quick introductions. When he said "mother ancestor" I felt my eyes start to well up.

"No Samsay, I don't pray at all."

"I will teach you. You must pray to mother ancestor and father ancestor."

Over the next months, Samsay would materialize on the porch seemingly out of thin air, kneel down facing the bamboo and begin to pray. Over the next months, I would learn to say the words that he had phonetically spelled out for me on a piece of tattered paper and kneel beside him and cry until the front of my blouse was soaked with tears.

We were an improbable pair. Samsay, a Cambodian-Thai-Hmong Buddhist and I, an atheist pastiche of eastern European and Anglo-Saxon genes.

After we prayed I would ask Samsay about his life. He was completely incurious about mine, although there was a deep flash of understanding in his sustained gaze when I told him at some point that both my mother and father were dead.

Samsay's stories were disconnected from each other by both time and space. One afternoon he told me about his grandfather, a revered shaman in the village who was regularly given elephants as gifts. Samsay gestured how he would come across snakes in the paddies in the village, quickly pull one up by its tail and whip it around his head, snapping its neck.

While this accounting of his conversation is true, it is not the way Samsay told it. "The people come and come and give my grandfather good man too many elephants." Samsay's English was halting and stripped down to its most essential elements—nouns, verbs in the present tense and the occasional adverb or adjective. His linguistic limitations made the stories he told all the more vivid and immediate, with a touch of the surreal.

Another afternoon he gave a disjointed account of how he was picked up along with some other kids by the Washington state police. Although he said he hadn't done anything really serious, his gun fell out of his pants and that was enough to send him to jail.

I learned that his father was an army officer who assured the loyalty of his subordinates by paying them with opium; that a huge fire that consumed almost his whole village one night gave him cover to escape the cruelty and indifference of his father's second wife whom he had married shortly after the death of Samsay's mother.

Samsay said, "I run and pray and cry and pray and cry." One day a Baptist missionary couple took him home with them to Washington. He found the strict household rules confusing and impossible to follow.

It was never clear what brought Samsay to San Diego, how long he had lived here or where he found the money to survive. He expressed disapproval of his roommate's slovenly habits and unappealing food choices and said he wanted to go somewhere else to live.

There were times when I suspected that Samsay was living in the streets, although he always appeared in clean clothes. I asked him if he considered living with the Buddhist monks in the area. City Heights has a number of temples and living compounds for the monks. Samsay had stayed with monks a few times but it didn't work out for him either.

The prayers and stories continued. We would both sit cross-legged on the porch and talk. I wanted to ask Samsay about the faint tracings of spidery tattoos I could see above the neck of his tee shirt and on his upper arms, but was either distracted or thought the better of it.

One day while we were sitting there I noticed a tent rising in the crotch of his shorts. "Samsay, what the hell are you thinking? Stop it." By the end of summer, Samsay seemed more and more untethered from whatever his life was beyond the gate of the house. I too was feeling some shift in my own life.

The deep wound created by mother's death was being cauterized by the insistent demands of life, which is different than forgetting. One day I asked Samsay where he would like to be, where he would like to live.

He told me that he had two sisters in two different states and said that he would like to go stay with one of them. I tried to make sure that he had their current addresses and phone numbers. "Okay Samsay, Rich and I are going to buy you a Greyhound bus ticket so that you can go to your sister's. Spend the night here and we'll drive you to the station."

Samsay didn't appear to spend any time contemplating the offer or what it might mean. He simply accepted it. The next evening, he slept on the couch and turned down the breakfast of eggs and toast the following morning. He did change his mind about which sister he wanted to visit, which sent us scrambling to determine the schedule for this revised destination.

Rich and I made sure that Samsay got on the bus. We waved goodbye to him with a mixture of relief and concern when we saw him seat himself next to a window, his expressionless face peering out at us.

Over ten years have now passed. Although I have absolutely no memory of Samsay's face, from time to time I catch a fleeting image of his familiar kneeling figure in my peripheral vision. In those moments I remember Samsay on the porch, send a prayer of sorts for his safekeeping into the heart of the bamboo.

"Samsay on the Porch" is based upon the essay "Ten Years On: A Dying Mother, the Invasion of Iraq and Samsay on the Porch" which appeared in the San Diego Free Press, *March 20, 2013.*

Ocean Beach | *Kelly Mayhew*

Frank Gormlie

The Story of How a Small Working-Class Coastal Community Within San Diego Spoiled the Establishment's Plans and in the Process Created a Revolution in Urban Planning

It was early afternoon on a hot July day in 2014 when then San Diego City Council President Todd Gloria gaveled the Council meeting to order. First on the agenda was a vote on the newly updated community plan of Ocean Beach, a small coastal neighborhood of the city—called simply "OB." The Council's action that day should have been a routine procedure, approving the product of a process initiated by the city's own planning department, ostensibly a process integrating the community plan of Ocean Beach into the larger General Plan of the City of San Diego.

Yet what was going on that day was anything but routine or ordinary. The cavernous Council Chambers, high up on the tenth floor of San Diego's City Hall, was swamped with people wearing blue T-shirts emblazed with large white letters saying: "*Keep the OBcean attitude.*" This visual statement to elected officials of the breadth of support for the community plan was worn by Ocean Beach residents, property owners, merchants and supporters. Leaders from every neighborhood organization in Ocean Beach had mobilized their respective memberships. The Town Council leaders were there, as were the local Friends of the Library, the OB historical society, other merchant leaders—they were all there. Community activists had mobilized dozens more through a petition drive in support of the plan—and signatures of thousands of residents, visitors and supporters had been collected.

What was happening that day was a showdown between a feisty, funky, working-class neighborhood and the San Diego establishment—a showdown over a blueprint for urban development—a community plan nearly four decades old, forged in the strong ecology-oriented, anti-development and populist grassroots activism of the 1970s. The "update process" by the City planning department had resulted in an official new planning document—the issue before the City Council.

Looking out over the "sea of blue" that afternoon in the bowels of City Hall was a scene that was very reminiscent of a scenario involving the exact same community, the same Council Chambers, and the exact same issue—the community plan—exactly 39 years earlier. It was the spring of 1975, when OB residents, property owners and merchants had mobilized in support of their new community plan. Then—as in 2014—the rebellious neighborhood of Ocean Beach faced off with the city's establishment and bureaucracy over the community's direction. The parallels would be eerily pleasing to those who had witnessed both scenes—but alas, no one had, except for this writer.

Tension and excitement were high as the San Diego Council members took their seats that day in July of 2014. Attentive Council members listened to the City staff reports and public presentations. But not everyone was enjoying the excitement. Standing opposed to the plan, a handful of small property owners and their supporters were challenging some of OB's historic restrictions on development. This small caucus, however, was not the only opponent in the Chambers that day facing off with the "sea of blue." Even though its presence couldn't be physically seen, its influence clearly was. The unseen entity was the powerful San Diego Planning Commission.

A month before the City Council hearing, the Planning Commission had reviewed the Ocean Beach Plan, the last stop for the Plan before Council. This panel of prestigious mayoral appointees represented San Diego's establishment more than any other body in the City's wardrobe of quasi-government committees, boards and agencies. Often these plum positions were rewarded to favorites by a revolving door of chief executives. In the minutes before the Planning Commission took their vote, many of the Commissioners praised the "uniqueness" of Ocean Beach, the community's funkiness and rich history. Then as a body they turned 180 degrees and voted to eliminate the very tools the community has used over the decades to ensure that uniqueness. The Planning Board in Ocean Beach has utilized certain mechanisms for years to limit over-development with city approval. This mechanism has allowed OB to be a haven from the three-storied behemoths that wall off the coast in other beach neighborhoods.

Specifically, the Commissioners wanted to remove any references in the Plan to what's called the "FAR"—the floor-area ratio. The FAR represents the ratio of how much floor space is allowed in new housing structures in relation to the overall lot size. Most of Ocean Beach—and particularly its coast—has a FAR of 0.7. This means a developer can only construct a building whose total floor space is 70% of the square footage of the whole lot. This relatively low FAR for OB has in most part prevented the construction of large single-family homes along the beach or other coastal stretches of the community. In contrast, most of San Diego has a FAR of 1.0 or more. Partially because of this, many coastal neighborhoods within San Diego and other towns along the coast have been inundated with the three-story structures, with massive footprints. Still, OB remains one of the city's densest neighborhoods even with a low FAR.

When the Commissioners' vote came down, many of the leaders of the Ocean Beach organizations who had attended the hearing were shocked. An urgent meeting was held by activists back in OB to map out a strategy to counter the Planning Commission's ploy to gut the FAR. They knew a showdown approached at the upcoming City Council hearing and they needed something to mobilize the community. What they came up with was a time-honored tactic of grassroots activists, a petition—which volunteers could circulate around OB, at farmers markets and at key stores—which would explicitly counter the Planning Commission recommendations.

As activists and Plan supporters worked out the language for their petition, the scene too was very reminiscent of what happened nearly 40 years earlier, when local OB residents began to write up and circulate petitions about the Plan. It was 1975 and the earlier petition called for the democratic election of the community planning committee, something not included in the city's scheme. Clearly, then, this wasn't the first time the community of Ocean Beach had to face off with the San Diego establishment over planning issues.

The Planning Crisis of the Early 1970s— Unbridled Construction

Today OB is described by city planners as the model "urban village within a city," a very "walk-able" small community one mile square. Sitting seven miles to the northwest of downtown San Diego, it's wedged into the sandy corner of the hilly Point Loma Peninsula, with about 15,000 residents—six of every seven of whom rent.

Ocean Beach, in the late 1960s and early 1970s, found itself like much of the rest of coastal Southern California experiencing higher density and congestion—the ugly consequences of decades-long unbridled apartment construction. The construction frenzy that engulfed residents at the coast was at the end of a chapter of the modern era of urban development in San Diego, and the curtain was closing on the stage that had been set by economic forces unleashed right after World War II.

OB has always been one of the more working-class coastal neighborhoods of San Diego, with its beginnings as a cheap beach resort. OB's small, narrow bungalows—once considered seasonal structures—provided the bedrock for the housing demands of aircraft workers and military families during World War II. Once the war was over, and capital freed up, the building spree hit its zenith in the Fifties and Sixties, the virtual heyday of the San Diego building industry. It was the boom time for apartment construction across the city and especially at the coast. For instance from 1967 to 1973 in the city of San Diego, only 31 single-family houses were constructed, while during the same period developers constructed 1,610 multi-family units. In Ocean Beach apartment construction was going full tilt as developers installed two, three and even four-story boxes with as little landscaping and parking as possible. In the process they tore down many old beach "shacks" that provided low-income housing, and squeezed their new tenants—often young and college-oriented—into every available inch of space on their lots.

The apartment builders were able to do this because at that time, there was no community plan, no 30-foot height limit, no FAR, and hardly any restrictions. It's no secret that during this period, developers, contractors and the captains of the building industry owned San Diego and its politicians. The effects of this unbridled construction were deeply felt by the community, a small working-class beach town, one of the very last coastal neighborhoods where the poor, young and retired could still live.

In OB, the population swelled with all the new apartments; less parking was available because of curb cuts by developers; due to the lack of mass transit most residents still had to go to work or school outside OB, which made traffic tighter and less manageable. Concurrent with the density increase and congestion, there were strains on the old infrastructure and land, as roads, streets, bridges, the ancient sewer and water systems were challenged daily. The recreation center and library, already inadequate, were strained over their limits. The old public schools were so crammed they had to bring in mobile classrooms.

Significantly, access to the beaches and cliffs by the public, both in terms of physical ability and visually, was being restricted by the new construction. With no height or setback restrictions, people's ability to reach or even see the Pacific Ocean became a huge issue, as fences, walls and large structures blocked from the public use a natural resource held in trust for all. With the quality of life diminishing in Ocean Beach by the early Seventies, OB came face to face with this crisis—a crisis in urban planning, of identification and character of the community, and ultimately, a crisis in democracy. Quality of life issues became paramount to denizens at the coast.

The Pen, Inc. Era

Even the local establishment knew something had to be done about the haphazard and chaotic building bonanza. And into the breach stepped the Peninsula Chamber of Commerce, an ally of downtown old money, a business-oriented group that formed a non-profit called Peninsulans, Inc., or simply Pen, Inc. Designated by the city to act as the "citizen's committee," Pen, Inc. had the exclusive authority to work with the city planning department to map out an urban design plan for the development of the entire Peninsula—including Ocean Beach. By 1968, the Peninsula Community Plan was the product of this marriage of the Point Loma elite and planning bureaucrats.

But who was Pen, Inc., exactly? Generally, it was an exclusive club made up of large property and business owners, apartment developers, contractors, real estate and insurance professionals, lawyers, and bank officials. They had breakfast meetings every two weeks at 7:30 a.m., and required membership fees to join. Most of the original thirty members of Pen, Inc. would not be recognized today, yet they included people of influence; Pen, Inc.'s chairwoman was appointed to the San Diego Planning Commission; its own lawyer was appointed as a judge to the Superior Court; its ranks listed a major restaurateur—who owned the Bali Hai on Shelter Island; the local owner of a series of family-named large markets; prominent realtors and developers who owned large apartment buildings in OB. It also included a vocal leader of a militant "born again" group called the Campus Crusade for Christ, who owned income-producing property at the beach.

It was a sub-committee of Pen, Inc. that drew up the specific plans for Ocean Beach. The finalized document vetted by city planning staff was called the "Ocean Beach Precise Plan." It was truly a blueprint for development written by the local blueblood. Of the 15 members of this sub-committee, only three actually lived in OB. The vast majority did own property in OB and, in fact, three-fourths of them or their spouses owned income-producing property in the seaside village. All of them would benefit by their land and properties becoming more valuable if their blueprint was implemented.

Just what did the Ocean Beach Precise Plan call for? Central to the Plan was a brazen design that called for the demolition of cheap rentals throughout the entire northwestern portion of the community, an area that included more than six residential blocks, all to be redeveloped as a glitzy, tourist-oriented waterfront with nightclubs and hotels. High-rises were just dandy for the cliffs and rest of the coast; green lights were on for four- to five-story apartments; a marina was pictured, dredged out of OB's waterfront; a 35% population increase was projected; it called for a paved road to be developed through a local regional park at Robb Field; it favored one-way streets crisscrossing OB, and the creation of a mall for the main commercial area of OB.

When the Precise Plan was released to the public during the summer of 1971, local residents were horrified and outraged. Clearly these plans—if implemented—would drastically alter the neighborhood, changing its character from a low-income working-class beach town to a high-end beach resort for the wealthy and affluent, favoring tourists over residents. The word wasn't tossed around in those days, but this was a clear case of gentrification—urban renewal where residents displaced by the demolition of the old housing cannot afford the new housing.

The release of this urban development plan—the Ocean Beach Precise Plan—to the community represented the opening salvo in a long, drawn-out battle between Ocean Beach and the San Diego establishment, a half-decade of power plays by the city's political leadership and planning bureaucracy against the residents of this small working-class neighborhood. Yet with each power move by the city, there would be a counter-move and push-back from the community. And it would be well into the mid-1970s before OB had a development plan that satisfied most of the different elements of the village, and before it had a democratically-elected planning committee to enforce it.

The Opposition Forms

For the first time in modern OB history, a community town-hall meeting was held in August of 1971 to get the word out about the Precise Plan and about Pen, Inc. It was organized by activists from three main groups, a militant environmental group called OB Ecology Action—that had successfully led a fight against the construction of a jetty by the City and Army Corp of Engineers the previous summer—the *OB Rag*—a feisty alternative newspaper run by anti-war leftists—and third, the Save OB Committee—a network of civic and counter-culture activists.

The resistance that formed to the establishment plan didn't emerge from a vacuum. Since the early Sixties, OB had been a strange mix of college students, retirees, surfers, sailors, ecologists, beatniks and artists. By the late-1960s it had morphed into San Diego's Haight-Ashbury, akin to the San Francisco center of hippiedom. Ocean Beach has always been a mostly Anglo neighborhood, reflecting the fact that it is part and parcel of San Diego—a city that historians have considered one of the most racially-segregated in the American West during the 20th century. OB's bohemian enclave sat alongside the cramped and transient "student ghetto" that sections of OB had become, off-campus housing for the numerous and nearby colleges and universities.

There had been serious signs of youthful dissatisfaction with the status quo in OB. The police-versus-youth skirmishes of Easter Day and Labor Day 1968, the week-long Jetty Battle of the summer of 1970, and the full-scale Collier Park riot in late March 1971, which had begun as an anti-Vietnam war rally and march. It was no coincidence that many OB residents were against the Vietnam war, raging at the time, and many leaders of San Diego's anti-war movement lived in OB. With the youthful energy of the counter-culture and anti-establishment politics, grassroots activism was in the air.

Opposition to the establishment's plan formalized in the late summer of 1971 with the formation of a coalition called the OB Planning Organization. Its main function was to formulate a populist mandate to resist the Pen, Inc. plan, and it did this by taking a survey of the neighborhood's residents. A dedicated core of a dozen volunteers began the polling, going door to door in the flatlands, and up and down the hills throughout OB and parts of Point Loma, asking residents questions about density, population increases, whether high-rise buildings should be allowed, on whether they supported a building moratorium. Surveys were given to 8,500 households, and by the end, there was a return of 2,805 of those polled—a stunning and significant 33% return rate.

When the City held public meetings on the Precise Plan during that fall, OB activists pushed back with a call for a "building moratorium" in Ocean Beach—a halt to construction until a plan that reflected the community was drawn up. The Committee to Save OB, an ally of the survey-takers, began to circulate petitions calling for a halt to construction and a moratorium on building. In conjunction with these efforts, OB's alternative newspaper, the *OB Rag*, published salvos against the Plan and Pen, Inc., educating residents about the crisis, Pen, Inc.'s designs and members—and how they would be enriched if their plan went through. One special issue of the Rag was hand-distributed to several thousand households in the northern end of the community. Inside was a large "green OB" poster, a solidarity symbol against development. Soon, green OBs were popping up in windows and doors across the neighborhood.

By early spring of 1972, the massive survey had been completed, and the results were presented to the community in a town hall meeting. Substantial and impressive, the results showed: 90.4% favored the small-town character of OB; 87.3% favored the building moratorium; 83.9% agreed with the use of down zoning to control population growth; 90% believed high-rise buildings should be prohibited and 60% felt apartments should be limited to two stories (this was before the 30-foot height limit); 75% wanted more neighborhood parks; and finally 88% wanted the results of the survey to play a major role in determining a community plan.

The survey results validated the concerns of the activists, giving them a political mandate. They kept up the pressure; poll results were sent out to politicians at every level of government who represented the OB area; the petition drive for a building moratorium continued—and thousands of signatures were collected; a "Stop the Apartments" concert was organized at a local house on the cliffs—attended by 600 young people, many of whom signed the petition.

The political pressure on City Hall appeared just too great. In May 1972 the City Planning Department announced that it had canceled or postponed all meetings or workshops on the Precise Plan. A collective sigh of relief swept over the community—for the planning and construction crisis seemed to have been averted, at least temporarily. Ocean Beach had awoken—its residents and small property owners having successfully mobilized in response to the threatened onslaught of development; meanwhile, the City and Pen, Inc. had backed off. The worst was over. Or so it seemed.

The lull ended six to seven months later. To the astonishment of locals, the City declared it was making plans to push the same old Precise Plan before the San Diego Planning Commission for approval. During that same time, the City Council passed an ordinance authorizing the creation of "community planning groups" for identified neighborhoods of San Diego. Activists in OB jumped at the chance to be first in the city to exercise this initiative, and wanting no ambiguity, founded a new organization called the OB Community Planning Group (CPG). It was the 28th of February, 1973, when 80 people in the auditorium of the local elementary school formed the new group. Over the next few months and through a series of large, open meetings and democratic elections, the organization elected a permanent steering committee. Faced with this more formal opposition from a group even calling itself a "planning committee"—the City once again agreed to slow down the process and wait for input from the newly formed group.

The push and pull maneuvering between one of the largest cities in the country and one of its smallest neighborhoods began again. True to form, the city countered the formation of the new grassroots group by announcing that it was going to bring all the different disparate elements together in something called the "Committee of 12." The idea was to hammer out a planning document that everyone could support, so from July to September 1973, representatives from CPG—including this author—the Town Council, and Pen, Inc. gathered around tables in the local Recreation Center for weeks of discussions. Shepherded by city staff, the Committee reached consensus on a number of issues, and the city issued a brand new draft plan, called the "Draft Revised Precise Plan," making it public in mid-January 1974.

Activists were elated again, at least temporarily, as this was the first formal repudiation by the city of the old Precise Plan, the one drawn up exclusively by

Pen, Inc. Gone were any plans for high-rises, or any indications of a planned "mini-Miami Beach"; off the table was any plan for whole-scale gentrification in northwest OB.

In the meantime, the grassroots Community Planning Group didn't sit still; it worked to expand its base. It published a newsletter distributed throughout OB as well as position papers on planning issues; it held spaghetti dinners at the Recreation Center to raise money; it hosted a benefit movie in the old Strand Theatre attended by 500 rowdy supporters. One of the group's core beliefs was that planning issues should be decided using democratic methods. To this end, in October 1973 the group hosted a community-wide election for its steering committee. OB was divided into five districts, with each district to elect three representatives to the steering committee. Polling places were set up in front of stores around the community and when it was over a total of 639 people had voted for candidates running for the 15 seats. The organization had held a genuine grassroots election. (Of note, local architect Rob Quigley, as well as this author, were elected to the Steering Committee.)

The city had the Committee of 12 continue to meet well into 1974 in an effort to resolve a number of contentious issues, such as one-way streets (CPG opposed them), low-income housing (CPG supported it), and the key issue of democratic community-wide elections for a review panel to implement the new plan.

A progressive voting bloc emerged in the Committee of 12 when CPG members and half the Town Council reps came to an agreement on a number of issues, including elections for a planning committee. They wanted to reach out to the community in order to achieve a wider consensus on the issues. But this endeavor was stalled by Pen, Inc. and the conservative town council representatives. And once again, the city tried to out-maneuver and water down this populist push by announcing it was expanding the Committee of 12 to 16 members by allowing a fourth group to enter the negotiation process, the OB Business and Property Owners Association.

As the tale unfolds of how a small community resisted the pressures of the establishment, one key element remained at the core of the organization that led the political fight against the plans of Pen, Inc. and the city bureaucracy. The Community Planning Group, formed in early 1973, remained in the middle of the battle for the right to have a community plan reflective of the wishes of the residents. Central to this organization's demands on the power structure was the concept of using democratic elections to form a planning committee with open voting by residents and property owners. Time and time again, the Community Planning Group fought for this type of community-wide election process. It was their persistence over a three-year period that paid off, as the group pressed for this new level of urban democracy.

While it participated deeply in the negotiations during the remainder of 1974 and into the next year, the Community Planning Group had enough depth to juggle its activism and successfully respond to new construction projects—mainly large, bulky apartments—still coming down the development pipeline. Over this period CPG was able to block the construction of eight five-story high-rise apartments, most of them aimed for the fragile edges of Sunset Cliffs.

With the limited consensus reached on certain issues by the Committee of 12/16, in Spring of 1975 the city published a brand new Precise Plan—complete with a colorful cover. This was the formalization of the earlier Draft Revision and carried more weight, and again, it confirmed the city's rejection of the worst of the original plan; no mini-Miami Beach, no marina, no high-rise along the coast. Yet, still it had major faults, and activists were disappointed that there hadn't been more progress between the Draft Revision published in January 1974 and the latest version, put out over a year later.

For activists, the chief problem with the new plan was the lack of an outline for the democratic selection of representatives to a committee that would implement the Plan. The revision also allowed a 33% increase in population density over a period of time—no one wanted to see that kind of massive growth. It called for a main north–south feeder street to be made one-way and directly connect with an extension of the I-8 freeway, OB's main link with the outside. From its beginnings, CPG opposed one-way streets as they become barriers to intra-community transit, cohesion, and "neighborliness." And no one wanted to see the large under-developed sports area, called Robb Field, sliced up. Finally, it lacked any plans for the development of low and moderate income housing.

Immediately, CPG launched yet another petition drive—this one to add its own amendments to the city's new plan, amendments to nullify some of the worst of that version, and one that called for a community-wide election process for a planning committee. After three to four months, volunteers had collected a hugely substantial 3,500 signatures from locals, in a community with only about

13,000 residents. Meanwhile, the Plan had gone before the Planning Commission in April 1975 and before a City Council sub-committee in mid-June.

July 3, 1975 was the fateful day the City Council heard the OB Plan. It was standing room only in the Council Chambers, which brimmed with residents, property owners and merchants from OB. It was the scene that mirrored that "sea of blue" showdown that came four decades later. In 1975, after all the public testimony and speeches, after more discussion among the politicos, the San Diego City Council—with Republican Mayor Pete Wilson at the ceremonial helm—took a vote and passed the OB Precise Plan—and with a number of CPG's amendments. The most important—the provision for a community election of a planning committee—was included. The City Planning Department was ordered to implement a Planned District for Ocean Beach, from the motion itself:

> [T]he new committee formed for the purposes of implementing the Plan, should be elected by the citizens of Ocean Beach in a democratic fashion, using a process monitored by a neutral party to be appointed by the Mayor and Council.

This was truly an historic vote by the San Diego City Council—for never before in the history of the city had a neighborhood been authorized to hold its own special election for its local planning committee. This was to be a first for any community in the city.

OB residents and activists returned home full of hope and pride that they had won a significant victory, a victory torn from the mouths of Pen, Inc. The sheer weight of their numbers, their signatures, their petitions, their persistence over four years had upended the establishment plan for the community. The people had revolted and had forced the implementation of a never-before-allowed element of community planning—an election of local planners; it was indeed a democratic revolution in the arena of urban planning, a furtherance of democratic rights for a working-class community. Any "citizen" could vote in this OB election—even renters, and of course, OB then, as now, had lots of them.

A month and half later, the Community Planning Group returned to the City Council and presented its ideas for the community-wide election, to be monitored by the League of Women Voters. City Hall—uncertain of what to make of this democratic metropolitan revolt—went along with the idea. And for awhile, it looked like the election would coincide with the November General Election of 1975—which gave activists hope for a large turn-out. But it wasn't yet to be. It wasn't quite time for OB to get its election.

The Effort to Derail the Election of the OB Planning Board

Back at home in OB, all wasn't peace and happiness. A small group of conservative politicos, dissatisfied with the new Precise Plan, colluded on a strategy to derail the election. They went back to the City Council, complaining that the July 3 hearing had been "unfair," and vehemently insisted that the City reopen hearings on the Precise Plan. This kicked the Plan back to the Council Rules Committee.

Who was this group? It had three key players; one was a very conservative former president of the OB Town Council who became notorious in 1972 for publicly denouncing demonstrators coming to OB and San Diego for protests planned for the Republican Convention—then coming to town but later moved to Miami. Next was an older, more reclusive extremist whose mother ran a breakfast cafe on Voltaire Street in OB. Both of these men wore a small silver hangman's noose on a chain around their necks—the symbol of the Posse Comitatus—a group whose core belief holds that the elected sheriff in each county is the only true and rightful governmental authority. The third was another former president of the local town council. The three had managed to be selected as the leadership of an ad hoc coalition made up of Pen, Inc.—the originators of the Precise Plan—a sympathetic faction of the fractured Town Council, and the Merchants and Property Owners Association. They sent out letters protesting the adoption of the new Plan, and complained that 2,700 property owners had not been adequately notified of the changes. They didn't mention however that in fact all three had participated in the Committee of 16 and had been part of the process that they now criticized as being corrupt. Their maneuverings forced the City to hold additional meetings with the result being more delays in the implementation of the new OB Plan. On September 25, 1975, the City Attorney ruled that the City Council hearing on the OB Precise Plan on July 3rd of that year was fair and legal.

This didn't stop the disgruntled dissidents. The three appeared in front of the City Council itself and demanded that it reopen its hearing. On October 16th the Council met on the issue and decided that the meeting of July 3 on the OB Plan had been fair; they refused to open up the hearing on it, and in effect, the Council passed the OB Precise Plan twice—once on July 3, and then again a second time when they validated their original vote. The three struck again. On December 11th, during a routine procedure to include the OB Precise Plan into the City General Plan, an attorney representing the ad hoc coalition sought a continuance on the grounds of their opposition to a Planned District. This caused even more delays.

Election Scheduled for Early May 1976

Finally the San Diego City Council set a date for the community-wide election of OB's first planning committee: May 4, 1976. All residents, all property owners and all business owners could vote, and it would be monitored by the non-partisan League of Women Voters.

The Community Planning Group spun into action and set up a process where local residents vied to be included on an organizational slate for the election. Out of a field of 35 candidates, 14 were elected as candidates to represent the group—including this writer. Internal discussions by the group resulted in a campaign platform that the official candidates had to endorse. This platform was very idealistic, very green, populist, and way ahead of its time.

The platform called the creation of the Planning Board "a step toward community self-government," and that planning included things besides density limits and traffic designs, that "economic, social, political, environmental and cultural aspects... are just as important. In a word, people." It stated community residents "should have the right to make decisions affecting all of their lives" which "includes public utilities, health care, the police and fire departments, social services, child care, educational and recreational resources." Further, the platform set the context, stating that the group and its candidates:

> see the fight for a decent plan and environment for Ocean Beach as
> a struggle between the vast majority of the people of the commu-
> nity, who are tenants, homeowners, and... small business people,

versus the small group of wealthy elite who would like to turn our community into a playground and resort area for the rich.

It called for a system to funnel citizen complaints about city services, for staffing for the Board, declared "child care is a right" and that "health care is a right." It called upon the Board to take measures to ensure a "balanced community" to include people of various income levels, of "different ethnic and racial backgrounds" and lifestyles. The platform stated:

> We believe that our society is suffering from its present degree of racial segregation.... We support efforts to increase the racial balance of the community. We endorse an effort to recognize cases of racial discrimination in the housing market and seek legal solutions as well as less formal community efforts to abolish this discrimination.
>
> We recognize that many other communities in our society are having serious racial conflict, however, we feel that because of the more open and progressive atmosphere of Ocean Beach, this could be a community where people of diverse ethnic groups could live together "and build a real sense of community."

These progressive views enunciated in the CPG platform of 1976 reflected the maturation of a grassroots movement that had evolved from protest to now projecting a vision for "community self-determination."

These views, however, weren't accepted by all, and once the campaign started, nasty edges emerged. A hate letter signed by "the Silent Majority of OB" circulated, denouncing the election and those involved. Fear-mongering rumors were heard that the radicals were taking over. Soon after, a slate opposed to CPG was formed, which included the president of the OB Merchants Association, a couple of prominent businessmen, a former City Councilman, and some property owners.

More roadblocks were thrown in front of the election. A lawsuit was filed a few months before, seeking an injunction against the entire election procedure. It was filed by none other than the same three who had earlier attempted to halt the Plan. The suit claimed that the City Planning Department had failed to send out adequate notices to all OB residents, property owners, and business licensees; it also asserted that residents and property owners who lived east of the community should also be able to vote—as they had an interest in the election. The City's response was matter-of-fact: it used three mailing lists to ensure registered voters, property owners and business were notified, it put out multiple news releases on the election, and plastered dozens of posters around the community. The City made the point that residents throughout Point Loma and across town in the Clairemont neighborhood had an interest in the election, but they didn't get to vote either. These were winning arguments, and the judge threw the lawsuit out. The last ditch effort to forestall the election and the Plan—the inevitable—was over. It was the end of the dreams for the commercialization of Ocean Beach—the final burial of the idea of turning the neighborhood into a mini-Miami Beach.

With finally all the obstacles removed, the election and the campaigning began in earnest. CPG candidates went door to door in their districts, distributing their individualized fliers and the group's brochure. As it was an election close at home involving the very neighborhoods people lived in, interest seemed to be very high. Dozens of volunteers were enlisted and trained to manage the election, register voters, and prepare for the vote and its count. By the time election day rolled around, it had been ten months since the City Council had authorized it. And if anyone had imagined that the passage of time would wear down the level of activism in OB, they were sorely disappointed, as there was an emotional intensity cresting when May 4th, 1976 finally arrived.

The village had been divided into seven voting districts, with one to two voting sites per district, mainly in front of markets, large and small. The balloting took place all day—and at the appointed hour, ballot boxes were taken to the OB Recreation Center for counting, with everything monitored by the League of Women Voters.

When the votes came in, it was apparent that the election and its turnout had been astounding. Thousands had voted. All told, nearly 4,500 ballots were cast in this special election. With a community population of 13,000, the eligibility rolls included 6,100 registered voters, 2,100 property owners (1,100 inside the plan area and 1,000 outside the area), and 600 business license holders. In District 1 alone, 851 ballots were cast. 1,108 voted in District 2. District 3 had 755 votes. Another 1,085 voted in District 4—the business district (where this writer lost by 8 votes). The lowest turnout was in District 5—with 696 votes. These were stunning numbers.

The big news of the day: candidates from the Community Planning Group had captured eight of the 14 seats on the Board, a clear majority. Some of those elected had been involved since the beginning in the battle for OB's community plan. They included a mix of Town Council types, counter-cultural radicals and anarchists, a "socialist," professionals and small business people. The sweep by the planning group candidates was empowering and historic; a small neighborhood organization had grown to be the majority on the first planning board democratically elected in the city's history.

After the first Board was sworn in, the members selected a woman activist as its first general chairperson, and then got down to the business of figuring out to how to proceed, how to operate. That Board and those that followed over the nearly four decades provide the modern history of development in Ocean Beach. By the time the first Board was installed in 1976, it had been a long, half-decade since the very first Precise Plan had been released in the summer of 1971. Over that time, there were numerous efforts by the establishment, through the city and its planning bureaucracy, to circumvent or out-maneuver the planning activists, to downplay their populism and demands for a democratic election. And all these moves were met with countermoves by the activists that often upped the ante on the table.

When at the midpoint of 1975 City Hall finally authorized a democratic election by the community for its planning committee, the establishment had accepted the concept that ordinary working people, renters, small property owners and small businesspeople have a say in a community's development and planning. This idea had been central to the grassroots activists during the entire lengthy battle for a community blueprint. And this is part of the legacy of the first planning board to all those that came later.

Stepping back, we can see that the creation of a planning review board for this small community back in the mid-Seventies was part of the "Revolt at the Coast"—a rebellion by residents up and down Southern California and San Diego, as quality-of-life issues became overwhelmingly paramount to unbridled urban development. The "Revolt at the Coast" included the passage of the signature environmental initiative of the time, the creation of the California Coastal Commission; it included the San Diego voter-initiated 30-foot height limit passed overwhelmingly by voters from all over the city—and enforced to this day. And it included the creation of the Ocean Beach community plan and its call for a democratically-elected planning committee—setting precedent for communities all over the city. When in 1976 the very first newly-elected Board for OB was installed, it also had the distinction of being the very first in the state of California.

The OB Planning Board Still Stands

A decade and half into the new century, the OB Planning Board still meets and is fully functional, reviewing projects, their setbacks, FARs, parking and height requirements, bulk and scale of houses, and whether they fit in with the character of the neighborhood. Since its inception, literally hundreds of OB residents, property owners and businesspeople have taken turns in the seats of the Planning Board—spending thousands of hours in keeping this grassroots, citizen-initiated, democratic institution and tradition alive. It is a testament to the people and character of Ocean Beach that the Board still lives, despite apathy, burn-out, construction upswings and economic downturns.

Over the years, there have been twists and turns, as interest and excitement over development issues have waned. Every decade seemed to bring its own mini-crisis, a push in the 1980s to raise density limits was defeated, a liberal anti-development slate won in the 1990s, attempts to build an Exxon gas station were quashed, and a progressive grassroots majority held sway for a few years in the early 2000s, even voting to oppose the Iraq war in 2003.

Ever since the very first planning committee was established in Ocean Beach, other neighborhoods within the city have organized their own, and in 2015 there are over 50 community planning committees. For instance, the very diverse community of City Heights had theirs organized in the early 1990s. And the planning committee for Barrio Logan was set up during the fall of 2014.

2014: The Showdown at City Council

And, nearly four decades after the OB Community Plan was established, in an ironic twist of history, its fate was again in question. The establishment—the powers that be—in the form of the San Diego Planning Commission, tried to undermine the essence of the Plan by eliminating a powerful tool the community used to maintain its working-class character. Thirty-nine years later to the month, the Community Plan of Ocean Beach was again in front of the San Diego City Council. It was July 1975 when the Council had originally approved the concept of the Plan and its Board—and it was in July 2014, when the Council again had choices to make on the OB Plan. The Council had to decide on whether to approve the Plan—again, albeit updated, but with its original restrictions intact, or accept the recommendations of the Planning Commission and gut the tool the OB Board utilized to inhibit over-development and keep some semblance of balance.

And likewise, a very similar "united front" assembled and mobilized at the City Council—similar to the one that had been organized in the summer of 1975 that had won the Council's approval for their Plan. Now, all these years later, the residents of the exact same village, from tenants to merchants in a "sea of blue," were again in a showdown with the city's elite. The grassroots pressure had been tremendous, with even the Republican mayor coming out and publicly supporting the Plan. Thousands had signed petitions; the eloquence of community leaders that day in their deliveries before the elected officials was memorable. Tension mounted in the Chambers, as the time for the vote came due. Ed Harris, the Councilman who represented Ocean Beach made the motion to accept the Plan as is—without the Planning Commission's recommendations. Harris stated the Plan was about "putting lifestyle and community above profit" and that it was his "firm belief that the San Diego Planning Commission got it wrong. And we need to right it today." Lori Zapf, the Councilwoman who would take over his seat a few months later, seconded the motion that day, and also praised OB, saying: "I think OB is the last authentic beach town in all Southern California."

The final vote came down—it was all green lights on the video screen—it was unanimous—the entire City Council voted to approve the Plan as it was, without the recommended deletions; the Chambers erupted in yells, applause and whoops, with the clapping sustained for many minutes. Smiles flooded faces that had been tense just moments before. The joy among the blue shirts was indescribable but palatable.

Ocean Beach, that little neighborhood that hugs the coast, cliffs and hills of San Diego's western peninsula had once again bucked the establishment— and had applied enough grassroots political pressure that the politicians were emboldened enough to go up against the powerful Planning Commission. The tools used by the community's own local planners to keep some rein on overdevelopment for nearly four decades had not only been left intact but strengthened.

This decisive victory for community planners, their supporters and all the various groups that came out in support, the camaraderie and solidarity experienced over much of 2014, again had expression at the end of that year. The Town Council awarded the title of Grand Marshall of their annual Holiday Parade in December to the OB Community Plan, and coroneted the chief planning activist as "OB Citizen of the Year." A contingent of fifty people holding signs walked at the front of the Parade as the Grand Marshall, to the applause of thousands who hugged the sidewalks along the main business street for the festive event. Once again, the OB Community Plan was celebrated.

The significance of these two parallel celebrated events, separated by 40 years, the original approval of a community plan for the community in 1975, and then the much more recent confirmation of the Plan and its celebration in 2014, cannot be understated. The story of how a small neighborhood resisted the plans of the establishment, not once but twice, in recent memory, cannot be a story that is lost because those who write history don't want to tell it.

And within the larger story is the tale of how an organized group of community activists consistently fought for, demanded and mobilized for the right to hold democratic elections for the local planning committee, for the right of a neighborhood's residents, even if they are renters, to take an equal part in the planning and development decisions that affect the neighborhood.

The small planning committee for Ocean Beach became of age when quality of life and grassroots democracy were the issues at hand. And this is the legacy that the OB Planning Board and all the community organizers who were involved in its creation leave to all other planning committees, across the city, and across the state. It's a legacy that includes the story of how a small working-class community bucked the system, fought for democratic control, and saved itself by successfully beating back the plans of the establishment.

This story hasn't made the history books and even city planners—suffering from an institutional amnesia—understate its importance to this day. But the stories of these two parallel movements—a generation apart—movements that saved this small working-class community—are etched like Native American petroglyphs on its sidewalks and in the social-memories of its elders.

OB Stairs | *Kelly Mayhew*

Steve Kowit

Joy to the Fishes

I hiked out to the end of Sunset Cliffs
& climbed the breakwater,
sneakers strung over my shoulder
& a small collection of Zen poems
in my fist.
A minnow
that had sloshed out of someone's bait bucket,
& that I came within an inch of stepping on,
convulsed in agony.
Delighted to assist,
I tossed it back into its ocean:
swirling eddies sucked about the rocks,
white pythagorean sailboats
in the middle distance.
Kids raced the surf,
a labrador brought down a frisbee,
& the sun sank pendulously
over the Pacific shelf.
I shivered & descended,
slipping the unopened book
into my pocket
& walked south
along the southern California coastline—
all the hills of Ocean Beach
glowing
in the rouged light
of midwinter sunset.
Even now
it pleases me to think
that somewhere
in the western coastal waters off America
that minnow is still swimming.

Mychal Matsemela-Ali Odom
Youth's Role in a City Becoming
Education, Black Power, and the Struggles for a Different San Diego

What we now call San Diego was first explored by the Spanish in the 16th century. Initially named San Miguel in the 1600s, the name was changed to San Diego following another Spanish expedition. The first permanent Spanish settlement however was in 1769. Until today, 1769 is celebrated as the year San Diego was founded. The story of San Diego is one of conquest, contest, and resistance. Honestly, San Diego has been inhabited by human beings for at least 9,000 years. The original inhabitants of this land, the Kumeyaay people, have always called the southernmost part of Alta California home. Much of what we know as San Diego history has been written on top of and over their histories.

San Diego's most storied cultural, political, and educational institutions reflect this complex past. Its most prominent universities were carved out of former indigenous land and burial sites. Interestingly, even the mascots of its three major sports teams—the Chargers, the Padres, and the Aztecs—reflect the military power, religious imperialism, and objectification of indigenous bodies that engulf much of the local history. San Diego's premiere public attractions, Balboa Park, Old Town, the Presidio, Cabrillo Monument, and Mission San Diego, reflect how its complicated history is linked to its everyday culture and public history. In 1969, people throughout San Diego celebrated San Diego's bicentennial with no reflection on its actually much more complicated history. Yet, instead of merely reflecting the domination of people of color, San Diego's public spaces also reflect an alternative history of resistance.

San Diego's bicentennial also exposes an important year in San Diego's social movement history—notably, one of student activism, Black Power, and Chicano Power. Instead of reveling in the past, these movements were focused on the future. In 1969, young San Diegans of color—along with their allies—struggled to create a new San Diego. This was a struggle that rejected the "whitewashed adobe" of San Diego's public history and aimed to form another society which valued the polycultural history of the city and made visible the contradictions on which the popular story of San Diego as "America's Finest City" had been manufactured. The construction of this popular view of San Diego was promoted by groups such as San Diego's Chamber of Commerce and other booster groups. This boosterism resulted in San Diego being awarded two All-America City awards, one in 1962 and the other in 1969. These civic distinctions erase, or some might argue highlight, another form of San Diego's exceptionalism.

In the 1960s, San Diego was the most segregated city on the West Coast. Nowhere else were Black and white lives more separate. In 1960, fewer than twenty Black people lived in San Diego's east county and almost 90% of Black San Diegans lived in Logan Heights and its vicinity. The rest lived in or near military housing areas such as Linda Vista and the Pioneer homes in Point Loma, which were also highly segregated. San Diego also had another more positive distinction, holding the highest rate of cohabitation between African Americans and Latinos in the Southwest. From California to Texas, no other place exceeded San Diego's rate of Black and Brown cohabitation. The resistance movements of 1969 engaged both of these realities. Education and youth politics were the primary site in which this activism took place.

Though the literature on San Diego and especially "the San Diego tourists never see" is still limited—the story of African Americans is the scarcest of the literature. For this reason, this essay looks heavily at the experiences of Black youth. However, this essay is not merely a history of Black San Diego. In fact, it actively challenges the ideologies that would allow us to imagine such an easy division of the history of Greater San Diego or Logan Heights/Southeast San Diego, where most of these events took place in 1969. In fact, all the events discussed in this essay remind us of the multiracial and relational history of this period in history. Education is a central theme to this essay because for all Americans it is the primary place in which they engage politics and citizenship. Remembering that it was not until the 1970s that the voting age was lowered to 18, it is a fact that in the 1960s education was the only place students could directly engage structural change in society. As we will see with the Lincoln High School walkouts of 1969, through education they battled residential segregation, biased policing, immigration policy, and the misrepresentation of the history of Black and Brown people.

Primary and secondary education students have largely remained invisible in Black freedom movement literature. When made manifest, as with the tales from *Brown v. Topeka Board of Education* to Selma, "they often function as walk-on players...but [are] not treated as serious political players."[1] Nevertheless, these student activists, through their actions and demands, articulated a challenge to the legacy of inequality in San Diego. The mobilization of high school students especially is an important place to begin to understand a larger history of struggles over education but also over political power. By examining the Black San Diegan experience, we see that students' demands reflected both ideology and practicality. They insisted upon education that reflected their history and cultural values but also adequately prepared them for the world—central to this was access to higher education. While students might have lived in racially homogenous neighborhoods and homes, their schools remained racially mixed. Through their alliance with ethnic Mexican students, student activism forces historians to reconsider the way both Black student and Black Nationalist politics were couched. This essay chronicles three important periods in the late 1960s: the creation of a cultural center, the formation of San Diego's first homegrown Black Nationalist organization, and student protest at Lincoln High School. These events present a challenge to the public history of San Diego.

Africa House

Opened in November 1964, the Africa House Cultural Center in the Logan Heights area, located at 438 South 37th Street, represents an early effort to organize youth for changes in education. "When a child is born...we would

---

1   This essay agrees with Jeanne Theoharis' proposition about the importance of understanding Black high school student activism as both a continuation of civil rights activism and complication of Black Power activism. However, this study adds to Theoharis' work by addressing the links of San Diego's walkout with Black Studies struggles. Jeanne Theoharis, "'W-A-L-K-O-U-T!': High School Students and the Development of Black Power in L.A." In *Neighborhood Rebels: Black Power at the Local Level*, edited by Peniel Joseph (New York: Palgrave MacMillan, 2010), 109.

like it to be here at the Africa House. In its work or play, as the child grows to adulthood, we want that work or play a part of this project and when that man or woman passes, let it be here—at the Africa House," the head of the African House Fine Arts and Cultural Guild, Eugene Peters, noted in his opening address.[2] Though it was a new organization, the Africa House maintained ideological and personal connections to an older Black Nationalist organization in San Diego called the Afro-American Association. In fact, the head of San Diego's chapter of the Afro-American Association (AAA), Joshua Von Wolfolk, attended the Africa House's grand opening.[3]

The Africa House embraced a diasporic and internationalist framework—the opening was attended by students and officials from Africa, Saudi Arabia, the West Indies, Panama, Mexico and other nations—while understanding the need for pragmatic professional training.[4] The structure contained a lecture room titled Exodus Hall and Paul L. Dunbar Fine Arts Gallery; the Africa House was also organized as a library and dormitory for visiting African students. The hosted lectures emphasized "the history of the Black Man in both America and Africa." However, Africa House also scheduled a 20-part course in Spanish taught by Chicana activist and former El Congreso member Julia Usquiano. With Usquiano as an instructor, the Africa House signified the long-standing relationship between Black and Brown people in Logan Heights. It also underscored the diasporic and international conceptualization of Africa House's meaningful curriculum. Indeed, proficiency in Spanish was central to the future success of Black students. In this accord, the Africa House also offered electronics classes. Offering Spanish and electronics courses alongside

---

2 "Sneak Preview Staged: Africa House Goal Told by Director," *Independent*, Logan Heights Edition, 11/19/1964, A1, Harold K. Brown Papers, Box 7 Item 10, SDSU Special Collections and University Archive.

3 Ibid. "Freedom Theater to Debut Play," *San Diego Union* 5/16/1965, E3. "Freedom Theater Presents Variety Show Today," *San Diego Union*, 8/22/1965, A13. Peters was also a member of the Freedom Theater Arts Guild, an urban theater company with which another local Black Power activist and CORE member, Ambrose Brodus, was also affiliated. As with the AAA, the Freedom Theater utilized public spaces—community centers, parks and schools—for their productions. Brodus later started his own local Black Power group called Soul Brothers and was a member of the San Diego Black Federation. It was later discovered that Brodus was also the minister of information for the local Black Panther cadre.

4 "Sneak Preview Staged: Africa House Goal Told by Director," *Independent*, Logan Heights Edition, 11/19/1964, A1, Harold K. Brown Papers, Box 7 Item 10, SDSU Special Collections and University Archive.

exhibits and history classes, the need for technical training was not divorced from the need for classical education nor was aesthetic art separated from propaganda in the Africa House.

The Africa House underscores the centrality of youth organization to the development of Black Power in San Diego and its implications on education struggles. While the Africa House, like the AAA, was dominated by young adult men, its structure and influence offered the place for future youth mobilization and much of the labor was performed by women of color. The city directory documents Africa House's existence until 1968. Yet, oral history suggests that its success came from its alternate role as an after-hours social space. Activists used these social events to fundraise for the daytime operations and promote Black consciousness. In fact, the longtime San Diego activist Vernon Sukumu remembers attending an after-hours event at the Africa House while he was still involved in the street life, and encountering Walter Kimble (Kudumu)— Kimble was a young member of the AAA. Interrupting the music and dancing, Kimble took to the microphone and addressed the crowd for about an hour on a variety of issues pertaining to African and African American politics and history. Be it at the official cultural and vocational events or the social gatherings, the Africa House moved this local movement out of the homes and parks to an education center. This campus was meant to represent Black culture and history as well as prepare to people for the future.

Black Power and San Diego

The national turn toward Black Power organizing, in 1966, made efforts at promoting "organizational unity" easier in San Diego. In spring 1966, Harold Brown, the chair of the San Diego Congress of Racial Equality and AAA member, organized the Black Conference. The Black Conference promoted cooperative activism by bringing Black organizations of diverse ideologies— even the Urban League and NAACP—under one umbrella.[5] The Black Conference represented an effort to organize the community across class, gender and age. Through this united front, the Black Conference brought together

---

5 Scot Brown, *Fighting for US: Maulana Karenga, the Us Organization, and Black Cultural Nationalism* (New York: New York University Press, 2005), 88. The organizational principles were similar to the Black Congress of Los Angeles, which Scot Brown identifies in his text.

The San Diego Community Patrol Against Police Brutality. The first three
members, Vernon Fontenette, Albert Heisser and Walter Kimble became
founders of San Diego's Us Organization chapter. (Vernon Sukumu Private
Collection)

and trained the next generation of local activists. The Black Conference's most
renowned young affiliate, Angela Davis, aligned with the group during her
graduate studies at University of California San Diego from 1967 to 1969.
During this time, Davis was known to many by the Swahili name Tamu
(meaning sweet), which she was given by another Black Conference member,
Vernon Sukumu.[6] However, in 1966, the Black Conference brought together
Sukumu (then known as Vernon Fontenette), Albert Heisser (Kazi), Joseph
Vinson (Chochezi) and Walter Kimble (Kudumu)—Kimble had previously
been a member of the AAA.[7] While heading the Black Conference, Brown
also directed the Self-Help Through Neighborhood Leadership community
action program. Primary to the leadership training was the objective to "instill
pride in being a Negro or a member of any racial minority" in its 35 "indigenous leaders" and, among many of its commitments, "to seek solutions to
de facto segregation in the San Diego School System."[8] Black Conference

6 Vernon Sukumu Interview. "Interview with Angela Davis," Eyes on the Prize II Interviews.
http://digital.wustl.edu/e/eii/eiiweb/dav5427.0115.036marc_record_interviewer_process.
html (accessed 3/1/2013).

7 Community Patrol Newspaper Clipping from Vernon Sukumu's Private Collection.

8 "Self-Help Through Providing Neighborhood Leadership," p. 3, Harold K. Brown Papers, Box 2

member Walter Kudumu was a training supervisor for the program.[9] As Robin Kelley notes, while War on Poverty programs like the leadership training as well as the Neighborhood Youth Corps project led by Leon Williams, and by extension the state-funded Teen Post, "might have failed to reverse the deteriorating conditions for the black poor, it ultimately played an important role in mobilizing them...and providing poor residents a greater voice in the affairs of certain social agencies."[10]

Union-Tribune Protest

A SCENE from a rally held last Friday at San Diego City College protesting editorial and hiring practices. The rally was sponsored by the Black Conference and was attended by about 75 students and faculty. Speakers included Joseph Vinson, Harold Brown, Clarence Irving, Vernon Fontenette, Walter Kimble, Albert Heiser and another City College student. The Conference has requested area stores to cease selling the Union-Tribune and residents to cease paying for the newspaper until more minority persons are hired and more minority news is printed. The boycott is now over a month old.

Led by Hal Brown and Joseph Vinson, members of the Community Patrol protest the Union-Tribune at San Diego City College. (Vernon Sukumu Private Collection)

In April 1966, the Black Conference organized the first "Unity and Leadership Conference," a three-day event held from the fourteenth through the sixteenth at Southcrest Park. The organizing committee consisted of veterans Harold Brown, John Johnson of the Urban League, and Tom Johnson of the NAACP. Still predominantly male, the Black Conference saw more women's participation than earlier efforts. Jacqueline Meshack, a long-time organizer, and La Verne Webb were two of the five women on the organizing committee. Sukumu and Vinson were the younger members on the committee. The convention was held at Southcrest Park because of the space it provided. The basketball court was used as an auditorium and the smaller rooms

Folder 7, SDSU Special Collections and University Archives.

9 Jamie Bryson, "Foreign Students Briefed on SD Racial Problems," *San Diego Union*, 12/29/1967, B3.

10 Robin D.G. Kelley, "Birmingham's Untouchables," *Race Rebels: Culture, Politics and the Black Working Class* (New York: The Free Press, 1994/1996), 95.

Speaking to the nearly 500 people gathered at Mountain View Park last Friday was Sukumu, San Diego State Black Student Union head. The program consisted of readings, speeches and music. Other speakers were Shaka, Cochezi, Tom Johnson (NAACP) and Jackman Le Blanc.
—Voice Staff Photo

Vernon Sukumu speaking at a Black Conference event held at Mountain View Park, 1968. Future city councilman, George Stevens (Shaka) was then a Conference member, Us ally and head of CORE. (Sukumu Collection)

were used for the break-out sessions.[11] Later named the Black Unity Conference, the meetings became an annual event. The 1967 conference hosted speeches from State Senator Mervyn Dymally, State Assemblyman William Greene and Ron Karenga of the Us Organization. The three-day event was attended by 1,000 people.[12] In his talk, Dymally urged the need for quality employment, affordable housing and better education.

The younger members of the Black Conference—Chochezi, Sukumu, Kudumu, and Kazi—formed the Community Patrol Against Police Brutality, the de facto militant wing of the Black Conference. In 1967, these members merged with Ron Karenga's Us Organization; Karenga had been a frequent speaker at the Black Conference meetings on Sundays at the park.[13] Chochezi was the founding chair but was succeeded by Sukumu when Chochezi left the organization the following year. As Us members, their work retained a connection to past efforts while adopting Us practices of consciousness raising. Like the Afro-American Association and the Black Conference, they continued to hold Sunday educational sessions at the park. They also administered their own learning center, the School of Afro-American Culture, from the Neighborhood House located at 44th and Market Street. On Saturday mornings they taught fifty boys and girls between ages 3 and 13 Swahili, Black history and literature,

---

11 Sukumu Interview.
12 "1,000 to Attend—3 to Talk at Negro Parley," *San Diego Union*, 4/15/1967, B3.
13 "Community Patrol Against Police Brutality Clipping," *The Voice*, 6/22/1967. CPAPB Union Tribune Protest Clipping. Vernon Sukumu Private Collection. "Black Power Talk Given," *San Diego Union*, 8/7/1967, B3. Brown, *Fighting for US*, 44.

African songs and African dances. Youth were trained as members of the *Simba Wachanga* (Young Lions) and the *Umoja* (Unity) and *Taifa* (Nation) dance troupes. Gender bias was prevalent in the Us Organization and as Angela Davis notes, when she helped organize with the Black Conference in San Diego she was criticized by Us members as "doing a man's job."[14] Despite Ron Karenga's writings that equated the women's role as submissive and complementary, as opposed to equal, to Black men, women in the Us Organization nevertheless made their own place and even challenged the misogynist ideologies of the male leaders. For females, known as the *muminina*, like Patricia Salimu, vice-president of San Diego State's Black Students' Council, and Maisha Kudumu, "the

School of Afroamerican Culture became one of the larger outlets for women's activism."[15]

The San Diego Us Chapter changed its name to the National Involvement Association (NIA) Cultural Organization. In Swahili, Nia means purpose. They still endorsed the Kawaida philosophy but aligned with Amiri Baraka's Congress of Afrikan People. Sukumu became the Western Regional head of CAP. (Sukumu Collection)

These were not top-down attempts to organize alienated and "impulsive followers"—as they are often described—but instead critical sites of youth autonomy and strategic planning.[16] Kazi served as the director of the local Teen Post One. With 200 members from the ages of 13 to 20, the center was run by the youth. With pool tables, arts and crafts classes and weightlifting, it offered an important place of recreation and self-governance for adolescents. For students like Otis Crockett, Teen Post was

14 Angela Davis, *Angela Davis: An Autobiography* (New York: International Publishers, 1974/1988), 161.

15 Jamie Bryson, "Negro Group Us Adopts Africa," *San Diego Union*, 3/4/1968, B1. "New School Stimulates Black Pupils," *San Diego Union*, 8/29/1974, B3. Scot Brown, *Fighting For US*, 56-57.

16 Theoharis, "'W-A-L-K-O-U-T,'" 109.

also where they began careers in political activism.[17] Students of Teen Post were taught about Black Power and trained around a plethora of progressive issues.[18] Such youth-centered efforts to reach the youth materialized into the creation of a youth-specific annual conference.

In spring 1968, the very first Black Youth Conference was organized at Southcrest Park. Albert Kazi was a co-chair of the conference and the theme was the "Youth's Role in a Nation Becoming." The idea was to allow for a forum where the youth could directly address their specific issues. As with the Black Unity Conferences, the Black Youth Conference was a weekend event, with registration held on March 1st and the workshops on March 2nd and 3rd. The Black Youth Conference attracted 1,000 attendees. Some of the workshop titles

Blur of Umoja Dance Company is reflected during performance yesterday at National Involvement Association's Community Cultural Center. There was singing, dancing and poetry.

San Diego Us/Nia Cultural Organization used the arts to organize and train the youth. Here the Umoja dancers perform the South African boot dance. The boot dance later influenced African American stepping. (Sukumu Collection)

were: "How to Build and Control the Black Community," "Black Consciousness," "Black Is Beautiful," "Police Brutality," and "Education as a Means." There was also a workshop solely on Black History.[19] Karenga, San Francisco State Black Student Union President Jimmy Garrett, John Floyd of Los Angeles' Black Panther Political Party and Joseph Chochezi all spoke. Karenga, who had

17 Jamie Bryson, "Teen Post 1—Center Means Many Things to Youths," *San Diego Union*, 10/1/1967, H1. Harold Keen, "It's Sock It to 'Em Time," *San Diego Magazine*, (April 1968), 52. Crockett went on to establish an anti-drug campaign in Southeast San Diego. However, his activism also made him and others associated with Teen Post frequent targets of police repression.
18 "Black Power Talk Given," *San Diego Union*, 8/7/1967, B3.
19 "Black Confer," *Good Morning Teaspoon*, 2/28/1968, 4. SDSU Special Collections and University Archives Digital Collection. Brian Behnken, "Introduction" in *The Struggle in Black and Brown: African American and Mexican American Relations During the Civil Rights Era* edited by Brian Behnken (Lincoln: University of Nebraska Press, 2011), 1-3.

the previous fall attended the Alianza conference in Albuquerque and signed the "Treaty of Peace, Harmony, and Mutual Assistance," urged the Black youth to give their movement "a shot in the arm" by uniting with Chicanos to fight against "the real enemy... the white races."[20]

The next month, Sukumu organized the first of many Kuzaliwa celebrations in honor of Malcolm X's birthday. In February they had convened a Dhabihu (sacrifice) in remembrance of his slaying. As Scot Brown notes, the public holidays created by the Us Organization reflected Black calls for commu-

Sukumu and his son at a Kuzaliwa celebration at Southcrest Park in the mid-1970s. (Sukumu Collection)

nity control and unity.[21] Yet for students from elementary through college, where these holidays had the largest resonance, these cultural events became a way to defy the most basic but fundamental of public school policies—attendance. The 17 May 1968 Kuzaliwa organized by Sukumu, San Diego Us and the Black Conference resulted in a de facto walkout. That Friday, 1,500 Southeast students skipped junior high school and high school classes and attended the festival at Mountain View Park.[22] San Diego became known for hosting the largest Kuzaliwa celebrations through the late 1970s. This eventually forced the district to close the Southeast schools for Malcolm X celebrations.[23] While such educational and cultural work challenged the administration of public education by providing alternative instruction and on some instances removing mass amounts of students, these students produced their own articulate critiques of the school system.

---

20 Ken Hudson, "Negro-Mexican Alliance Pushed," *San Diego Union*, 3/3/1968, B6.
21 Brown, 75.
22 "Negro Students Mark Birthday," *San Diego Union*, 5/18/1968, B3.
23 It is my contention that the cultural events and official student walkouts acted as general strikes that both removed the most valuable labor from the school system while calling for further democratization of public education.

The Other Lincoln High School Walkouts

Through cultural production and public discourse, students criticized the limited progress in educational reforms since the early 1960s. In 1968, KEBS (now KPBS), San Diego's public broadcasting television station, aired a three-hour documentary chronicling the issues of "academic and counseling preparedness" at Lincoln High School titled "Nobody Knows the Trouble I Had." The third segment, a dialogue between students and counselors revealed efforts to improve public education in San Diego by groups such as the Citizens Committee for Equal Educational Opportunities years earlier. As a result, students and community members became further radicalized.[24] If there were any advances, they had only come in "the last year or two," the students felt. Mostly though, faculty and administrators retained negative views of Black student aptitude and aspirations.[25] Describing what was referred to as being "counseled down," one student explained, "The counselors degrade you, channel you down.... This type of thing boils down to the same ole racist bag. Blacks are suppose[d] to be inferior and teachers actually teach you to be inferior psychologically."[26] One student actually remembered being told not to attend UCSD, despite being offered a scholarship. To counter such attitudes, students began to support themselves.[27] These students actually began to teach younger African American children. One student stated, "This summer I taught young black kids. This first thing we did was make sure that the student had a positive identity of himself: (1) This is a feeling of pride, a feeling that he can learn.... (2) These kids were only 6 or 7, but they already had feelings of ingrained inferiority."[28] As a part of the change needed, the students suggested that teachers and counselors at Lincoln be educated in Black history. The students also saw the need for more African American teachers and counselors but noted a difference between "Negro" teachers and "Black" teachers. Negro teachers "know no more about their culture than [whites] do."[29]

On Friday 11 April 1969, this discourse turned to action, and for the next ten days the students at Lincoln High School united to wage the most effective

24 CIC, "Part IV," *Special Report on Education* (1968).
25 CIC, "Part IV," p. 5 & 1.
26 Ibid, 1-2.
27 Ibid, 2.
28 Ibid, 5.
29 Ibid, 6.

challenge to educational disparity. That morning, San Diego Abraham Lincoln High School senior Roy Lee Johnson arrived late and was not permitted to enter his classroom but was instead ordered to the principal's office.[30] According to Lincoln's regulations, an admittance slip was required for exceptionally late students. While sitting in the principal's office awaiting disciplinary action, Johnson decided to leave the office. At approximately 8:40 a.m., Johnson arose, left the main building and dashed across the campus to the campus auto body shop.[31] At the auto body shop, he met with fellow students including another senior, Frank White. Expressing his anger about the situation, Johnson asked for a tool he could carry with him back toward the administration building—White suggested a pry bar.[32] Johnson initially intended to return to his classroom and hit his teacher but instead ran through the halls using the pry bar to break windows and the main display case. While Johnson was ultimately persuaded to cease by fellow students, the commotion caused other students to leave their classes. At around 9 a.m. one of these students pulled the fire alarm, and the remainder of the 1,000-plus student body left their classes. For the rest of the day, about 250 students gathered on the campus patio, refusing to return to class.[33] This was the beginning of a ten-day protest which also spread to other local high schools.

The administration, school board and law enforcement depicted this protest as an isolated incident when in reality it followed a decade of struggles over inclusion and equity in San Diego. At Lincoln, Black teachers such as mathematics instructor Alfreda Smith had secretly supported the idea of student walkouts, as they had the parents' protests years before but had been unable to act. As elementary-aged children in the early 1960s, these teenagers had matured in the movement and served as a vital connection between civil rights, Black Power and higher education activism. What is more, the genuine links between Black and Chicano students in this protest offer a story rarely told about Black and Chicano freedom struggles.[34] In an interview, Carroll Waymon stated that

30 "School Hit by Walkout, Mass Rally," *San Diego Union*, 4/12/1969, B2.
31 Ibid.
32 Personal Conversation with Frank White, December 2012.
33 "School Hit by Walkout, Mass Rally," *San Diego Union*, 4/12/1969, B2.
34 I agree with Jeanne Theoharis' assessment of Los Angeles walkouts that suggests that Black high school student walkouts complicate our understanding of Black Power's development through its connections with civil rights as well as Chicano activism. Theoharis, "'W-A-L-K-O-U-T,'" 109.

the protest was caused by "the inability of the school district and the school board... to hear the parents and the students over the five to eight years and what they were saying about the schools."[35] In this instance, the students became the leaders for educational change in Black San Diego while older activists played a secondary role. Then head of CORE and Black Conference member, George Stevens (at that time known as Shaka Zulu) issued CORE's public support for the students that Friday.[36] Bob Russell, a former school teacher and president of the Black Educators of San Diego, also gave the students their backing.[37] The CIC, NAACP and Urban League participated as mediators. Members of the Us Organization, Black Panthers and Brown Berets ensured the safety of the students.

Just blocks away, Mountain View Park became the gathering point for the students. On the first day, African American and Chicano students drafted a list of 22 demands which they ordered be met before they returned to campus. The core of the list mandated better education, including Black Studies and Chicano Studies curricula, decreased policing of student mobility and more equitable administrative policies. They also demanded control over the programmatic and culinary operations of the school. Students demanded better education. Articulating a "Third Worldism" generally ascribed to colleges like San Francisco State or groups like the Black Panthers, these demands also engaged transnational policy. These students demanded a school that reflected the diversity of their cultures and their histories but also their region.

The first demand was for "higher education standards"; the seventh demanded "an education relevant to Black and Brown students"; the seventeenth demanded that the school stop "taking the cast-off books of other schools," and the nineteenth demand ordered that "Black and Brown studies" classes count toward graduation credit.[38] As the students had already been in contact with the Afro-American Association, the Black Conference and the Us Organization's initiatives, been taught by Bob Russell and others in school and

---

35 "Lincoln: Racial Crisis in San Diego Schools?" *CURE* Newsletter, Vol. 1 Number 2 (May 1969). Citizens United for Racial Equality Papers, Box 2 Folder 14. SDSU Special Collections and University Archives.

36 "School Hit by Walkout, Mass Rally," *San Diego Union*, 4/12/1969, B2.

37 "Stern Action Promised at Lincoln High," *San Diego Union*, 4/14/1969, B1.

38 "Lincoln Student Walkout," Leon Williams Papers, Box 107 Folder 13. San Diego State University Special Collections and University Archive.

knew of the teacher training the CIC tried to implement, change would only require the school board to act on proposals that had laid at their feet for five years. With demands three and four, the students moved beyond the classroom and asserted the right to programmatic control over campus events, and the fourteenth point mandated: "That there be more holidays to honor black and brown heros [*sic*]." As opposed to someone who would "tell us only what the administration wants us to hear," it was necessitated that students regulate cultural events and guest lectures. Their demands crossed the lines of ethnicity as well as radical formations. With the fifth demand, students called for Black Panther Kenny Denmon, Us member Albert Kazi, and Mexican American Youth Association leaders Carlos LaGerrette and Bert Rivas to be advisors on campus. They also requested that Black Panthers, Us members and Brown Berets replace the campus police.[39]

Far from superficial, the seemingly mundane nature of some of the demands is a testament to the systemic problem the students challenged. The ninth demand ordered "better food standards" and "Black and Brown cooks."[40] Locally, food services had already been a tool for political engagement with the Black Panthers, with their free breakfast program administered from the predominantly-Black Christ the King Catholic Church and the Us Organization's weekend school.[41] Hence, with the ninth demand the students engaged economic circumstances and ideological shifts. As the League of Women Voters reported five years earlier, Blacks went virtually unemployed in the kitchen staff of Black schools—the students addressed that discrepancy. However, beyond employment, the ninth point represented the attempt to generate policy and structure which affirmed students' value systems. Reimaging foodways was how Black activists asserted a new consciousness and challenged old ones. In the 1960s, African American cuisine became known as "soul food," but instead of its genesis being in slavery the origins were traced to African traditions.[42] Elijah Muhammad, as early as the 1950s, mandated new dietary practices as necessary for conversion—beyond traditional Muslim restrictions, many of the items

---

39 Ibid.
40 Ibid.
41 "Black Panther Friends Hold Rally Here," *San Diego Union*, 7/11/1969, B2.
42 William Van Deburg, *New Day in Babylon: The Black Power Movement and American Culture, 1965-1975* (Chicago: University of Chicago Press, 1992), 201-203.

Muhammad forbade, such as collard greens and catfish, were meant to unfasten African Americans from southern and slave traditions.[43] However, Dick Gregory later countered by suggesting that the food slaves ate, "soil food," was organic vegetables and fruits as well as dairy-free. While there was no official doctrine, cultural nationalists such as Vernon Sukumu promoted Afrocentric vegetarian diets.[44] To create a more equitable educational experience meant modifications at all levels.

With their critique of the dietary options, the students articulated a keen evaluation of immigration policy and its effects on local administration. The policing of the schools, as with Johnson's tardy violation, was connected to the militarization of the borders and the constraints on immigrant students. The tenth point mandated that students be allowed to leave campus during lunch because of the poor food selection while the eleventh demand ordered that students on immigrant visas not be forced to return to Mexico because of their dissatisfaction with the school system.[45] Historian Martha Biondi notes that the Black Studies movement was always internationalist and critical of American Exceptionalism and that in places like "Los Angeles and San Diego, Black student leaders welcomed" Third Worldist efforts to educational reform.[46] While Lincoln was a predominantly Black school, ethnic Mexican students made up most of the remainder of the student body. Evinced in these demands, African American and ethnic Mexican students took seriously the calls for alliance and mutual struggle (in fact, off-campus a group called Black-Oriental-Mexican-Brothers (BOMB) was created).[47] Reconfiguring how the story of Black and Latino educational struggles have been told, these students displayed continuity with past struggles in San Diego and the contemporary alliances being made on the college campuses. The biased policing of Johnson,

43 Edward E. Curtis, IV, *Black Muslim Religion in the Nation of Islam, 1960-1975* (Chapel Hill: University of North Carolina Press, 2006), 98.

44 Doris Witt, "From Fiction to Foodways: Working at the Intersections of African American Literary and Culinary Studies," in *African American Foodways: Explorations of History and Culture* edited by Anne L. Bower (Urbana and Chicago: University of Illinois Press, 2007), 114-116.

45 "Lincoln Student Walkout," Leon Williams Papers, Box 107 Folder 13. San Diego State University Special Collections and University Archive.

46 Biondi, 249-250, 265.

47 Leroy E. Harris, "The Other Side of the Freeway: A Study of Settlement Patterns of Negroes and Mexican Americans in San Diego, California" (Ph.D. diss., Carnegie-Mellon University, 1974), 106, 137, 139, and 144.

a Black student, on campus produced a public discussion on education and immigration policy.

The Lincoln Walkouts represented a struggle for equal education in Greater San Diego. A parents committee that was formed insisted that the boycott of Lincoln High School be extended to all Southeast San Diego schools if the school board did not address the need for change at all schools servicing Black and Brown students.[48] Significantly, these students demanded "a change in the attitudes of the faculty and administration" but actually did not request a mere shift in hiring policy.[49] While not all of their demands were met, they provoked the most immediate reaction by the school board and achieved, in ten days, what the community had struggled for throughout the decade. On May 7th, Dr. Ernest Hartzog, a local educator and former San Diego State star, became Principal of Lincoln High School, making him the first Black principal in San Diego.[50] While not as radical as Harold Brown and many of his other friends, he had long worked with San Diego's youth of color, since his graduation from college. A week later, Hartzog announced former Charger Earl Faison as the first Black head football coach for Lincoln.[51] By the next February, Lincoln Black Student Union president Dianna Toliver admitted that some change had occurred but more was still needed. "It's been like moving up steps but I sure didn't realize last spring how many steps there had to be." Some of the demands, such as a guarantee that the police would not be called, more holidays and an open campus were not met. However, Black Studies and Chicano Studies classes were implemented. What is more, additional people of color were added to the non-teaching staff, the food was improved, and facilities were made available for student use.[52] That February a fifty-student ensemble presented a performance on the history of Black people from Africa to America in the school's auditorium.[53]

---

48 "A Planned Response From the Community When School Opens," Citizens United for Racial Equality Papers, Box 2 Folder 14, SDSU Special Collections and University Archive.

49 "Lincoln Student Walkout," Leon Williams Papers, Box 107 Folder 13. San Diego State University Special Collections and University Archive.

50 Charles Davis, "Principal at Lincoln, Aide Gets New Posts: Transfers Effective at Once," *San Diego Union*, 5/7/1969.

51 "Faison Gets Hornets Jobs," *San Diego Union*, 5/17/1969, C2.

52 Ken Hudson, "Lincoln Student Leader Accepts Gradual Change," *San Diego Union*, 2/10/1970, B1.

53 John Stewart, "Negro History Presented at Lincoln High," *San Diego Union*, 2/10/1970, B1.

Conclusion

In 1969 local business and civic leadership celebrated San Diego's exceptionalism. By 1969 San Diego had been honored with two All-America City awards. As well, on 16 July 1969, the bicentennial was a cause for rejoicing and multiple public ceremonies. However, not all San Diegans were celebrating. Instead, these celebrations underscored the contradictions in Greater San Diego's society. In Logan Heights and beyond, African Americans and Mexican Americans, as well as their allies, mobilized in opposition to the history San Diego publicly celebrated. In fact, that summer, the local movement took a more radical step as Black and Brown community members openly challenged the legacy of racial segregation and conquest in San Diego. While many people know about the Chicano Park movement which began partially in response to the construction of the Coronado Bridge in the summer of 1969, few people know about what is officially known as the Mountain View Park Disturbance. As noted in this essay, one way in which people in Logan Heights challenged the de facto segregation in San Diego was by converting the public parks into political and cultural rallying points. While many public parks and tourist attractions beyond the vicinity of Logan Heights remained off limits to Black and Brown people, places such as Mountain View Park (often called Oceanview Park) and Southcrest Park became important meeting points. Political rallies, athletic contests, and everyday cultural events were a common occurrence at the neighborhood parks. Located on Oceanview Boulevard in close proximity to Lincoln High School, Mountain View was the most popular destination for African American families. It was a normal occurrence for thousands of people to pack the park on Sunday afternoon.

This high density of Black people also attracted police surveillance and harassment. While the community relaxed, listened to music, and barbecued, scores of San Diego police officers would observe from the hills and across the street. Oftentimes they would descend upon the park, breaking up crowds. The youth, and especially the lowriders, were the primary targets of police abuse. On Sunday, 13 July 1969, local residents fought back against that repression. That Sunday, the police attacks were met with a militant response from the community. Following the police attack on a lowrider, a crowd of "mainly youths…surged out of the park" and began to fight the police around 5:30 that evening. By 7 p.m.

over 200 officers had been deployed to the area as San Diego's urban rebellion escalated. With a crowd estimated at around 500, youth exchanged gunfire and Molotov cocktails with the police. The public response to police harassment was reported by all accounts as swift and organized. Also, just like the protests at Lincoln and the Black Youth Conference, this community struggle was largely Black but not entirely Black. Just like a local uprising two years earlier, Chicanos were among the crowds of protestors. This resistance however was not contained; reports suggest that it spread toward College Grove, a few miles northeast of Logan Heights. For the next ten days, as the city celebrated its bicentennial, Logan Heights and Southeast San Diego remained under occupation by local police forces as skirmishes persisted.

Like the struggles over education, the Mountain View Park Disturbance is an important part of San Diego's public history that has been forgotten, lost, or hidden. It offers an alternative relationship between citizens and local government. It also shows the importance of youth to the local struggles for equality. In actuality, the rebellion did not begin at Mountain View Park. It was instead a part of a long history of community response to exclusion in San Diego—exclusion from public resources and local history. With the exception of the African House, all of the places discussed in this essay still exist and many of the activists are still alive. The goal of this essay is to bring the people, places, and events back into public consciousness. It is my hope that the readers of this essay actively engage this history as I have.

Michael Billingsley

The Civil Disobedient

The morning of January 15, 1976 started out just like any other in the Skyline neighborhood of southeast San Diego, but there were two special things that set this day apart. For one, it was the day before my 14th birthday. Second, it was the birthday of Dr. Martin Luther King Jr.

There had been a movement to make MLK's birthday a national holiday—in fact, African Americans all over the country started celebrating before it became a legal holiday. One of the things that appealed to me was that my birthday was on January 16, one day after Dr. King's and the day before Muhammad Ali's. Civil Rights had been a favorite topic of mine because of growing up in San Diego and living in predominantly white Pacific Beach followed by Skyline, a largely African American community and then being bused to school in Anglo Serra Mesa. I saw firsthand how blacks were treated differently from one side of town to the other. My parents came from Birmingham, Alabama in the 1930s to '50s. They were not vocal activists, yet they never stopped reminding us how different life for us would be as black people, especially in dealing with police and authority figures.

I used to question my mother about life under the Jim Crow and segregation laws, but her answers stayed vague. It wasn't until years later that I realized this was a sore subject for her. One day while watching old news footage of the police in Birmingham using dogs and fire hoses to control black protesters, she said, "There he is." When I asked, "Who?" She said nothing else, but a tear was about to fall from her eye. The more I snooped all I would find out was that many of those were her neighbors and close relatives. In 1955, my father left Birmingham to join the U.S. Navy where he served the next 20 years. As much as I admire those who fought for equal rights, I must say people like my parents were also heroes for protecting their families and securing a good future for all.

But on that day in 1976, without the knowledge of my parents, I planned to ditch school for a special event. Luckily I lived in Skyline and only had to walk about two miles to Martin Luther King, Jr. Park to take part in my first expression of civil disobedience. After pretending to leave for school, I met up with my friends and as we walked to the park, we laughed, made fun of each other, and bragged about who would pull the most girls. Not only that, anyone we came across would say things like, "You guys ready to make history? This will be the next holiday." There was a sense of pride in the neighborhood that was seldom seen or felt in Skyline. It was a welcome distraction from the usual news of shootings, arrests, overdoses and fights that were so commonplace.

As the day went on, hundreds of people flocked to the park. Some were skipping school, some work—whole families participated. The smell of barbeque filled the air. There were local bands playing, along with ministers, politicians, and my favorite, plenty of girls. The park itself never seemed more manicured than on that day. Freshly cut grass and from the eastern approach, the eucalyptus trees seemed tall and the branches reached out as if they welcomed everyone coming there with a big hug. Folks were feeling good about it and with as much fun as I was having, I kept wondering how my parents were going to react when they found out I had skipped school for this.

The only bad part of this day was that I was still poor. I had no money to eat and as it grew later, I knew I would never be able to walk home. My plan was just to ask anyone I saw to help me with some change so that I might be able to ride the bus home. While I was out panhandling to achieve this goal, I looked across the street. At this time there were no homes on Skyline Drive across from MLK Park, just very high canyon hills. And along the tops of these hills were lined with what looked like every police officer in San Diego, standing next to their cars, holding rifles, and surveying the crowd through binoculars. Minor feelings of regret and fear began to seep into my brain that only a few hours earlier had channeled the mentality of Dr. King, Malcolm X, Gandhi and even Nat Turner all rolled up in one.

Then I got really afraid. By the time I finally had enough money to get on the bus and go home, darkness had enveloped the hills of Skyline. The music groups had disbanded, the barbeque pits had been extinguished, and all the politicians and ministers had left for the safety of their homes. But I had done it. It took nearly four hours to panhandle and to scrape together 50 cents to ride the bus, but I finally had it!

I waited for the eastbound number 11 bus, confident that after I explained to my parents the reason for and meaning of my disobedience that they would be proud of me. The bus began its approach to MLK Park. I reached into my pocket to organize my measly 50 pennies, not noticing that thugs, drunks, junkies and all-around bad-asses were the only ones at the bus stop with me. The driver, a young Mexican woman, was as surprised as I was once she opened that door. About 30 people rushed into the bus without paying, all the while yelling obscenities at the driver—"Move this bus, bitch," "What the fuck you waiting for, *ese*? You must want yo ass kicked!" I even heard one brother say, "You don't move this motherfucka, I comin' up there and do it myself."

I thought, "Who the heck are these people? What happened to the spirit of the unborn holiday? What would Rosa Parks do in this situation?" I believe she would have done what I was about to do. I was the last person to enter the bus, and I took all that change I had procured during the day and put it in the receptacle that showed I had paid for this ride. Right behind me was the San Diego police department, in full force. I took the last seat available right behind the bus driver, feeling good about myself because I was the only one who had paid on that bus. I hadn't said a word; I just hoped this would be over soon so I could go home. I took out my Afro Pick, the one with the black fist, and began shaping my afro. By this time, the police were receiving every indecent verbal insult imaginable: "Fuck you, ya swine, muthafuckers," "Pigs ain't shit," "Get you cracker ass out of here".... The barrage went on and on for about five minutes.

Then, very quietly, an officer was standing right in front of me. I'll never forget him for he had the pinkest skin I had ever seen and his full, fat face sported a mustache that look just like walrus tusks. His angry contempt for the rebelling crowd was becoming tangible, and if the lighting had been right, I'm sure I would have seen steam whistling out of his ears.

He also had "the look." There is a look that white people have when they hate black people. This look I don't believe can be controlled. It's as though the person is possessed by the ultimate evil—piercing eyes that degrade you just by a glace. Stonefaced, he looked down at me and said, "What did you say?" and since I hadn't said anything, I tried to ignore him. Again, "What did you say?" I looked him dead in his eyes and without any expression said, "Nothing.

I didn't say a...." And before I could get the rest out of my mouth, he had me by the neck, forcing me off the bus with his brute strength. At the same time, the people on the bus exploded into violence, kicking windows out, running each other over to get off the bus, and trying to avoid the all the other police.

I had paid and thought I had left no reason to antagonize the police. I figured I would wait them out and then go home. The officer who grabbed me finally wrestled me off the bus, where I thought he would let me go for I had done nothing wrong. I was the only one who had paid yet I was placed in another chokehold and had my face bounced off the side of the bus a couple of times, then I was handcuffed, and thrown in the back of a squad car about 20 feet behind the bus.

In those days the buses had a rear window that wrapped around the back of the vehicle so I could see everything that was happening. Now this was the scariest thing I had ever seen in my life. There was one brother left on the bus all the way in the back with about ten cops approaching him. He took on the most convincing karate stance I'd ever seen—the cops hesitated, but kept approaching. The lead cop seemed scared, but inch-by-inch, closer and closer, he came. Right behind him was the only female cop on the scene. Once they were close enough, the brother took the offensive and then threw a straight right at the lead cop. He ducked and the female cop took the punch square in the jaw.

From that point on all I could do was pray for that black man. They beat him with clubs, guns, boots and whatever else they could hold and swing. I could hear every blow that man took from those angry police officers. Every blow to his body made a blunt thud that reverberated through my eardrums and the sound of the wooden clubs against his skull cracked like the sound of a baseball bat connecting with a 90 mph fastball. Before they finished, I felt as though I had received each blow on my own body. While in the back of that police car, I squirmed and tried to move out of the way of every strike. And then the strangest thing, the world went silent. The screaming faded out; all the people darting away in fear kept running without making any noise. The only sound was the thud and crack of those clubs connecting with that young man's body and head. "Thoomp! Thoomp! Thoomp! Crack! Crack!" for what seemed like an eternity.

It was not until he seemed lifeless that they stopped. After a couple minutes in which I thought he was dead, the police picked up his beaten body and dragged him to the car I had been detained in. After literally throwing him on the backseat on top of me, this brother mustered up enough strength through countless bumps and bruises that I could literally see growing from under his skin to say, "Whaddup, lil' homie?" With amazement and relief my trembling voice replied, "Wassuup."

The next morning, I woke up on my 14th birthday inside a concrete room painted dull white over a standard brick pattern along the walls. What caught my attention was a stainless steel toilet sink combo that sat way too close to the bed. When I saw that, I said to myself, "Michael, you are really in trouble now." I trembled when I thought of how long I would be locked up in there. Fear began to grip me like a chokehold and barely let me breathe for what seemed like hours after I had woken up. Just as a sense of hopelessness began to take over, the loud clang of keys rattled outside my door and it swung open. A guard looked in and asked, "Are you Michael?"

"Yes, I am," I replied.

"Follow me and stay to the right of the yellow line and don't say a word."

The officer led me through a series of hallways, one looking exactly like the other. All of a sudden at another doorway just like the hundreds or so I had been seeing, he stopped me, rattled those keys again, opened the door and it was like the gates of heaven greeting me. There sat my mother and father alone with a white man in a cheap suit and old briefcase. I sat down across the table from my parents while the public defender stayed at the end of the table. I kept my head down for as long as I could, fearing the looks I would get from my parents. Would it be disappointment? I could live with that. Or would it be that look both of them had just before the belts came off and the serious ass whipping started? I didn't believe I could ever look them in the eyes again. I had lied about ditching school, found myself in the company of thugs, and been arrested. I knew they would hate me for life.

Finally, I glanced at my mother whose eyes were red from crying, with tears running down her full cheeks. Then I glimpsed at my father, who didn't say a word, but the look in his eyes gave me a sense of calm. I saw no disappointment, only relief that his son was all right. This opened my own floodgates, and I began to cry like a baby. At the end of the best and worst day of my life my parents still had nothing but love for me.

Eventually life returned to normal. Even though I was charged with inciting a riot, disturbing the peace, and resisting arrest, the charges were dropped. But the way I looked at the world would change forever. To this day, I have never fully trusted any police officers. I began to see them as an occupying force in my neighborhood—more of a street gang than law enforcement. And my view of black people changed as well. It is hard to attend any event such as a concerts or play without thinking, Which one of us is going to fuck up this peaceful event? As far as that man who got beaten on the bus, I hadn't ever seen him before and haven't since.

Mario Lewis
At the Chargers Game

Mario Lewis, 46, Black, San Diego, California, Owner—
Imperial Barbershop.

"In the mid- to early '70s my sister and I went to a Chargers game with my father. We (are) actually Raiders fans. My father, is a nice—nice-size man with some nice-size arms and everything and we were enjoying ourselves at the game and at the end of the game these four white guys were following my father out of the game calling him the n-word. Calling US the n-word, I should say.

"I was a youngster. I was maybe about 10 or 11 years old, if that. And so my father had a van and so my father, I guess he knew that he was about to get into a confrontation with 'em because they followed us all the way to the car. My father told us—he said 'Run and lock yourself in the van.' Right. So me and my sister ran and we locked ourselves in the van.

"And my father had one of those belts that had the two buckle things back in the day and he took the belt off, wrapped it around his fist and my father commenced to try to kill them dudes. My father socked them all up. And that was the first time I really experienced the n-word in that magnitude, and that manner in which my father let them dudes have it. Like really let them have it. And me and my sister were crying and screaming because we didn't know what was going to go down. You know what I mean? So that was my very first experience with the word."

[Harris asks what Lewis thinks about the use of the word today.]

"I think it's totally disrespectful. I think the youngsters now that utilize the word, they don't understand the significance of it on how people died while yelling that word while their bodies were swinging on trees and how the word is just negative. They try to put a positive spin—you can't put a positive spend on something negative. That' straight negative energy. It's definitely wrong. They try to use it as a term of endearment and make it exclusive for brothers to say it and all this other stuff like that.

"Me, personally: 'n-i-g-g-a' is 'n-i-g-g-e-r'—STILL. It's still the same thang. Ain't nothing changed. It's just slang."

The preceeding was originally published as "'N-i-g-g-a' is 'N-ig-g-e-r'—STILL" in The n-Word Project a website put together by Professor Frank Harris. On the site Harris notes that, "This project involves collecting narratives from a range of people across America about their thoughts, feelings and experiences with the n-word, as 'nigger' and 'nigga,' and whether its growing use might lead to it becoming the new standard reference for Americans of black African descent. It is part of my larger research on the evolving name-descriptions of Americans of black African descent over the past four centuries."

Kinsee Morlan

"The Nigga Project Experience" Wants to Have a Talk

San Diego Couple Continue Their Modest War Against the Rise of the N-Word

The staff at Jones Brothers BBQ in Encanto go about their business serving up ample helpings of pork ribs, beef brisket and other smoked meats and sides. Mulemvo Nianda is hanging up a handmade poster board with the word "NIGGER" written boldly above a blown-up, black-and-white photo of a lynching of a black man, with other blatantly racist imagery peppered below. The poster keeps slipping off the barbecue joint's sweaty walls, though, so Nianda settles for placing it on a table.

A crowd of about a dozen finish their meals and look toward the slightly nervous young man at the front of the room.

"I'm a spoken-word artist and a documentary filmmaker," Nianda says. "I'm here to present to you today a project, but before we get to the documentary, I just want to give you a quick spoken-word piece, which is what I do—it's my specialty."

Nianda, who goes by Inside Nianda Speaks when it comes to his creative work, clasps his hands and takes a deep breath, launching into a piece that includes lofty lines like, "One nation, one anthem, one people, one color; we're all equal" and "I have to learn to be a man and stand for one thing; live for something."

After the piece, he switches on his documentary, *The Nigga Project Experience*—a rudimentary video he shot with his smart phone—and folks begin shifting uncomfortably in their seats. The film features man-on-the-street interviews asking people what they think about the word "nigga," spliced with shocking, historical photos of lynchings and other civil-rights-movement imagery, plus a few clips from mainstream hip-hop videos, like rapper YG's 2013 hit, "My Nigga."

After it's over, he gives people a survey, asking for their thoughts on the n-word. Then he opens things up for discussion.

"I don't really get offended by that word," says a young black woman in the audience. "I just feel like, as long as we understand that the people who are using it are ignorant; honestly, it mostly just makes me feel embarrassed for the people using it."

An older gentleman speaks up.

"Well, I'm from a different generation than a lot of you young folks here today, and the word is *highly* offensive to me," he says. "The word has become so white-washed now; we use it so much. Nobody is offended by it—it's just another word to young folks, but it's still an offensive word to a generation that endured a whole lot more than this generation has."

Eventually, an uncomfortable disagreement breaks out between a white woman and a black man, and the charged, racist feelings forever linked to the word "nigga" are unleashed.

◆ ◆ ◆

"Yeah, I definitely remember that moment," says Nianda of the argument that broke out at the summer screening he hosted at Jones Brothers. He's sitting in a study room at the Malcolm X Library in Emerald Hills with his girlfriend and collaborator, Juanita Boyer. "That was intense."

Nianda and Boyer have been screening *The Nigga Project Experience* and hosting community discussions at barbecue restaurants, hair salons, libraries and community centers throughout southeastern San Diego since the beginning of 2014. They try to incorporate spoken-word, music and art into the events, and they always conduct surveys so they can continue collecting and analyzing people's thoughts and feelings about the word.

This year in particular has been monumental in exposing the nation's festering racial tensions. Earlier in 2014, Nevada rancher Cliven Bundy's and former Clippers owner Donald Sterling's racist comments made the rounds. More recently, the killings of unarmed black men by white police officers in Missouri and New York made the issue of race in America impossible to ignore. Nianda and Boyer have used the momentum and renewed focus on race relations to help engage the local black community in their discussions about the n-word. They want people to think about why it's become so pervasive, especially among the younger generation, which uses "nigga" almost as a replacement for "brother"—a term of endearment.

The project "started with a spoken-word piece and just carried on from there," says Nianda, a former Marine who's studying sociology at San Diego City College, where he regularly does flash-poetry performances by standing on top of tables or chairs to deliver his original compositions to crowds of unsuspecting passersby. "I asked someone from class how he felt about the word one day and just decided to make a documentary and interview him. Then I started asking different people, walking up to them and asking, 'How do you feel about the n-word?'"

The Nigga Project Experience is broken into three short parts. Nianda and Boyer are currently wrapping up Part 3, which focuses on interviews with young black men. The project has inspired Boyer to create another DIY documentary, *My Community*, which tells her story of growing up in a Los Angeles ghetto and attempts to show a different, more dynamic side of southeastern San Diego. She believes that negative portrayals of the black community dominate in mainstream media, and she wants to offer an alternative....

All of the couples' videos are scrappy. The sound and video quality is bad in parts, and the two are completely self-taught with limited resources.

"But we work with what we have," Nianda says. "We would love to have the better equipment, but, at the end of the day, it's not going to stop us from the goal we want to accomplish."

The goal, Boyer and Nianda say, isn't to eradicate the n-word; they think it's too ingrained in black culture. Instead, they want to make their peers more aware of its original intent by making graphic visual connections to the word's hateful history and opening up a dialogue. Ultimately, they'd like to see more people use more discretion when unleashing "nigga."

"We might think we're taking the power away by reclaiming it but, at the same time, it's still perpetuating the same cycle of racism and portraying a negative image and we don't really seem to see that," Nianda says. "We don't see that it's a huge detriment to our culture."

Kinsee Morlan is the Arts Editor for San Diego CityBeat, where this piece was originally published.

Raymond R. Beltrán
From Imperial, Up Euclid

Give me the streets, the concrete streets
any day. I've paid high prices to be in touch,
in touch with curls, black curls and
brown heads gleaming at the rising sun,
gleaming through housing projects in The Dip.

Black-fisted murals, black eagles encircled in red flags,
give me the streets, the poor contrast,
colorless streets, where green outshines the gloom.
The green of bling bling, big bodies
rollin on twenty inch chrome blades, making
that hustle through Little Africa.

Why don't you go ahead and give me Sundays,
those Euclid Ave Sundays in front of Fam Mart,
the ride or die, do or don't, watch me…nah fuck that!
Picture Me Rollin mentality.
We do anything nowadays to take our minds off reality.

I want that bus stop in front of Federal Ave,
Nubian Queens with vestiges of royalty in their beauty,
y mis mujeres, dry chocolate tone, indigenous nose,
tight eyes of experience, and about five little hijos behind,
holding their own.

Give me the wisdom that Kwame walks among,
selling the best incense on the block
ready to talk for a while, fighting the power, mighty icon
of this black and white collage, like
a movie that was filmed way before my time.

Give me the holy ghost through choir harmony
coming from the Light of the World,
watching the streets through a cracked windshield,
praising my own providence, bumpin Lucy Pearl,
and by all means give it to me with some sense of soul.

Pinch me off a piece of cotton candy
from long, golden brown, sweaty stems of swollen feet.
I'll pay three dollars. If you ask me, that's cheap,
a bit too cheap for the conquest of El Norte.
The taste of a tired nation is…what they call it?
Bitter sweet?

Give me that hop scotchin, hip hoppin, b boppin
I'll take this hip hop renaissance back in time and
bring back rhymes of Solitary Reapers and beauty inside.
If I can have now, I can find reason in rhyme, and
give it back to you on a platter in a pink box with a bean pie.

Maybe you can give me the mural of a white Jesus
on a wall that street warriors dare to decorate with words of hate.
Or maybe you can give me that tired old black man's blow horn.
He's been standing all life long and ready to return home,
dying for you to realize the brass tone of the feet of our lord.

Give me the streets, please, from Imperial up Euclid.
I'll take all of it, tough looks, ho's and crooks.
Let me have that seven deuce caddy with
three wheels laid tilted on a sugar daddy.
I will take those golden brown, bald heads packed in a Regal,
maybe a sign of defeat, but…
Give it here.

DeJe Watson

C203 (Office Hours)

In my office I abandon geometry
        stare: at comical dimensions of a former self institutionalized time
traveler   moving at warp speed (circa 1950) / these walls salivate minstrel
tongues   academic jibba / jabba hibernated phrases unfazed by Jim Crow
rhetoric sworn
        in on quadrants as I walk the trail of tears to the mail room an
abandoned torture   mask free floating spikes in any given direction as
ground signs hopscotch   everywhere a fetish figure's *gin-gin-gué*
                    SHOUT OUTS
            across concrete vévés
            lacquered leaves below //
            decode the invisible world
            of my sandals' sufi
I / darkest juju
        speak & spill ink from my sequestered pen as light years refuse me lift
off   run-on   sentences the lover/s fusion mocking idol creativity again I
leaf through student   papers for poetry conjured beneath the rough draft
of subverted logic skunk on   dark circles of midnight palm oil a bull/s eye
redundancy ring-shouts   decentering the fool in the mirror
I have become
        music bending beneath corridors down the hallway facing hi rises of
what used to   be Coronado // *A Love Supreme* riffs of the Alhambra inside
my garret heaves a   shuffle stepping giant ghost on a smoke break recalling
the maafa stranded on   the bridge of Dolphy's isle of unhatched
dissonance // longing for dousn guni   strings   attached
During office hours
        Nicole asks about the literature of black love: my face a jigsaw puzzle
instead   we talk about Sierra Leon the missing pieces of women men
and children the   affair between an artist and her medium never promises
literary love // only focus   in the midst of school—two jobs her baby/
daddies fist caressing the flow of   a bandied universe

I slowly decompose
    inside daydreams peopled in high def deeper than blood brothers //
poets   dancers & musicians appear and disappear / butterflies struggling
against the open   mic of   mediocrity the space bar my Jun-Jun exuding
Gorée gamma rays
    the computer screen a landlocked vagina full of untapped letters scatted
across the   keyboard/s pelvic floor
After two years
    Eszlam brings me Baklava & Bahai an Iranian refugee studying pre-med at
    ucsd he gravitates above Muslim fundamentalism missing our nightly
sojourns   to central Africa // Dustin drops in before leaving for San
Marcos / he promises to   stay the gravity of his grandma's life fluttering
between studious fingers
Baptize me
    inside a ghetto of bright moments left over lightening bugs arrested in
the   buttoned lip of a mason jar // this future composition of canned
jams an   intermediary offering of strawberry summers buttercuped
until death do us funk   the slow drag recoiled inside the fall terminal of an
Ethiop/s ear
I am the living slave
    tossed overboard a hybrid thing sunken treasure of diaspora // viral-spam
    survivor beneath the coral reef of email soft-shoed between pop-ups
in this   hinterland of phonemes an abandoned bottle tree head bobs
through krio letters   discovered as cyber spirits junkanoo // ancestral low
riders falsetto playing the   fatted hand of
FALLACY
    the empire/s pork pie hat waxed on jazz 88s
    scientific paradise of enemas dj'd by Miff Mole
    the faithful administrator's chair declines to know
    an empty closet of suits and pantyhose
I am the liquid trance
    dancer detangling words // the Senegalese woman knitted inside the
door of no   return breathing vapors of those naked children gone before
bathed in the   shackled tight pack of necessary tubs / the complacency of
idle fingertips vomits up the memory of my daughter/s slender cheek as we
slumber on sheltered   afternoons a tangerine silhouette where fragile
flesh meets shattered hambonista
Hope—the tangled umbilical
    a heavenly hunchback poised designs the master plan: a venus flytrap
    of curried cosmograms remixed over the coming years as carats

of tenure hang in my face and I am completely erased
C_2O_3 asphyxiates
      fear grown zigzag from the underbelly of headless haints / the wave
function of   keloids branded lightly matching shadows on the exterior
door an unstable gibbet   hangs in plain view of those who impregnate the
knowledge of proffered bones
I pedagogy
      under the influence of four walls plastered inside this linear sojourn
/ the tutelary   whip impregnates ivy refusing the laws of brick face and
intellectual blues
      in my office there are at least 203 kinds of practical spells to grammar
check tears   spilled on personal narratives buried next to the missing
picture of palm wine a   hole drilled in the chalk tray ties down the projection
screen beneath budget cuts   and dusty erasures of the working class
In overcrowded classrooms
      a barrier reef of hungry eyes seek higher education where proletariat
dreams   mingle with the privilege of nightmares at the piper/s cost during
evaluations
      I focus on the broke-winged words of my translated colleagues
      Igbo-Mende-Gikuyu horoscopes fly from their crooked-tongues
Coltrane sits behind me
      redesigns me reminds me of the music I am not playing the poetry I am
not   writing the songs I am not singing // I am the portrait of an artist
in the four   cornered room of Baldwin/s absurdity a pseudonym for the
dreaded F# my fingers   trembling as the twilight ascends on a glass blown
chalice searching for an   oasis from which to take the perfect drink

Sarah Saez

San Diego's Underground Economy

San Diego is known for being a top tourist destination but it's also home to a diverse and vulnerable population of immigrant workers who serve the residents and visitors of America's Finest City. For the past five years San Diego's community of taxi workers have been mobilizing for change. Once here in America many of them encountered extreme barriers including language, cultural differences and social and economic hardship. In addition and in contribution to these issues they often have an almost complete lack of political power to make a real difference in the neighborhoods they live and industries they work in. If you want to know who holds power in America's Finest City you don't need to look much further than the taxi industry which has been referred to as "a key indicator of the true nature of local politics" here in San Diego.

Issues in the taxi industry go back for decades. Since the late 1960s San Diego's largest player in the taxi industry, Yellow Cab Company, and others have been putting money down on politics by making donations at one time through illegal, laundered money. After San Diego's District Attorney Ed Miller made a point to crack down, various politicians including the Mayor at the time and councilmembers ended up being indicted for conspiracy and bribery. Yellow Cab thought it would be a good idea to pay off politicians in exchange for a meter increase. Even after Yellow Cab sold off its over 300 permits following the indictments they still remain a political influence to this day and as a result, for the past three decades the San Diego taxi industry has changed very little. That is until hundreds of African immigrant taxi drivers from City Heights decided to fight back.

On December 18th, 2009 over 200 taxi drivers went on strike to protest abusive practices and high lease rates stemming from the underground sale of taxi permits. The strike led to the formation of the United Taxi Workers of San

Diego (UTWSD). The neighborhood a majority of taxi drivers live in, City Heights, is very different from the downtown clients they serve. City Heights is home to one of the densest populations in San Diego County with a population of over 15,000 residents per square mile compared to San Diego with only just over 4,000 residents per square mile. Even with three times the population density, City Heights residents have become disenfranchised with their lack of political influence.

City Heights isn't a tourist attraction and isn't often treated as an equal part of America's Finest City. But neighborhoods like City Heights are in fact the lifeblood of San Diego and its tourism industry. Its residents get you home safely when you've had too much too drink on New Years Eve, they drive the grandmother whose kids don't come to visit to the grocery store, they clean your hotels and work hard throughout the night to keep San Diego clean and ready for the day's influx of business people, tourists and commuters. And all this only to make an average of $23,172 less a year on average compared to the rest of San Diego. And for Taxi Drivers it's even worse.

A study conducted by San Diego State University and the Center on Policy Initiatives found that Taxi Drivers only earn an average of $4.45 an hour. These low wages, mistreatment by permit holders and the downsides of simply living in City Heights helped to fuel the taxi drivers and their communities to fight for change.

On November 10th, 2014 the City Council voted to lift the cap on taxi permits, enabling thousands of drivers to have the opportunity to own their own business and no longer pay exorbitant lease rates to permit owners. But when the City Council voted to lift the cap on taxi permits they not only changed the lives of taxi drivers, they showed an entire community that you can change your future for the better.

There's still much more work to be done until San Diego can really lay claim to being America's Finest City while so many of its key stakeholders are still not being heard, but we're getting there. The day when San Diego's workers are the ones making the decisions about their workplace, neighborhood and City, I'll know we've arrived.

Susan Duerksen

Living and Working in Poverty
Grim Reality in "America's Finest City"

"Living in poverty" is one of those shorthand terms that rolls easily off the tongues of news anchors and politicians before they turn to the next topic. We all tend to glaze over the full meaning of the phrase, the grinding day-to-day misery of hunger, worry, discomfort, exhaustion, and despair.

In the city of San Diego, the proportion and number of people living in poverty edged up in 2013. It should have gone down. Instead, 7,000 *more* people in the city live in poverty now, in addition to the 202,000 who remain in that dire situation from the previous year.

Statistically, it was a small increase, nothing drastic. When the Center on Policy Initiatives reported it in an analysis[1] of data from the U.S. Census Bureau, the main response from local media and others was a yawn.

But consider what that statistic means. It counts only the people whose household income is below the federal poverty threshold, an absurdly low measure in high-cost places like San Diego. The threshold is the same everywhere in the U.S. and varies only by family size; for example, it's about $12,000 for a single person and about $24,000 for two adults with two children. That's per year.

People living in San Diego can have incomes substantially above that level and still be quite poor—but not officially counted as poor. To live here with income lower than the poverty threshold is to be destitute.

To fully grasp the obscenity of the situation, consider that we are four years into a recovery from the national recession. Local industry is doing well; the San Diego region's economic output has rebounded above pre-recession levels. People are working hard and companies are making money.

---

1   http://www.onlinecpi.org/poverty_earnings_income_city_of_san_diego_2013.

But wages, here as elsewhere, have not kept up. The recovery in profits is not being shared with the people doing much of the work.

Marie Kaio has worked in fast food restaurants for 35 years and still makes minimum wage. When her husband died suddenly this year, she had to borrow money for the burial and couldn't afford a full funeral. By the end of each month, she and her teenage daughter survive on bologna sandwiches and food from her church.

Marcus Nichols, 31 years old, works more than full time at two minimum-wage jobs as a security officer. Unable to find a place he can afford to rent in San Diego, he lives in his car and occasionally gets a hotel room to take a shower.

Marie and Marcus each get up and go to work every day. They and many others like them earn their pay, yet remain miserably impoverished.

What's an Employer's Responsibility?

When CPI researchers crunched the census data, we found that among all San Diegans of working age (older than 16) who live *below* the federal poverty threshold, more than 41% are employed.

Remember, that's the same income level that's considered poverty in small towns in Alabama, and they are trying to live on it in San Diego. How can it be that *anyone* is employed and yet in such deep poverty—let alone 41%?

About 135,000 jobs in San Diego pay at or near minimum wage, now $9 an hour in California, which amounts to $18,720 a year for full-time work. When people in those jobs have any family to support, they are impoverished. With one-bedroom rents here topping $1,000 a month, that full-time income leaves precious little for food, transportation, child care, medical bills, and all the other costs of living.

And of course, many workers are denied full-time hours, often so that they can also be denied healthcare and other benefits.

Do employers have a responsibility to pay enough for a person's time that the employee can live? If they don't, then we all as taxpayers pick up some of the tab, and people who are working hard to support themselves live without things most of us would consider necessities, including family time, private living space, and three meals a day.

To paraphrase one of our greatest presidents, that's unacceptable and un-American.

> No business which depends for existence on paying less than living wages to its workers has any right to continue in this country. By living wages, I mean more than a bare subsistence level—I mean the wages of a decent living.
>
> —Franklin Delano Roosevelt, 1933

The Income Gap Widens in San Diego

Within the City of San Diego, a total of 144,968 adults and 64,077 children lived in official, rock-bottom poverty last year, with household incomes below the federal poverty threshold.

How many more San Diegans are poor but not below the official cutoff? One reasonable measure is double the federal poverty threshold. A full third of the city population—443,584 people—live with household incomes below that level. That's still too low to independently meet the basic costs of living in this region. Without the money for basic needs, every day is a struggle to get the family enough food, maintain some kind of shelter, and juggle bills.

That's how a third of us live in this sunny, wealthy city.

And it's getting worse. The median household income in San Diego—the level at which half the households make more and half make less—was nearly $6,000 *lower* last year, adjusted for inflation, than it was in 2007, before the recession began.

That's certainly not because of shrinking incomes at the top. In fact, the rich in San Diego, as elsewhere, keep getting richer, so the drop in the median is driven by deep pain at the lower end of the scale. If you lined up all the households in the city in order of income and divided the line into fifths, the top fifth took in 51% of all the income in the city last year—more than the other four fifths combined. The bottom fifth—we're talking about 96,146 households—had only 3% of the total income.

The recovery also has been good for local businesses. In 2013, the regional Gross Domestic Product, a measure of economic output, grew to $1.2 billion above the pre-recession level.

Corporations and the wealthy are doing well. The problem is a hidebound resistance to paying wages that reflect reality and allow a hard-working person to get ahead.

Wages are lowest, and most often below the cost of living, in some of San Diego's largest and growing industries, particularly hotels, restaurants and retail stores. In the hotel and restaurant industry, median 2013 earnings in San Diego bottomed out at $25,632—for full-time, year-round work. And that's the median, meaning half the employees make even less than that.

Not Really Getting By

How do we expect people to live here, where they work, on those wages? In CPI's latest *Making Ends Meet* report,[2] we found that even a single person living alone needs more than that—at least $27,655 a year—to meet the no-frills cost of living in San Diego without help from taxpayers or others. For working people raising children, of course, the costs zoom up from there.

We profiled Adam Carcione, a cook at a large, popular San Diego restaurant, who spent his workdays preparing gourmet meals for strangers yet struggled to afford healthy food for his own 3-year-old son. His wife worked as a pastry chef at another restaurant, and the family got by only by living with her mother.

They were finally forced to leave San Diego to find jobs that paid enough to get their own apartment. Before he left, Adam said that despite two incomes at higher than minimum wage, "We're not really getting by. We're not on aid, but we would be if we weren't living with my mother-in-law."

Lisette Orosco makes $11 an hour working full-time for a law firm, but must share a bedroom with her two school-age children in a house she splits with two other adults. Even so, as much as she wants to be self-sufficient, she said her family wouldn't survive without food stamps.

Ivan Jimenez works at a downtown San Diego restaurant and a fast-food joint, and dreams of going to college and becoming a doctor. At 21, those dreams are stuck in the hopelessness of long hours for low pay, because most of his meager wages go to help support his mother and three younger sisters.

---

2   http://www.onlinecpi.org/making_ends_meet.

One Step Forward, Yanked Back

This summer the San Diego City Council took a crucial step to alleviate the worst of the city's working poverty, voting to raise the local minimum wage to $11.50 over three years. The amount was compromised down, but a meaningful improvement. And the ordinance also gave all workers in the city the chance to earn up to five paid sick days a year.

However, the local Chamber of Commerce and other business interests then poured nearly $500,000 into a deceptive petition drive to block the Council's action. Professional petitioners, paid up to $12 per name, went door-to-door and stood outside stores telling potential signers the petition would provide "a chance to vote on raising the minimum wage," not mentioning that the unnecessary vote would freeze an already-approved increase. By deceitfully convincing people to sign who actually wanted the minimum wage to rise, they were able to finagle the necessary signatures—only about 6% of registered voters—to yank back the desperately needed wage increase. It is now a referendum on the June 2016 ballot.

Opponents don't dispute that 63% of San Diego voters favor increasing the minimum wage and providing earned sick time.[3] Over the next year and a half, those voters will be subjected to a Chamber ad blitz of misinformation seeking to harden their hearts.

The minimum wage increase would mean a raise for an estimated 200,000 San Diegans, including those who make slightly more than minimum wage but less than the eventual goal of $11.50 an hour. That compromise wage level, while not sufficient, would give hard-working people a better chance to keep a roof over their heads and food on their tables.

In October, just two days before the Chamber's misbegotten signatures were verified, the U.S. Bureau of Labor Statistics issued a report declaring San Diego the fourth most expensive place to live in the country. The only cities where it costs more to live are Washington DC, San Francisco and New York City.

The local NBC affiliate posted the news of San Diego's high-cost ranking on its Facebook page and got hundreds of comments like this one:

> PLEASE everyone that doesn't like [sic] here—MOVE THE
> HECK OUT!!! Then we'd have more jobs available and more

---

3   Greenberg Quinlan Rosner Research poll, 2014.

happy, smiling people.... Work hard and budget your money and
you'll be just fine.

The grim reality that people in our community *are* working hard and yet
impoverished remains hidden to those who don't want to see. Some people do
leave the city and some eventually manage to find better jobs, but the pover-
ty-wage jobs will still be here, ensnaring other people, until we force a change.

For too many of our neighbors, low wages are destroying the American
dream of rising above poverty through work. We must demand better than that.

Marianne S. Johnson

Courthouse Portrait, East Main Street

East County files through metal detectors
where the bailiffs jaw and ignore
the silver-tipped boots and bolo ties
worn by the suits, setting off
the scans. "Jackets off," one brays
but stays focused on the double Ds
in tank tee, spaghetti straps and *Jesus
Saves* tattooed on her shoulder.
Pistachio green hobo bag,
and a yellowed bruise
under her left eye.

Jesus Saves follows Bolo Tie
to the elevator, sits with him
outside courtroom seven.
At the far end of the bench,
a stroller, a toddler, a third
on the way, and a hand clenched
with a temporary restraining order
rolled like a cigarette. Monday
morning after the Santa Ana,
dried blood and tears, scorched beds
of El Cajon, burnt grass,
and spent shells in Santee,
the TROs pour in like a sudden
summer storm, dragging their tots
behind them.

Jesus Saves leans her shiner
toward Bolo Tie scratching
on his legal pad, yellow

as her eye, and says "More paper
won't protect me."
"This is all I can do."
Lawyer's answer—
comes with the suit.
To his boots she states
"I need a gun."
In the courtroom, women line up,
fill the room—wait, come and go,
come wait go, come and go.

"Courthouse Portrait, East Main Street" was originally published in The Far East
Project: Everything Just As It Is.

Justin Hudnall

Eastern Lights

It was like salvation when the Chaldeans started opening up hookah shops. They knew us all by name. I'd walk through the door and into a handshake, always someone's friend, a title fairly purchased along with a little bit of tobacco and coal for the hookah at fifteen dollars a pop. Underage in a town full of nothing but utilitarian drinking bars, we needed a place to congregate or go crazy. At the Muslim hookahs, poor white offspring of dust bowl Oakies like us would send the Arabs and Somalis into a wild west silence before the screen door whacked shut behind us. So we'd happily scrape the money together and hand it over to the Chaldeans, like Mike, who welcomed rent payment for a table from whoever was offering it.

Mike's place, The Zodiac, was wedged in a stripmall right between a Soup Plantation and a Chinese buffet, still within the East County Radiation Zone, as the more coastal people referred to our semi-rural side of the tracks. My friends and I were trash to plenty other folks, of that we were reminded often enough that we strayed into foreign territories only for notable reasons, but we banked our pride on knowing at least we weren't the monster truck-driving twats, the self-branded Metal Mulisha, replete with WWII German death's head as their emblem.

We were the ones old enough to start working on cancer but too young to start psoriasis—goths, middle-class punks, the young and struggling sober looking for a place between AA meetings, gay Christian kids who wouldn't come out until they'd moved outside the reach of their parents' evangelical damnation; the Zodiac was our clean, well-lit place and I thought I knew everybody in it until Jennifer arrived.

Almost as tall as me and my six feet. Ink-black hair all the way down to the top of her tailbone with about a half-inch of brown roots grown out. Pale the way you have to work at in Southern California. Skipped-meals skinny.

"I'm going to ask her out."

That's the first thing I said when I saw her.

Jennifer sat down at a table near enough that it wasn't weird when I started talking to her. She'd just come from a concert by The Cure. This was 1999.

"They still sounded good," she said. "But it was depressing to see Robert Smith so fat he could only squeeze into a hockey jersey."

It wasn't until the cafe closed that I worked myself up to ask for her number. She gave it to me without pause or ceremony and told me anytime, day or night, was as good a time to call as another.

Either her mom or Grandma answered. You never can tell age over the phone with a woman of a certain lifestyle. The line was passed to Jennifer who said I'd have to come pick her up if we wanted to go out. She'd never learned to drive.

She didn't want me to know where she lived. I was to park and meet her at the Arco on the corner of Douglas and El Cajon Boulevard. Neither of us had cellphones, just an agreement on a time and place, so I showed up on time. She walked out of the dark in my rear-view mirror fifteen minutes later, just appearing all at once under the gas station's corpse-blue, florescent lights wearing a backless shirt, mid-thigh black denim shorts, and two-dollar flip-flops. She got in the passenger side of my un-killable sedan, said hi, leaned back and put her feet up on the dashboard. Daring me, just daring me to say something about the jagged red weal of scar tissue, half a finger wide, that ran up alongside her egg-white calf.

So I asked, "What did you do that with?"

"Broken glass I'd heated up with a lighter."

"Well, now you have to tell me the story."

Jennifer must have thought I was a good listener because she went for it, told me all about how when she was fifteen, her upstairs neighbors would let her come over and hang out with them, two dudes in their twenties. They'd all get drunk and watch movies from the dudes' VHS collection. One night she passed out and woke up to them raping her and videotaping it. It wasn't hard for the DA to convict them. They'd kept the tape.

"The State set me up with some counseling and my therapist gave me some pills that made me tired all the time, but all that ended once I turned eighteen."

She'd been to jail a few times. Public intoxication. Drunk and disorderly. Assault. Things had been going good for Jennifer recently though. She was starting to feel more in-control. No problems with the law for awhile. She'd never moved, still lived in the same apartment building. She hadn't wanted me to see it. Too close to the county welfare office, and she said she was ashamed of it.

I parked in the Zodiac's lot. We sat in the car while she finished her story, appearing as divorced from the harm it referenced as if it had happened to somebody else. The only part that felt weird was why she'd thought to tell me about it in the first place, as casual as beating dust out of a rug.

"You asked."

"Do people not ask?"

"No, they just say, 'that's a hell of a scar.' They point it out to me like I never noticed it and move on."

Boy, did I feel flattered, I really did. I wanted to ask her loads of questions then, but Jennifer figured the best way to end her story was to smile, get out of my car and walk inside without looking to see if I was following.

By the time I'd caught up with her, she'd already recognized a troupe of three guys sitting at an outdoor table. All of them were in their late teens or early twenties, all of them wearing black the way guys like them do in Southern California: black shorts, black-death metal band t-shirts, black hoody, black shoes and black socks pulled up leaving a village idiot space of hairy white leg, their too-long wallet chains dangling off the chair seats. The worst combination of wannabe tough guys and Anne Rice fans.

Since I never got their names, I'll make some up. The short & fat one who constantly found something to chuckle at but never with, we'll call him The Great Pumpkin. He was referred to by his friends as, no shit, "Prospero," but no one has a nickname like that unless they give it to themselves, so it doesn't count. If it wasn't for the little bit of goth in the room, he'd have never got away with it.

The little acne-scarred twig with translucent white skin and a flap of yellow hair above sunken eyes, we'll call him Scarecrow. The stand-out shit-kicker that ruled the roost in his big black Doc Martins, the edges of steel toes starting to wear through the leather, he just gets to be Shit-Kicker.

Scarecrow invited Jennifer to a party back at a condo they were just on their way to. The Great Pumpkin thought that was a great idea. Shit-Kicker just stared, first at Jennifer, then at me.

"Do you want to go?" Jennifer was excited.

"Do you?" I was not excited.

She nodded and squeezed my hand. We went.

Our directions led to a complex that could have been designed by Soviets for a warmer climate: decomposition-green sameness with a legislated ugliness, like so many other apartment complexes scattered all over the El Cajon valley floor.

We parked right in front of the party and climbed the cracked slab stairs up to the front door. Jennifer stopped me before going inside, turned right around and put her hand on my chest.

"Don't leave me, okay?"

In case she was flirting I smiled, but she sounded serious so I said, "Of course not."

There were about thirty kids in their early twenties, some still in their teens milling around in a living room area and small kitchen. The ceiling was covered in spray-on stalactites of an off-white pallor that was shifting toward the yellow, like the skin of one of my friend's mother who'd been diagnosed with lupus. Beige wall-to-wall carpeting showed the pockmarks of dropped weed embers. Blankets and pillows wadded up on an overstuffed brown couch suggested that one of the apartment's renters slept there.

Most everyone was cycling through to the apartment's small "backyard," a plot of cracked concrete gated by a prickly untreated wood fence. A couple of drink coolers sat leaking next to some dirty white plastic chairs, an ancient plastic patio table with a hole in the middle for an umbrella that wasn't there, and a bicycle that had sat ignored longer than it had ever been ridden.

Scarecrow handed Jennifer a Budweiser upon our arrival. He wasn't pointed about ignoring me. It just didn't cross his mind to do otherwise.

Holding court beside the coolers, Shit-Kicker was instructing The Great Pumpkin how to do push-ups.

"You just keep bringing your hands closer together over time as you get stronger."

Great Pumpkin said it didn't matter, all he'd ever have were sausage tits.

"No, no you've just got to keep slowly moving your hands closer together and keep doing it every day."

Jennifer set to knocking back beers and fast, reloaded by Scarecrow as soon as she clinked down an empty. She seemed to know everyone and paid me less of a mind with each familiar face that came around. Her voice, so soft and melodic during the ride over, fell away after her fourth beer and ninth cigarette to reveal that East County accent, one that some people acknowledge and some swear doesn't exist, a kind of off-the-wagon dust-bowl gypsy drawl, or else the ghost of one who'd taken possession of her now.

"Hey Hooker, haven't seen you in years!" she called to a girl who looked like every girl who worked behind the makeup counter of every lower-middle class Macy's ever.

When Jennifer got up to sit in Scarecrow's lap. I found an excuse to go for a walk. A Mexican kid named Angel announced he was going up the road for cigarettes and I just followed.

"She's a strange girl," he said.

"I don't really know her."

"None of us do. But some of those guys are dangerous around a girl like her."

He looked at me like he wanted to make sure I understood what he was saying, and I looked at him in a way that said I did. I bought a pack of cigarettes even though I didn't really smoke back then.

On the return trip, we stopped across the street from the apartment to smoke. Out here, all the street lights are a dim orange-yellow, of a shade like a dehydrated dialysis patient's urine. It strains your eyes to look at anything they light for too long. The color kills your depth perception, but the cornea never stops trying to focus. They showed up when the astronomers on Mount Palomar discovered they could see the stars better through their telescope if our light wasn't in their way.

Angel flicked his butt in the street and blew out a long lungful of air.

"Why do you hang out with them?" I asked.

"Don't really know anybody else."

"Got to know somebody."

"Got to know somebody. Exactly."

Nobody was on the back patio when we returned through the wooden gate, even though the beer was, which was a bad sign. There was a ruckus coming from the living room. I thought about turning and leaving, then I thought about how she made me promise not to, and I thought about whether or not that mattered any more, and I decided that it did. I pushed through a wall of youth clutching beers that were forgotten for the spectacle they'd surrounded in a circle: Jennifer, naked, dancing, whipping her long black hair around like a mad pony, no thought to cover the triangle of light brown hair between her legs.

"Oh, man," said Angel. "You should get out of here. Nobody has your back."

Jennifer went down to her knees on the worn wall-to-wall carpet and crawled over to our host, this Great Pumpkin who wanted everyone to call him Prospero, who was the only one sitting down on the couch. He had a dumb nervous smile on his face and his affect said he found it all funny, but his eyes pled out-and-out panic.

"You want me to suck your dick?" she cooed to him.

And Shit-Kicker was yelling for him to stop being a pussy or get out of the way and lemme at her and such, all swelled up like there was nothing more to him than cock and a want to punish that combined announced, "dishonorable discharge." My hand reached to take hold of her shoulder, but when she felt my fingers graze her skin she spun and raked her nails down my arm.

"Don't you ever fucking touch me you fucking faggot! I'll fucking kill you, motherfucker!"

A hand on my shoulder pulled me back into the obscurity of the circle's outer ring.

"Don't fucking try to do anything," Angel said. "You're going to get stabbed."

Then Jennifer went right back to backing Prospero further and further up the couch. He was kind of swatting at her until she reared up over him, triumphant. There was nowhere left for him to go when her hand slid up onto his crotch.

And paused there, all of her did, confused at first then smiling. We all knew the poor guy was soft. It kind of endeared me to him. Nobody with a conscience wouldn't be soft in that moment. But Shit-Kicker was the first to laugh, and Great Pumpkin shoved her off him, a little harder than he probably intended, yelled for her to fucking stop it and get off him.

It was like he'd let the air out of a balloon. She hit the ground ass-first. All the fight went right out of her. She managed to turn even paler. For a moment I thought she'd woken up from whatever trance she'd passed into and discovered herself, suddenly modest, but her eyes weren't focused on anything happening in that room, not even in that year.

She seemed so small then, curling around and trying to disappear into herself, her hair almost covering her small pink nipples, murmuring, "You don't think I'm attractive. You think I'm ugly. I'm disgusting."

Shit-Kicker said he didn't know about that faggot but thought she was looking just fine.

I shouldered around him and knelt down low, right in Jennifer's ear where no one else could hear, and I asked real nice if she wouldn't talk to me for a moment in the bathroom.

"Okay," she said back like a sad little kid, exactly like a sad little kid, and she rose and led the way.

Shit-Kicker was not pleased. He moved to put himself in our way, but Angel stepped in front of him.

I locked the bathroom door behind us.

"Listen, if we don't get out of here right now I know something really bad is going to happen. Please. Please come with me."

She smiled like an older girl would at the nervous overtures of a younger suitor, like she was going to let me in on a secret, like she wasn't naked and the priest at her own sacrifice.

"I'm glad you were here. Thank you for staying. But I think you should go now. I'll be okay."

I left.

I wasn't raised to stay after a woman says to go and I wasn't looking for a reason at that point. I walked out of that bathroom to the hallway, where most of the party had run back to the coolers to beer-up for round two. Angel said for me to move my ass because they were gathering even then to kick it, so I turned without saying goodbye and walked quickly but without panic, like how I think you're supposed to do around untrusted dogs, past the landing where Jennifer had told me not leave her, down the concrete steps to my car across the street.

They were coming, spilling out of the living room through the open screen door. Silhouettes framed by an orange rectangle. Open doors out here can look like a keyhole in a wall of night. "That's pretty," I thought.

Back in my mother's house, I locked myself in the bathroom, lay down on the cold tile and turned the faucets on to fill the tub. I never got in. I just laid with my ear to the floor and listened to the water rush through the pipes underneath.

One night, some skeeters drove by and shot up the Zodiac's front patio with paintball guns. Then, after 9/11, the FBI dropped in on Mike to interrogate him because two of the hijackers had been his frequent customers. He gave up after that and closed shop. Thankfully, by then we'd all gotten old enough to start drinking.

Before he ended the Zodiac though, I saw Angel again. I had to ask him three times before he finally told me how after I left, Jennifer had taken two guys upstairs at the party and fucked them after finding a video camera, and she'd recorded herself doing it. He said people have that video. He said there was nothing I could have done about it. There wasn't a point I could see in telling him the story about why it had all gone down the way it had. She'd told me her reasons before she'd done the act and I didn't want to share. I never saw Jennifer again, but not for lack of trying.

Steve Kowit
Jacumba

I am sitting in the restaurant of the spiffy
new air-conditioned Jacumba Motel
& Health Spa, sipping a root beer
& staring out at a desert
so blazingly desiccated & stark
it's hard to imagine that anything
other than lizards & buckthorn survives here,
& wondering where the old Jacumba Hotel
disappeared to,
that rambling, stucco monstrosity
where one summer night we....
Well, what's the use. Without that hotel
this town is nothing at all of the crumbling,
moth-infested ghost-town it was,
blistering out in the Anza Borrego,
halfway to Yuma,
exquisitely shabby & brooding.
Ah, Time—with your ferocious improvements!
Your infernal, confounded meddling!

Tamara Johnson

A Drought Is Not a Desert
Landscapes of Denial and Other Speculative Fictions

> *Lower, always lower than I am—such is water.*
> —Francis Ponge, from "Of Water"

We used to be a forest. When I was a girl, a white deer lived on the boundary of a disappeared terrain of "tall and straight oaks and other trees, some shrubs resembling rosemary, and a great variety of fragrant and wholesome plants."[1] This is the offical story. A 1602 survey party found the Mediterranean climate here to be "a fine site for Spanish settlement" and estimated the heavily wooded area on the northwest side of the bay to be "three leagues in length and half a league in breadth."[2] Because European explorers were known to exaggerate, and because any corroborating evidence of tall trees was mostly anecdotal (derived from the narratives of laborers such as the women who remembered sitting in the shade of tall oaks as they washed and mended, the tanners who used wood to fuel fires as they smoked hides near trading vessels, and the men who cut roads and had their progress impeded by many large stumps), our forested past can seem as made up as the story of the white deer. But my father had seen her. As children we were as enraptured by the telling of her sudden, and surprising, emergence as we were by any ghost tale.

---

1 From the journal of Father Antonio de la Ascension, a Carmelite priest who was part of the Viscaino's original survey party. This quotation, and the one that follows, is found in William Ellsworth Smythe's basic history of San Diego called simply *History of San Diego*. Smythe covers the evidence for a Point Loma Forest on pages 27-36. His primary sources are good and his conclusions sound. Much of the text, however, is maddeningly Eurocentric. If you aren't familiar with the idea of a wooded San Diego, and can stomach the overt colonial cheerleading, I recommend taking a look at his book online through the San Diego History Center's website: http://www. sandiegohistory.org/books/smythe/1-1.htm.
2 Ibid.

I'm less interested, however, in whether a forest actually existed than I am in the impression that a forest existed. The way we see *what we see* necessarily depends on a kind of *déjà vu*, or preternatural understanding of the thing before us. For example, the Atlantic pilgrims were starving in the winter of 1621 not because there was no food where they were, but because they didn't see the abundant lobsters, oysters, and mussels *as* food.[3] The Puritans were obsessed with corn, however—a generic word for any edible grain or cereal—and so they raided Wampanoag homes and burial sites for maize, arguably the largest kernel in the abundance of indigenous grains.[4] Like the so-called explorers Cabrillo and Viscaino, the Mayflower refugees didn't actually venture much beyond the immediate harbor. Instead, they pointed cannons in the general direction of any standing trees or brush—an understandable precaution to take, perhaps, after a long day of looting. The Indians eyed the self-imposed famine with curiosity: indigenous gourmands had shown the immigrants where to find the tastiest clams, how to open the hard-shell quahogs, how to trap the massive lobsters that virtually walked into awaiting baskets.[5] Still, even the descendants of these newcomers avoided shellfish well into the eighteenth century. They avoided, too, the visually unpalatable forests, usually attempting to raze them completely.[6]

Having been an island, becoming a forest must have been a letdown. And what an island we were, with our dark queen, trained griffins, and a surplus of men with which to feed our pets.[7] Deep in the recesses of our collective memory we must pine for this lost empire, so nostalgic are we for all things islander: sway-

3 "The waters were so rich in lobsters that they were literally crawling out of the sea and piling up inhospitably on the beaches." Mark Kurlansky from "1620: The Rock and the Cod" in *Cod: A Biography of the Fish That Changed the World*, New York, 1997; p. 69.
4 Charles C. Mann, "Why Billington Survived" in *1491: New Revelations of the Americas Before Columbus*, pp. 31-36. To see how French colonists, by contrast, feasted, see John Mack Faragher's excellent history of the French-Acadians, *A Great and Noble Scheme: The Tragic Story of the French Acadians From Their American Homeland*, New York, 2005.
5 "In 1622, Branford reported with shame that conditions were so bad for the settlers that the only 'dish they could presente their friends with was lobster.'" Kurlansky, p. 69.
6 The clearcutting of forests as one of the general labors of colonialism is well-documented in Peter Linebaugh and Marcus Rediker's *The Many-Headed Hydra: Sailors, Slaves, Commoners, and the Hidden History of the Revolutionary Atlantic*, Boston, 2000. In reference to the island of Barbados, the authors write: "It took four decades to clear the island's xerophilous forest, with its ironwood, rodwood, tom-tom bush, and hoe-stick wood," p. 125.
7 From the preface of Elna Baker's *An Island Called California: An Ecological Introduction to Its Natural Communities*, Berkeley, 1984, p. x. "Know ye that on the right hand of the Indies there is an island called California…."

ing palm trees, tiki torches, and Hawaiian shirts. It could be said that we are a kind of island still, with the border wall to the south, Camp Pendleton to the north, the mighty Pacific to the west; and, our various mountain ranges boxing us in on the east side. We sometimes behave as islanders, or what we imagine islanders look like. It is often observed that San Diego is a very small town for such a big city, by which is meant that not only are we provincial, but insular and narrow-minded. People are always arriving to improve us. Early in the twentieth century, eugenicists became obsessed with fallen empires and began to envision a superior civilization emerging from the rubble of European decadence. A new, sturdier, race was to arise out of westward expansion. Suddenly, the majestic redwoods symbolized this new supremacy. The artist and the poet waxed rhapsodic.[8]

One September morning, hot and windy enough to trigger the red-flag warning that signals severe fire season, I stepped out of my second-story apartment holding two chilled colas aloft. The gas-powered motor cut suddenly and with it the deafening roar. As a huge dust cloud arose, a young man in a blue bandana removed his earplugs and wiped his forehead with the back of his hand. I ducked back into my home momentarily and hastily removed the bottle-tops from the old-fashioned glass containers, then descended the long red staircase thrusting one bottle ahead of me. Both of us—the long-term gardener and the long-term renter—drank warily, silent for so many reasons. The space we surveyed together was a small one. Nicknamed "the wilderness" by a former neighbor, the grounds indeed harbored a dizzying array of animals and vegetation, including my attempts at three-sisters gardening, the remains of which were weed-wacked beyond recognition. That the entire neighborhood had come to this was dispiriting. We had all meant well, covering our brownish lawns with plastic landscape sheeting, punching holes for tasteful succulents, carefully raking the decomposing granite into zen-like patterns the better to emphasize a few, carefully-selected (and expensive) boulders. That these synthetic deserts, these drought-tolerant topographies, were so easily despoiled came as a surprise. Less water wise than dirt foolish, we had disappeared our lawns, and then victory gardens, only to replace them with what could best be described as a giant cat box.[9]

---

8 See "Redwood Empires" in Dana Frank's book *Local Girl Makes History: Exploring Northern California's Kitch Monuments*. See, especially, the section called "Virility and Virginity." San Francisco, 2007, pp. 15-21.

9 "I suspect this landscaping will have some fans because it is 'tidy' and 'low maintenance.'"

The opposite of an enclosure is not a better enclosure. A national wilderness, for example, is no true commons. A park is simply a wilder garden and, as such, necessarily contains the legacy of displacement. Once cleared of homesteaders and the indigenous alike, recreation areas serve as a silent endorsements for development elsewhere. The labors of civilization remain, as they have been for centuries, the clear cutting of forests and the draining of fens.[10] Tending a garden is by such definition not labor, but leisure. Wilderness remains undeveloped, virgin, unexploited. The essence of the progressive fallacy is that the only mature path is the forward path, through industry—which is to labor as cleverness is to intelligence. To be slow, by a broader definition, is to become familiar; familiarity is not complacency. Still, in the kind of self-fulfilling journey that circular logic always takes, a landmark may in fact offer indication of how lost one is.

When the representation of a place is built on top of an existing place, the representation (French bistro, Brooklyn nightclub, English garden) erases, in effect, the thing that came before. Like a vast Etch-a-Sketch, Missions become Ranchos, New Spain becomes Old Mexico, Californios become Californians, orchards become vacation spots and so on. San Diegans have long been chided not only for failing to be early adopters (not Seattle enough, or Portland enough, not suitably Silicon Valley), but also for failing to scale upward. That people in Des Moines, or Los Angeles, do not imitate our style is seen by branding advocates as a failure of action, but we should remember where the idea of branding originates. When we speak of something as "being on the map," or (more often, perhaps) "not being on the map," we are not speaking of an actual thing but of a representation of a thing. If we are discussing a representation of a thing, we are talking about perspective. It is important not to mix up these ideas—the thing and the idea of the thing—if only because representation is what being on the map means.

For many people, poor people, people who like where we are currently standing, the idea that we should exchange a real place for the idea of another place is

---

True. It is also devoid of life and actively hostile to nature. Landscapes *speak*," writes Kelly Coyne, as Mrs. Homegrown, on her excellent blog *Root Simple*. Also included with this entry is a snapshot of the almost comically bad "model landscape" around the grounds of the Los Angeles Department of Water and Power. "Can Our Landscapes Model a Vibrant Future? Not According to the LA DWP," July 7, 2014. http://www.rootsimple.com/2014/07/can-our-landscapes-model-a-vibrant-future-not-according-to-the-dwp.
10 "The Labors of the Hewer and Drawer," Linebaugh and Rediker, pp. 43-49.

too ridiculous to consider. If we resist the attempts of outsiders to make us into "a world-class city," it is because we already live at the end of a very long view. "Older than dirt" is a figure of speech rarely leveled as a compliment, but humus and humans share a common root with the word humility. To be of a place is to be of the soil, or earth. Dirt is not dead; or, more accurately, soil is made up of many living and non-living bodies—just as the world above it is, as the human body is. The word *terroir* rightly connotes the taste of a place, its flavor; but, it might better be translated as someplaceness. That we give so little thought to what's under our feet should give us pause. Local land management systems that have been in place for at least 12,000 years were once dismissed as primitive; but, the dirt on which I stand is now understood to be an intricate collaboration between animals, plants, fungi, bacteria, nematodes, protozoa, and insects. The anthropogenic soil of the Amazon has been called "among the finest works of art on the planet."[11]

To continue to treat properties as empty stage sets on which to project fantasies is the opposite of sophistication. It is not only naïve but dangerous to ignore the ingenious carbon capture system that may be the best human survival strategy that is happening despite us. Healthy soil holds water, too; tiny organisms cluster around the deep roots of plants, building honeycomb-like structures that trap both moisture and gas, which in turn control the underground flow that is our best defense against both drought and flood.[12] We know, of course, that a good way to jumpstart the desertification process is by cutting down trees. Suddenly, however, in the name of drought, we are being told by seemingly credible news sources that it's "Trees vs. Humans,"[13] and that Nature is "winning the water wars"[14] by failing to release, as runoff, the precious water we humans need to fill up our depleted reservoirs.[15] These

11 Mann, p. 305.

12 See Kristin Ohlson's *The Soil Will Save Us: How Scientists, Farmer's and Foodies Are Healing the Soil to Save the Planet*, particularly her section called "The Marriage of Light and Dark," New York, 2014, pp. 23-47.

13 "Trees vs. Humans: In California Drought, Nature Gets to the Water First," NBC News, October 17, 2014. http://www.nbcnews.com/science/environment/tree-vs-humans-califonia-drought-nature-gets-water-first-n2288276.

14 "Trees May Be Adding to the Misery of California's Extreme Drought, Soaking Up a Lot More Water That Normally Might Fill Reservoirs, Researchers Say," MSNBC Business, October 17, 2014.

15 "How Too Many Trees Contribute to California's Drought" from KQED's *Morning Edition*, replayed on NPR Stations around the country on October 14, 2014.

so-called news items (which read like pre-packaged releases from the timber industry) are alarmist and ridiculous, but they wake up our limbic brain with battle metaphors in a two-faced strategy of personification (selfish trees, they deserve to die) while maintaining the posture of scientific detachment. Headline-grabbing strategies such as "the war on squirrels," "the fight against global warming" and even the ubiquitous "losing a long struggle with cancer" elevates our supposed foes into a kind of cartoon animism in which nothing really dies because nothing was ever really alive. Unlike the better children's stories such as *Charlotte's Web* or *Make Way for Ducklings*, no one is ever really in danger because there is no personhood, therefore no sense of kinship or empathy. These news stories read worse than children's stories; they read like personal gaming devices.[16]

On the many trips and road tours I've taken, a favorite way to pass the time is a game of Would You Rather. The entertainment value lies in the absurdity of the false dilemma: "Would you rather spend a week at Burning Man or an hour at open mic?" Digital gaming is often a more advanced form of this diversion albeit a diversion that occasionally masquerades as serious business: "If you were traveling through an unfamiliar galaxy and encountered hostile drone fire, would you…?" While the online versions *seem* infinite, they are quite literally an exercise in going along with the program. This morning, the local radio station congratulated residents for "falling in line" with water conservation efforts and it reminded me of these kinds of serious programs.[17] Public radio listeners are generally good-hearted people: we want to make the right choice. But, by obeying the commands of various agencies to "water wisely" or "waste not" it's easy to forget that 80% of California's water supply is allocated for highly inappropriate irrigation practices and that most of the remaining 20% is used, not by thirsty consumers, but by the military, private industry, and state and local facilities. And anyway, a command is not a choice at all. Thus, our individual synthetic deserts serve mostly as individual survivor narratives—the literal embodiment of, "If you were stranded on a desert island and could only take one potted plant with you…?"

---

16 See Douglas Rushkoff, *Program or Be Programmed: Ten Commands for a Digital Age*, New York, 2010.

17 KPBS Radio, January 7, 2015. I'm not sure if the line about residents "falling in line" was scripted or not; it came in between stories and may have been improvised by the announcer.

Perhaps I'm the naïve one, holding on to a time that should never have existed, my memory clouded by the taste of home-cured olives, the smell of ripe figs, and the snapping sound a pomegranate makes before you wear the red stain on your fingers all day. Perhaps I'm too caught up in the history of a terrestrial paradise that never actually happened. Or perhaps the nature of progress really is in the naming of lost things, the parade of perpetual mourning that the Buddhists call samsara: Oak Park, Lemon Grove, Spring Valley. Here, we proudly wave the flag of an extinct bear after all. Anyway, the choice is not between forest or desert, humans or aliens. If we want to make it through the rest of the Holocene, with its projected Sixth Great Extinction, we would be wise to consider hybrid locations—and to enlist the help of hybrid companions—be they cyborg or wild-domestic.

Diogenes, the slave philosopher, was asked where he came from and replied that he was a citizen of the world, or *cosmos*. This identity, from which we derive the word cosmopolitan, is not the vantage point of the elite traveler but, rather, the humility of the multitudes. Frequently used as a shorthand for the heavens, the cosmos could just as easily refer to dirt, or mud. A handful of healthy soil contains more life than all the humans who have ever lived; the simple life forms in an acre rival the number of stars in the sky.[18] When I walk through my Uptown neighborhood during the workweek I am often struck by how abandoned it feels, how empty of human life. Mostly it's just me and the gardeners—although with the rapidly rising rents and the water-tolerant landscapes our kind might be displaced soon. Sceneries change, of course, and I am mindful of the fact that I come from a wilder, hairier, past and may simply be prejudiced by a different aesthetic. If the soil is, as William Jennings Bryant wrote, "the ecstatic skin of the earth," why shouldn't topographies reflect the obsessive sculpting and grooming that accompany current bodily preoccupations?

Here above the line, or border, in a place sometimes known as *la tierra de las reglas* by those below it, I am treading on the orderly restraint of the personal, low-impact, model of consumerism that liberals embrace with a vigor, but which tends to accomplish little. To be fair, I know only second-hand the pressures homeowners are under to conform to and maintain codes, having opted out of the mainstream early by studying poetry. But the desertification

---

18 "The Marriage Between Light and Dark" in Ohlson, pp. 23-47.

of San Diego is troubling to me not because it offends my tender sensibilities with its bad taste, but because San Diego the city is bordered by actual desert— the kind that does the hard work of soaking up the blood and shit that is the result of so many bigoted and misguided acts.[19] This real desert is a beautiful, but harsh, landscape that is frequently exploited by those who would use their power to enforce a crude pantomime of conformity by local smallholders. Side by side with synthetic turf, the toy deserts of the urban gentry are play islands upon which to await our collective, but fictional, rescue. In the limited options presented by boy wizards in their genius bars, human guard dogs monitor the passwords meted out to obedient members of small, gated, communities with the promise that the ghostly white apple of knowledge really does lead to forbidden images of beautiful naked women hidden deep within a singular cloud. Technology is not new, but common and old.[20] The slickest hand-held device has its origins in dirt—in the coltan mines of Ethiopia, in the national wildlife refuge of the Congo with its international bootleg operations. In the words of science and tech journalist Annalee Newitz, "I don't believe in The Singularity for the same reason I don't believe in Heaven."[21] Progress doesn't move in clean lines; it isn't tidy. We can't yet make sense of what we still haven't encountered.

---

19 One might say that from a particular vantage point, San Diego has always been a destination spot for the wrong type of person: the working person, the poor person, the person of color. Perhaps the most notorious example of vigilantism by the elite happened during the free speech fights of the last century as is documented by Jim Miller in "Just Another Day in Paradise." Here he quotes "Codger" Bill Lewis, among others, who experienced torture rituals that often preceded the deportation of so-called undesirable citizens: "They kilt two and ya' don't know how many more bodies they mighta dumped in the desert for the coyotes since a lot of us were what ya' might call foot-loose, without family or connections if we was to disappear" (From *Under the Perfect Sun: The San Diego Tourists Never See*, New York, 2003). But there is no reason to believe workers aren't meeting similar fates today, as documented by journalist Roc Morin for *Vice* magazine: "Oftentimes, the identification happens after the cremation, but at least in those cases we can give the families ashes. In California, there have been [...] laws passed where they actually scatter the ashes at sea. So there's nothing left to give the family. Which is re-traumatizing for the family." *Dead Migrants Are Vanishing at the Texas Border*, December 16, 2014. http://www.vice.com/read/dead-migrants-are-vanishing-without-a-trace-at-the-texas-border-1216?utm_source=vicetwitterus.
20 Kevin Kelly makes this case in his book *What Technology Wants*, New York, 2010; Kelly, however, defines technology in such as way as to exclude lost indigenous practices such as the "built environments" that, according to University of Pennsylvania archeologist Clark Erickson, make up "most, if not all, neotropical landscapes" (Erickson quoted in Mann, pp. 305-306). For more on indigenous cultural practices *as* technological practices, see M. Kat Anderson's *Tending the Wild: Native American Knowledge and the Management of California's Natural Resources*, Berkeley, 2005.
21 See "Why the Singularity Isn't Going to Happen" http://io9.com/5661534/why-the-singular-

Northeast of San Diego, in the hills of Riverside County, is an oak tree (*Quercus palmeri*) that is at least 13,000 years old, but perhaps much older. A recent image of the scrubby botanical reveals nothing special—just a tangle of branches rising out of a literal garbage heap. At its roots are the mycorrhizal fungi that in another time and place might be re-branded as a unique truffle and hunted with the help of domestic pigs, a human–animal partnership centuries in the making.[22] If we believe, to paraphrase Derrick Jensen, that water comes from the tap and food comes from the grocery store, we will defend places of commerce and transportation to the death; but, if we believe that food comes from the soil, and water comes from rivers and streams, we will defend these places because we know that our lives depend on them.[23] When environmental and political activist Wangari Maathai was beaten unconscious for opposing development in her native Kenya, then-president Daniel Arap Moi called her a "a mad woman" and "a threat to national order and security."[24] But, she was right to link desertification, deforestation, and a water crisis with other, more pedestrian, concerns. As the novelist Junot Diaz puts it in his essay "Apocalypse," about the Haitian earthquake: "We must refuse the old stories that tell us to interpret social disasters as natural disasters."[25] If a drought, by definition, is a temporary disturbance, why (instead of preparing terra firma for the coming floods, the inevitable El Niño or La Niña) would we entertain the curious fantasy of escaping (literally or symbolically) to other, more exotic, environs? The answer comes, as it often does, in orthodoxy—complete with authority in triplicate, the chief executive officer, whose acolytes conduct elaborate stagings of personal virtue and compliance. But there is no virtue in self-negation. And in the event of disaster, one should surely not count on being selected for transportation at all, let alone to any celestial body. If history is clear about any one thing it is this: The future is underground, and always has been.

---

ity-isnt-going-to-happen.

22 Rachel Sussman, *The Oldest Living Things in the World*, pp. 42-51.

23 I know Derrick Jensen has spoken about this idea elsewhere, but I first heard him discuss it in a private conversation at UCSD's Che Café in the summer of 1996.

24 I first encountered these quotations in her autobiography *Unbowed*, but since the awarding of her Nobel Prize in 2004, it is a rare biography that doesn't use the Moi quotation or a quotation by her former husband, who when he filed for divorce in 1979, called her "too strong-minded for a woman," and complained that he was "unable to control her." Both Moi and Wangaai's former husband are quoted, for example, in the most recent Wikipedia entry, keeping her acts defined, to a certain extent, by the two presumed authority figures who opposed them.

25 Junot Diaz, "Apocalypse: What Disasters Reveal," *The Boston Review*, May 1, 2011.

Addendum

As this anthology readies for press, a friend of mine—a good guy, a smart and interesting guy, a guy who has lived in San Diego his whole life—posts a link on his Facebook page with the following comment: "San Diego has made the cut as a promising place to live. Sweet!" The link is to an article in the so-called "paper of record" that still, apparently, serves as the authority on geographic desirability. Young college graduates are moving here in droves. I have not a thing against young college graduates, I used to be one; but, if attracting young people is the mark of success, it explains the other local story of the week: the giant Ferris wheel proposed on San Diego Bay. I like carnival rides as much, or more, as the next person. Still, if such diversions are the focus of our attentions it's no wonder that other stories are getting so little traction. I asked one of these new college graduates, one of the so-called movers and shakers, for her opinion on a local writer. "No one outside San Diego cares about San Diego," she responded, by which she meant that she doesn't care about San Diego, and why should she? She doesn't know the place, having arrived here only recently from the Capitol area. Her position in branding is with a firm that specializes in creating online images, the location selected based on an algorithm. But the job wasn't what it appeared to be: the chief advisorship was actually a low-wage position, her office a fancy cubicle. This new resident is settling in, however, and starting a family in an old neighborhood. I wish her and her new family the best—and by the best I mean I hope she settles in for a long spell.

Steve Kowit

Dusk in the Cuyamacas

It was that tangerine
& golden
sepia light
spilling over the Cuyamacas
—each leaf
of the manzanita
chiselled in space—
that shook me out of my dreams
till I woke again
to my own life:
everything shimmering
everything just as it is.

Jill G. Hall

No Such Thing as Global Warming?

The overhead fan starts
to twirl even though no
one has turned it on.
An orange oriole smacks
into the window stunned.

A distant siren screams.

It's 90 degrees at the coast
and 110 in El Cajon while
slate-colored ash sifts
over San Diego and Santa
Ana fires flame once more.

Soon to be bloodshot eyes begin
to burn. Folks hose down their
yards, pack cars and watch the
endless news stories of blazes
that shoot up, over and over again

and tickertape words scroll
across the bottom of their
screens listing neighborhoods
being evacuated hoping
it's not their turn this time.

Diane Gage

Peace in Our Time

Not so easy in this suburb to make the crops rejoice.

One neighbor does it with raised beds, good mulch.
Several have turned to palm trees, or hired pros.
Most have learned over this tract's fifty+ years
which plants can be happy here
with our particulars of soil, water, sun,
wind, temperature. It's not a thin or colorless mix:
jasmine, jacaranda, bougainvillea, fescue, iris, fig,
roses, of course, mimosas, gazanias, impatiens, sage,
alyssum everywhere, avocados, geraniums, euryops, daisies.

Just add water, borrowed from towering mountains
hundreds of miles north and piped controversially down.

So many soldiers came home from hell hungry
for a slice of paradise they could hardly bear,
but build it they could, engineer it, pave it, wire it,
secure it, improve it within an inch of its former natural life,
then lock it up so they could roam the desert in monster RVs,
their kids parked in front of various flickering screens—
some of them in armored vehicles, bunkers, tents,
gone to keep a war going halfway around the world.

Sylvia Levinson

Sorrento Valley

Rolling hills, swells, like soft breasts,
once stretched along this cleft of freeways,
passage between city and beach. Now slopes
terraced, excised, like lost body parts. Now,
building upon box-like building; colonies of
humans who spend their mornings swarming
to freeways, their evenings creeping back.

The ground was never good for growing much—
volunteer mustard in spring, a cheery yellow lift
for homebound drivers. In winter, dead grasses
waved, long and dun-colored. Once, horses grazed.
Fox and rabbit, snake and mouse, long displaced,
deprived of home. Fragile fossils crushed by scuffed
leather work boots. And, above the earth, we lose
our home, our center, natural curve of land, the trees.

We live on traffic and adrenaline, re-contour the land
which molds us, scrape away the very shapes our bodies crave.

Megan Webster

Ambling Around Lake Murray

There's something about the lake—
the way it trembles into shimmer,

the way ducks paddle wakes of silver
& water siphons gold from the sun;

the way it runs in tandem with the sky,
gathering pools of purple cloud;

the way it drowns the face of war,
the sunken orbs of drought & famine.

There's something about the lake—
the fisherman hooked to his bowing rod,

still as a Hogarth painting,
the heron stilted on its island rock,

eyeing both halves of the world.
Something not found in the raging

throb of ocean. Something
that sinks your eye in the prow

& keeps your paddle pulling.

Sandra Alcosser
Because the Body Is Not a Weapon

In this town of date palms
and expensive pastry
everyone wears pastels.
Everyone owns a sports car
and speeds. I leap with blondes
in a gymnasium of steely leotards.
No one speaks to me.
No one catches my eye.
I eat ill-conceived
Mexican takeout—
pasty beans with
chopped beef.
In my dreams
all the creeps of my life
call me. I swear the only person
who spoke last week
had three-inch toenails
curled over his sandals.
Oh yes, and at the grocery
a little girl in coveralls
studies me when I smile.
You're not my mother,
she kicks her thick legs
through the cart rails.
You're not my mother.
Still I pass lightly
as a dust diamond
through my pink sea cottage.
And how should I take this omen:
stalled in traffic, a van of boys
barks at me. Twelve years old,

they lick the windows.
They moon their half-formed buttocks.
They wiggle their shell-like genitals.
Do I laugh?
Have I become a foreign country?

Jeeni Criscenzo
When the Purple Arrives

It's here so briefly…
Those precious days
when San Diego springs up purple!

When the morning mist
coats the coast in pale lilac.
Sea lavender and purple sage
line the bike path to OB.
And jacaranda trees sway
in a delicate violet dance
along the streets of downtown.

When the marine layer slips away
unveiling sun-drenched geraniums and bougainvillea
meandering on front-yard fences,
a bit of a breeze flaunting their facets
of amethyst and mauve
in the midday light.

When the angle of the evening sun
picks out the indigo in the Chicano Park murals,
and the woven shawls pulled snug on the shoulders
of weary women chatting at the picnic tables.

When May days die
with the sunset's last gasp,
of a deep, dark, purple prayer…

By June, jacaranda droppings
will litter the sidewalks.

And the canyon breezes
will plead for your attention,
with parched sage breath.
And the purple fades away.

Those who come for the winter,
declare there is no change of seasons here.
Seeing only the peeling eucalyptus,
browned sea lavender,
succulents in slumber.
All dull as the Anza desert in December.

True that little that's lush lingers
after that orgasmic burst of purple is spent.
But we,
the watchers of gardens and skies,
We wait.
Through autumn and winter we wait.
We wait.
For those brief days in May,
when the purple arrives!

Kevin Dublin

How to Fall in Love in San Diego

Eat blackberry brie bites
between two fingers
at a crashed Hilton party
between the harbor
and Convention Center.
Dance to an all-white-
Otis-Redding cover band
in Hawaiian shirts.
Foot it to the dueling piano bar
after Security checks lanyards.
Give the bartender a large tip
and advice that changes her life.
Flirt with a Swedish accent.
Pretend you're here
for a wedding
—unless you're here
        for a wedding
—then pretend you're here
        post-divorce.
Whisper in a cute brunette's ear
that her girlfriend is gorgeous,
but hug the doorman.
Learn his name
the way Goldilocks
tastes porridge—tenderly.
Tap three strangers.
Ask for the restroom
in a foreign tongue
from *perdon,*
dónde está el baño?
to *have you seen the loo?*

Be a noble experiment.
Tell all hostesses Liam sent you.
Ask why they don't know him.
Text any number in your phone
and change the name to Liam.
Get addresses of the cutest girls
and never visit them.
Snag the Uber app.
Ask where the driver's
pink moustache is.
Tell him you heard
Hillcrest was fun, but
you'd rather drive
to an apartment—
any one he has the keys to.
Stir gasps in distant rooms.
Heed cabbie's command:
Make me forget
we swoon in a desert.

Katrin Pesch
Dictionary Hill

A gravity hill is an anomaly. It's a place where the law of gravity doesn't apply. Objects can be seen to roll uphill. Water flows uphill too, and cars, when put in neutral, magically ascend slight slopes as if pulled by invisible strings. It's not gravity that is suspended, though, but perception that is being tricked into believing that what's actually downhill is uphill. This optical illusion occurs if the horizon line is hidden and the relative incline of a slant or slope is thus obscured. There used to be a gravity hill in Spring Valley, on La Presa just off of Birch Street. People from as far as LA drove here to experience the sensation of defying gravity. So I make the trip too. But gravity seems to be firmly in place again, thanks to the construction of houses that drew the horizontal back into the landscape. No sensation of rolling uphill, just amazement about the sheer steepness of the terrain. At the end of La Presa, a Thomas the Train ride-on toy lies shattered next to the interlocking concrete barriers that separate the cul-de-sac from the rugged hill. It may be that Thomas' breakdown was caused by exertion from rolling up hill in the heat, but really the collapsed toy looks as beat-up as the area around it is run-down. Or maybe he is just stored by the driveway, waiting to be assembled by the kid who lives there for another fun ride.

◆ ◆ ◆

The hill that once defied gravity carries many names. Some are known, others forgotten. Lookout Mountain is one of them. Today the little mountain goes by Dictionary Hill. In 1910, a development company had bought 480 acres of federal land and established a subdivision called San Diego Villa Heights. The subdivision was created for promotional use by a San Francisco-based publishing company. Small building lots were given as premiums with a $109 subscription to a 25-volume encyclopedia, the *Library of Universal History and Popular Science*,

View South

bound in half-leather. Upon full payment of the installments, the owner was to receive a deed for the complimentary lot at no further cost. "It is guaranteed," the order form reads, "that these lots are high and dry, free from swamp and damp, wet land." Located on the southern side of the hill, the lots were indeed free of swamp. But the surveyor who had laid a perfect grid over the land didn't account for the topography. At 50x120 feet, many of the narrow plots were crammed onto ridges and steep slopes and proved unsuitable for building construction. Almost none of the subscribers took ownership of their lots, nor did the developer take steps to provide the necessary infrastructure. Literally and figuratively, the few new owners who arrived on the hill were left high and dry.

Downloaded from the internet, volume 1 of the *Library of Universal History and Popular Science* comes as a digital scroll of 435 pages, made from pixels instead of parchment paper. I skip over the nondescript cover, but before I get to the title page I linger over the two pages of marbled endpaper. Paper made from colors floating on water, pulled into ornamental shapes with fine tools like hair or fiber. Colors absorbed by a sheet of paper leaving a watery design on the surface: a perfect way to fix the wetness of water onto the dryness of a page. Less than marble, the endpaper's shades of earthy brown and red remind me of the red volcanic rock that forms Dictionary Hill, a toxic fluid dried into stone. It seems as if a piece of the terrains' rocky surface has been mapped onto the marble endpaper, a secret trace of the complimentary plots of land that were given away with the encyclopedia. The repeating undulations of the pattern resemble the contour lines that project Dictionary Hill on the region's topographical map, which was compiled much later in the 1950s. On the map, the winding brown lines show the hill's elevation, while the straight street grid of the original surveyor is superimposed in white. Over the course of the century a neighborhood did develop on the hill, and the red color shading the contour lines on the map marks not rocks, but the built-up area that covers them.

After scrolling down a six-page stretch through a desert of empty, yellowing pages, I arrive at another rock formation. A photograph of a monumental statue of Ramses II, carved into the sandstone cliffs at Ipsambul temple in Egypt, foreshadows the specific historical and geographic focus of the *Library of Universal History and Popular Science's* first volume. The encyclopedia's introduction, it turns out, is written by none other than Hubert Howe Bancroft. The famous California historian was no stranger to the area. In 1883 he had bought a small adobe building at the bottom of the hill and established his Helix Farm there, a summer residence and olive and citrus farm. The two-room adobe was the first white settlement in east county San Diego, built on the site of a former Kumeyaay village. Tucked away in a dead-end street and not exactly well known, the Bancroft Ranch House is a small museum today with an ever-growing archive of historical artifacts, mundane objects, community life, and personal stories.

Titled "The Educational Value of the Study of History," the encyclopedia's introduction reveals Bancroft as a compelling writer. He situates all things known as equal members in a vast confederation that he calls the republic of science, in which each member depends on the others. There's the parliament of things, the democracy of objects so frequently evoked today, *avant la letter* in a place where one would least expect it! But Bancroft soon takes a different path, when he describes the task of history to discriminate from the vast amount of facts about the past the ones charged with historical valence. "It can hardly be wise to make the memory serve the purpose of an old-fashioned garret in a country house,—a receptacle for all sorts of odds and ends of property, precious and worthless. Surely, such indiscriminate memorizing must be a waste of energy, and the perversion of a noble faculty."

Surely Bancroft didn't envision his country house to be a small-town museum one day, filled to the brim with all sorts of odds and ends, precious and worthless!

Rather, he associates the study of history with the approximate and probable, compared to science's claim to absoluteness and exactitude. Learning to discern

Mountain View

the truth and gain understanding of the causal relation between pertinent historical facts is the very training that the study of history may provide. More than merely expanding his mental horizon, it will make man more modest and more temperate. And tolerant, too. What separates the writing of history from contemporary commentary, Bancroft muses, is the advantage of the retrospect and the allegiance to unbiased and non-partial presentation, "with respect to all subjects whatsoever." In short, the study of history just as much as the writing of it is nothing less than what makes man a complete human being.

Or at least some of them. As Bancroft lays out his understanding of history, he also reveals himself as a man of his class, time and social horizon. "We commonly think of American History," he writes, "as beginning with the year 1492." But patriotism, he goes on, should not fall into the trap of narrow-minded provincialism. It is therefore important to look to the European forefathers and their ancient predecessors in order to achieve full self-understanding. The more strongly he argues for a universal approach, the more he qualifies as to whom this universalism applies. For "[a] nation emerging from savagism, until it has a written record makes little advancement." Bancroft's word's adumbrate what the series editor spells out a few pages later in language plain and unmistakable: "The only race which has figured in history is the Caucasian. The history of the civilized world is the history of the Caucasian race."

Bancroft brings up a beautiful image of history as a bow of light: "[I]t flashes its rays far back over those rough waters through which our ship has been ploughing, and it throws at least some illumination forward upon the deeps of time toward we are about to sail." One can imagine how the original inhabitants, their willow bows shouldered in skeptical anticipation, stood atop the hill and watched the ships of Juan Cabrillo arrive at the bay in 1542. The Portuguese explorer sailing under Spanish flag was the first European to voyage the coast of present-day California. While Cabrillo's ships were sailing into the unknown, the Kumeyaay had learned about the arrival of white men already through messages passed on from tribes in the interior and related the news to Cabrillo's crew. "And in another day following in the morning came to the ship three Indians large," the expedition's log states, "and by signs told us that walked by the inland inside men like us bearded and dressed, and armed like the ones on the ships, and they showed that they had ballistas and swords, and they made gestures with their right arm as if they were spearing, and they went running as if they were on a horse, and that they killed many Indians of the native, and for that reason they were afraid; these people were well proportioned and large." Three layers of mimetic action are compressed into these lines. There is the double description of a testimonial that is first acted out and then written down; the third step is performed much later in the verbatim translation of the log from Spanish to English. Along the way, the actions of victims and aggressors become eerily conflated into a string of past events: they showed, they made gestures, they went running, they killed, they were afraid. The Kumeyaay's gestures capture a past event; Cabrillo's log keeper describes the Kumeyaay's gestures. Unspoken, both reports spell out the atrocities

Coronado Bridge

committed by the men-at-arms traveling with conquistador Francisco Vasquez de Coronado, en route through the New World earlier the same year.

The Kumeyaay's social structure entailed an extended system of lookouts and runners. Early white settlers, too, had dubbed the hill Lookout Mountain, and came up here to spot their cattle or to check if the steamer had come in, before making the 12-mile trip to the harbor. The name Dictionary Hill came later, a twisted residue of the encyclopedia that some of the new settlers stacked on their shelves. A lookout becomes Lookout Mountain; Lookout Mountain becomes Dictionary Hill. The small hill's change of name relates to a larger shift in the way historical knowledge is captured and produced. In terms of local history it marks the shift from looking to reading, from *looking at* something to *looking up* something. In terms of historiography it parallels the movement from oral testimony to written account; from local to global; and from particular to universal. Historical events cease to be embodied knowledge; at the same time the writing of history is written out of history.

Skyline

Wind hits the microphone and transforms into roaring thunder. The audio drags the image with it turning the sunny hill into a high desert plain. Vibrant reds faint and subtle shades of green are muted by noise. The open space mocks my normal-range lens and recedes behind a screen of dust. It all looked different when I hauled my equipment up the hill. The wind brushed lightly over the costal sage and caressed my bare arms getting heavy with the weight of the tripod. I stop to rest a couple of times and look towards the ocean, my eyes squinting in the sun. The higher I get, the more familiar features appear. There are the high rises downtown that make up San Diego's teething skyline and the elevated curve of the Coronado bridge soaring across the bay, 200 feet high and tall enough to allow passage for the ships of Pacific Fleet stationed at the Navel Base nearby. 12 miles east and 1,000 feet above sea level, I climb the final stretches to the peak. A flurry of butterflies breezes by. These are the visitors who truly defy gravity, floating swiftly on wind currents and thermal uplifts to save energy for future engagements. Atop the hill males compete for the best spots to impress the arriving females. First documented in the 1960s, the "hill-top-ping" mating behavior of insects on Dictionary Hill has since been threatened by other's competing for prime real estate with a view. A string of developers has proposed building projects crowing the peak. The last such plan sought to raze 35 feet off the top of the hill in order to built a subdivision of 211 homes. The planned gated community would have cut across the open space, turning the last wildlife and plant habitat in densely populated Spring Valley into a land-scape shaped by concrete trenches and retaining walls: Welcome to Highland Ranch. The development fell flat in 2010, thanks to the efforts of the Dictionary Hill Open Space Advocates (DHOSA), a community group that called atten-tion to the project's massive environmental impact.

Stamped out of the ground as a promotional gimmick of a publishing company, the Dictionary Hill neighborhood has been ill conceived from the very begin-ning. But rock is more enduring than paper. And more valuable, for that matter. While the *Library of Universal History and Popular Science* is long outdated and spends its digital afterlife in the public domain, most of Dictionary Hill is still parceled into lots that are privately owned, though hoping to thrive, one day, as a public space.

Cesar E. Chavez in Barrio Logan | *Juanita Lopez*

Brent E. Beltrán
Livin' La Vida Logan

Barrio Logan is one of the oldest neighborhoods in San Diego. It used to be one whole community called Logan Heights, named after congressman John A. Logan, but the creation of the Interstate 5 freeway that bisected the neighborhood changed that. Then the building of the San Diego–Coronado Bridge changed it again. Thousands were displaced from building the freeway and the bridge. Now Barrio Logan encompasses a relatively small patch of land sandwiched between the San Diego Bay and the I-5 freeway and north of National City and south of San Diego's East Village.

Fewer than 5,000 people inhabit my barrio. Thousands more come during the day to work here in the shipyards, the Port of San Diego and the other companies that line the bay side of Barrio Logan. Of those 5,000 barrio denizens about 85% of them are non-white, most of which are of Mexican descent. But things are changing. There are demographic shifts as property values rise and the proximity to Downtown San Diego is realized. Developers are drooling to take over the land to build condos and hipster bars. A showdown over the future character of my community is on the horizon.

Barrio Logan is one of the most stereotyped neighborhoods in all of San Diego. People who don't live here have negative thoughts about my barrio. That it is crime ridden. Full of gangs. Violence plagued. But Barrio Logan has gotten a bum rap over the years. It is not the crime-infested slum that people think it is. Things have changed for the positive and Barrio Logan has become a place where working families can once again raise their children in a positive, culturally affirming way.

Barrio Logan is home to Chicano Park, the largest outdoor display of murals in the world. It's also home to the militancy that created Chicano Park. A militancy that won't ever go away, even as the Chicano Movement generation grows older. Barrio Logan is also home to a burgeoning Barrio Arts District. If Chicano Park is grandaddy to San Diego's Chicano arts scene then places like the Voz Alta Project Gallery, The Roots Factory and The Spot Barrio Logan are its wayward grandchildren ready to rise up and share this generation's vision of Chicano art and culture.

Barrio Logan is home to the Barrio Station and the Barrio Logan College Institute. Las Cuatro Milpas and Blueprint Cafe. Centro Aztlán Marco Anguiano and the Paradise Senior Center. Don Diego VFW and the Logan Inn. We are churches and one liquor store. A community with taco shops, carnicerías y fruterías galore. We are San Diego Public Market and Mercado Northgate. We roast fine coffee beans at Ryan Bros., Cafe Virtuoso and Cafe Moto. Murals blaze colors on walls throughout this neglected, working-class neighborhood. Barrio Logan is one of the poorest communities in the city of San Diego. Yet we shine on. We are the embodiment of a living, breathing culture going about our lives. We live la vida Logan.

Reprinted from the San Diego Free Press, *April 3, 2013.*

JUNCO'S JABS by Junco Canché

Jerry Sanders and Kevin Faulconer share their disdain for Barrio Logan residents.

Brent E. Beltrán

The Rock: Resistance Barrio Logan Style

Juanito held the rock firmly in his hand—almost too firmly, as his knuckles turned white from the pressure. He stood there shaking, and tears slowly fell from his reddened eyes. A wheezy cough escaped his tight lungs as the eleven-year-old stood on Harbor Drive facing the towering cranes that loomed over this toxic barrio. Every breath he took was a challenge. The setting sun cast a powerful glow of purples and oranges across the radiant, polluted sky.

He had grown up on these neglected streets, a Barrio Logan native in more ways than one. He stood there with rock in hand as semi trucks rumbled past, hauling bananas picked by people that looked just like him. The vehicles added more pollutants into the atmosphere as they traveled to various points north and east. That rock, smooth from centuries of ocean water beatdowns, weighed heavy in his trembling hand.

Juanito was tired. Tired of his father slowly dying from a cancer brought on by harsh chemicals he had used to clean with while working on the very site his son now stood in front of. Tired of his madrecita working too many hours at the various jobs she had to endure to pay the rent on their dilapidated home since her husband could no longer do so. Tired of his older brother Beto not being around anymore. Cops had caught Beto tagging after a shipyard security officer saw him hitting up a wall with anti-pollution slogans. He was doing five years to make an example for any other potential anti-shipyard taggers. The District Attorney received campaign donations from the maritime industry, and in return she made an example of this barrio kid to prevent future incidents like this from happening. Juanito was also tired of his younger sister, Maria Elena, always being sick, lungs wheezing much worse than his. She'd missed more than a year of school, setting her back a grade level.

As Juanito stood there, he thought of all the pain, agony and frustration that he'd had to handle at such a young age. He thought of his formerly strong father's treatments that had left him weak, a shell of his past self. He thought of the greasy, old, white landlord making passes at his mom, knowing his father couldn't do anything about them, saying he'd lower the rent for a "little something." Mom always politely said no, hiding the fury deep inside her proud soul. He thought of his sister gasping for air with every attempted breath, lungs too tight to fully oxygenate her blood, her lips sometimes turning blue. He thought of Beto doing time for writing "All We Want is Clean Air" for all to see.

As he stood there with rock in hand, all these thoughts of loved ones done wrong came racing through his prepubescent mind. The suffering of his family and community weighed on him. Something must be done, he thought to himself. But he had no power, no connections. He was just a kid from Barrio Logan, after all. Still, he thought, something must be done.

Juanito clutched that rock as if the universe depended on it. As if life itself were at stake. And for him it was. His dad dying, his mom slaving away while fighting off harassment, his brother locked up, his sister gasping for air with every breath. He felt they all depended on him to do something, anything for the barrio they called home.

With every ounce of energy and will his eleven-syear-old body could muster he let the rock fly. And fly it did, like a cannonball coursing through the dusky air. And when that cannonball struck the glass window, shattering it into a million shards of broken bits, with a powerful crash, Juanito saw it all in slow motion. As though time were barely moving. It seemed like an eternity before the crash of glass ended. But when it did, there was no more trembling; there were no more tears. Just Juanito standing there, staring forward with the biggest smile to ever cross his beautiful, brown face.

Michael Cheno Wickert
Gato Chito

Footprints through sunset parks
Dorado sneaks calm between
Treetop leaves reaching forth
White-noise freeways swish past
Otro momento negado
Vestido en dusty grey haze
rebozo mudo
Cada paso gnóstico
Sin miedo de reproche
The sidewalk sage scuttles
Toward sun beat
Ashing lime-green liquor store
En la 22 y Broadway
Completamente enterado
Chito
Parado en espera
Vuelve a su amante
Y le dice en voz de gato
—no hay placer a vivir entre aquí
y el paraíso.

El gato rambla de esquina a callejón
De basurero a porche en silencio
Debajo el pozo oro blanco
Contra la rayada y cansada oscuridad
Sí, rambla
Sí rambla porque sí
Él ya peleó en las guerras de
Arena y selva
Ya durmió en el amparo de la puente del autopista
Sobre banqueta dura y viva con fiesteros

Él ya
Ahora con ella
Su teonontzín
Su Guadalupe
Su Malinche
Su Adelita
Amorosa
Mano en mano
Ellos ramblan
Sí, ellos juntos
perfectamente ramblan
por allá y por aquí

Aquí en el sur del norte
En el norte del sur
La esquina del mundo
Derramado con sueños destripados
Sangrando esperanza por la boca
Fertilizando brotes insignificantes
Aquí en el entremedio
Paisaje extraño
dicen que todo se permite
Que todo es posible
Que nuestro amor puede crecer
Al lado del liquor verde-limón
Donde se conoce la canción del
Aire sucio
empujado del camión
lleno de caras perdidas
mirando los amantes
ojos cariñosos
labios
dulces
infatuados
contigo
precisamente
abrazando
nuestro destino.

Camino contigo, mi amor
Tu corazón y lo mío palpitando

Mientras los carros suben y bajen
Nuestros dedos intertwined
We stumble medio borracho
Tripping on cracked slabs of concrete
Crushing broken glass cahuama dreams
Underfoot
Esta vez yo te miro sin ojos
Unlike always
Aquí in the muddle
on a southern california street
confessing
hoping
standing
here
tangled in a kiss
where you and I
become nosotros.

Michael Cheno Wickert

We Were Born

We were born from break beats
Shoving their way
Past Sunday morning mariachis
Grandma in her slippers slapping
Sliding across floors
Complaining
—ay, qué frío
the clean sun blooming dorado
above mountain tops
—allá mijo,
allá 'rriba uno se conoce—me dijo
morning slumber sueño
wrapped in swap meet
Amor Azteca blanket
Shivering off last night chills
Where we sprung up along
Avenues
  Grand
    Imperial
      Coronado
And crowned ourselves kings
Of the mix that is the mezcla of
Market Street bandits borrachos
Bouncing philosophy on the
Turntables of J St. Dj's
Jousting Black Uhuru
And Biggy
Up slopes
Broadway bares Winos on rooftops
Digging Sly Stone on a roll
To Ramón Ayala

Dancing mica-less
Silhouettes
In a bomba stove kitchen
        Una velita
        Mano poderosa flickers
        Rosary beads
        Jaycees Market calendar
        On the refri
        Smell of Ariel and Pinol

A calloused palm
Su sonrisa todavía enamorado
Reaches for her lower back
Another slips into her dry cracked hand
Cupped in prayer
A plume of smoke
Swirls his words
        —chaparita de mi vida
chafes her slippers
in perfect time
two-step tempo recuerdos
chispas
her momentary youth
regained
a cat swaying on fence-posts
below faded diamond sky
orange
twirling
between beats and beatings and revolutions
leaning dizzy
against alleyway walls
graffiti shouts
        —Presente, mi general
        —a sus ordenes
        —ahí, le espero
esperando
escuchando la noche
pensando
        en ti
solito me dejaste

drinking in liquid dreams
slurring epiphanies
passed out in wood-clad garages
drunk on crooked talk
had by halves of ourselves
just not quite us
not quite them
disallowing the other, siempre
beyond meztizo
mulato
mvarioisunderstood
beyond remnants of allá
those old bones rebirthed
on these sandy shores
remain within the gaze
of grandma
su duende bailador
su radio
those slippers
smell of fresh coffee
warming the morning
air
with a breath
her words
those smiling thoughts

a vision

a prophesy

a sunrise

in this new tierra
        de santa sangre

Impeach the System, Golden Hill | *Vince Compagnone*

III. MEMORY AND LOSS

Doug Porter
My Days at the Door

The *San Diego Door* and its antecedents were a big part of the alternative media scene in America's Finest City over an eight-year period starting in October, 1966 when the *Good Morning, Teaspoon* published its first edition.

By December, 1971, when I first climbed up the steps of the paper's Victorian stick mansion at 2445 Albatross Street just north of downtown, the paper had gone through "free love," hippie-druggie and counterculture phases and a half-dozen names. It had evolved to become a publication with anti-establishment news and alt-culture reviews, featuring powerful graphics and color.

Solid support from local businesses, regional concert promoters and national record companies meant the paper often published in two sections. Two hundred fifty or so vending machines around the city combined with regular radio advertising on local rock stations gave the *Door* a higher profile than one might expect for an "underground" newspaper.

I came to the *Door* via the *OB Rag*, a spunky and radical underground paper with a strong neighborhood bent. The collective publishing the *Rag* was scattering to the winds (it was re-born several times and exists as a blog today). As a blue 1964 Plymouth Valiant cruised by our Muir Street house on the evening of January 6, 1972, a gunman fired two shots through the front window, wounding one woman and narrowly missing another.

Although it would later turn out that the driver of the car was an FBI informant, the local daily paper and at least one television station ran stories suggesting the shooting was staged by our group to gain sympathy for San Diego State economics professor Peter Bohmer. He was part of the group and, as the highest-profile radical in the city at that point, subject to attempts to gain his dismissal from the school along with regular harassment from various police agencies....

The shooting was the last straw for the collective and our landlord; we'd endured months of threats and small acts of vandalism by a group calling itself the Secret Army Organization.

On the night of the shooting I was meeting with a *Door* editor about becoming a contributor. They had questions about me being too radical; I was concerned about sexism in the paper's classified ads.

I guess it worked out. A week later I was living at the paper's headquarters. My first story concerned Black Panther Huey P. Newton. Soon after, the women working on the paper brought about the end of the offensive classified ads.

The house on Albatross was part office, part group house and part meeting place. The popular notion of the hippie commune being an oasis of sex, drugs and constant parties was a million miles away from the reality of the *Door* house.

The Victorian structure dated from the 1870s, we were told, and came complete with a widow's walk outside the west-facing master bedroom overlooking the harbor. Little work on the interior had done since the 1920s, when Mr. F.O. Carlson acquired the property. There were chandeliers in three of the first-floor rooms equipped by both gas and electric. The overgrown yard gave it the image of being a haunted house.

City directories show the property being unoccupied starting in 1966, and we presumed that was when the widow Carlson died. More than one *Door* staffer reported seeing or hearing strange things in the house.

Then-publisher Bill Maguire rented the property in 1969. It was cheap, centrally located and had plenty of both space and privacy. The only downside was noise from the jets flying in on what was then the approach to the airport. You could literally see treads on the tires as the planes flew over.

There were usually kids underfoot—several women with children were senior staffers—and the constant smell of paranoia kept the aroma of burning ganja to a minimum. The big-time social event at the house was the Friday-night Risk board games, where all of us anti-imperialist types got to hone our strategic military skills.

The steep flight of aging wood steps up from the street functioned as an early warning system, so when the authorities stopped by to visit we knew they were coming. The house was raided by the cops a handful of times on the pretext of a search for AWOL sailors. None were found.

They never did look in the backyard tree house where (unbeknown to most of us) Sam, the staff cartoonist, had a crop growing. Eventually the police settled in with an unmarked car parked down the block; on occasion the FBI suits would park their car on the opposite side of the street. I don't think we ever locked the front door over the two years I lived there.

Although the *Door* had as many as three dozen staffers at times, only eight to ten of us lived in the six-bedroom house. The oversized living room on the first floor served as a production room with homemade glass-topped light tables lining the walls. The room I always imagined as the Victorian library served as our office, with meetings and meals taking place around an oversized dining room table next to the barely functional kitchen.

People came and went from the *Door* and the house with great frequency. One of our ace reporters and his significant other simply disappeared one night, not long after telling us they were working on a blockbuster story about organized crime and land developers. They eventually surfaced in the bay area. And those of us remaining pieced together the story from notes they'd left behind.

The *Door* had its lighter moments. In 1973, the paper published a parody edition of the *San Diego Union*, complete with the headline "Nixon Declares Martial Law." We responded to a letter from the daily's law firm asking us to cease using their logo with a note of condolence, regretting that so many of their attorneys at the firm were deceased. And when fast food king Ray Kroc bought the local baseball franchise from the Copley newspaper empire, the team was promptly dubbed the "San Diego Big Macs."

The subject matters that the *Door* took on, given its finite resources, look all the more impressive after four decades. Issues that were given regular and unstinting coverage included the war in Vietnam, the struggles of the Farmer Workers Union, abortion rights, energy prices, U.S. intervention in a wide variety of third world nations and sexism in the educational system. Anti-war protests large and small, along with every trial of protesters (and there were lots of trials, this being good ol' reactionary San Diego) were reported on.

Lots of other local stories found their way onto the paper's pages, news that the local establishment press omitted or buried. Stories about (libertarian) tax protesters, police harassment of local Chicanos on immigration charges, community opposition to development plans, sources of funding for local political races and even sub-rosa tactics being used by the city government to evade controls on municipal sewage discharge (something that's still going on!) into the Pacific Ocean all graced the pages of the *Door*.

Over time, some of our best sources turned out to be reporters from the daily paper who were disgusted by the openly reactionary agendas espoused by their bosses. We'd go downtown to the Press Room bar across the street from the *Union-Tribune*, drink a few beers and keep our ears open. More than one front page story started out that way.

News editor Bob Hartley and I had a Sunday talk show on KSDO radio. After a few months of death threats—their regular audience was sorta right wing—our broadcast careers came to a screeching halt after we interviewed Jane Fonda.... Or maybe it was the track from the Firesign Theater album for the "Famous Judges School" we ran as an ad.

Movie, record, book and concert reviews appeared throughout every issue of the paper, sometimes competing with "hard news" for front page headlines. Writer/Director Cameron Crowe's role as a 15-year-old music reviewer at the *Door* was chronicled in the movie Almost Famous.

The paper featured many interviews, including one with Mohammed Ali. Reporter Bill Ritter interviewed local radio and television station people and got their take on the state of the electronic marketplace—which was ironic, as he went on to become the anchor for ABC News' New York affiliate.

The handwriting was on the wall by late 1973 as changes in the publishing industry and the political landscape impacted the *Door* and other papers around the country. Pressure from the Federal Bureau of Investigation on the music industry dried up an important source of ad revenue. In San Diego, a free and apolitical weekly (*The Reader*) appeared with support from some of the same businessmen the *Door* had offended with its investigative reporting.

In November 1973 we got word that our Victorian mansion on Albatross Street was slated for destruction. A half-block long wall of condominiums now takes up that side of the street.

The *San Diego Door* lasted for another year or so, publishing out of another house in Golden Hill. I left the paper in the spring of 1974 to seek my fame and fortune in Washington, D.C. as an editor for *CounterSpy*. To this day I cannot drive up the steep hill on Laurel Street from Little Italy without thinking wistfully about life in the days at the *Door*.

Parts of this story were published in the OB Rag Blog *in 2009.*

Boycott Gallo | *Vince Compagnone*

Arthur Salm

Into the Blue Again, After the Money's Gone

At least Roosevelt had something else going for him. "At night I work the door at the Comedy Club in La Jolla," he said as we bounced along to our first pickup. "I've been bugging them to let me do five minutes. You know—in the middle of the week, when hardly anybody's there. Man, I can do five minutes. Anybody can do five minutes. *You* can do five minutes."

That was generous, because Roosevelt had hardly known me for five minutes. He was driving a mini school bus, something not much bigger than a van—five rows of seats, and a seat-bench in back—and I was riding along to learn the route, which I was to take over the next day. The school district must have been *really* short of buses or drivers or both if it was contracting out to this dicey-looking outfit whose ad I'd answered the day before: "Laine's People Movers." Mostly they drove people to and from the airport, so when they got a school-district gig they had to scrounge up some certified school bus drivers. Like me.

I'd gotten my school bus driver certification a couple of years earlier, snagged by a 3x5 card on the bulletin board at San Diego State's employment office. It promised decent part-time wages—perfect for someone drifting languidly through graduate school. The California Highway Patrol issues the certification, so the classroom part of the course is taught by a Highway Patrolman. The material was straightforward, common-sense stuff, so much so that I remember just one detail:

"Only certified school-bus drivers," the no-nonsense, stainless-steel-gray-haired instructor informed us, "are allowed to transport students."

A guy raised his hand. "What if you're already doing it?"

The CHP instructor said, "What do you mean?"

"I'm driving for a private school," the guy said, "and I don't have my certification yet."

"You're transporting children? For a school?"

"Yeah, every day."

"Well," the—and here I should add, *uniformed*—CHP instructor, said, "all I can tell you is, cease and desist. Don't drive any more students until you're certified." He looked down at his notes to continue with the lesson.

"But I've already got the job," the guy said.

The officer looked up. "Cease and desist," he said. "Okay? Cease and desist."

"Is there any way I could get in trouble?" the guy wanted to know.

"Keep talkin', chump," a guy in the seat behind him suggested.

I got my certification, drove school buses for about a year, then managed to get a job with what was then known as San Diego Transit, the city bus service. The pay was so good—this was 1981, mind you—that I was able to stay in school and support myself in a small Pacific Beach apartment two blocks from the ocean while working just 25 hours a week. *Barely* able, but still: not a bad way to live for a single guy on a slow trip to nowhere in particular. I drove early-morning routes, 4:30–9:30 a.m. or 5:00–10:00 a.m., hours when thieves, killers, and lunatics are asleep; there was never anything even approaching an incident on my bus. After the first couple of weeks of psyche-shredding nervousness I slipped into a groove and the job became easy, even fun, and never for a minute boring. (*Riding* a bus is boring; piloting a 40-foot vehicle through traffic is not.)

Not long ago I read a *New York Times Magazine* piece on Portland, Ore., saying that Portland was where young people go to retire. That's exactly what was being said about San Diego back in those (to me) sun-dazzled days. My friends and I would spend whole afternoons sitting on the decks of Mission Beach bars, beer-hazed by 2:00 and drunk by 4:00, listening to the stereo implore *Don't fear the Reaper*, and believe me, we didn't.

Driving a bus was so easy, as was life, that I stopped going to grad school. Just stopped. I'd completed my coursework for an M.A. in American Studies and had gone to see my advisor to talk about writing a thesis. The conversation inspired my one and only out-of-body experience.

My advisor was leaning back in his chair, talking and talking, when in a jolt of insight I realized that I would never write that thesis, or any thesis. I was through. What I had to do now was get out of his office. I'd stopped paying attention, and when I tried to latch on to his monologue in order to look for an opening in which to inject a polite "Gotta go!" I could not understand what the man was saying. I got each word, in isolation, but words strung together were making no sense. It was at that point that I floated straight up, then over to the corner of the room, where I watched him gibber gibberish and watched myself pretend to take it all in.

Eventually he stopped. I slid back into my body, told a rock-solid-believable lie about how I'd stop in next week, and walked out the door, off the campus, and away from higher education forever.

Then I got laid off.

Seems the city was short of funds, so it was cutting back on bus routes. Last hired, first fired, and since I hadn't been there very long I was one of those 86'd. My great regret is that I didn't save the written notice, because I've yet to come across a more unintentionally appropriate (if ungrammatical) use of the passive voice: "It is with great sadness that it is necessary to lay you off."

Unemployment compensation, I learned, runs out. My net worth, which had been hovering in the high three figures—I liked to say "five figures" because I included the numbers to the right of the decimal point—plummeted. Then I saw the Laine's People Movers ad.

"It's transporting handicapped kids," Laine himself told me when I showed up for the quickie interview. "You don't have a problem with that, do you?"

Of course not, I told him, and asked him to show me how the bus's wheelchair lift worked.

"No," he said, "these are mentally han… mentally *challenged* kids."

No problem, I assured him.

"Now, Maria," Roosevelt was saying early the next morning, glancing over his shoulder at me as the bus bounced along, "she's a sweetheart—I take a right here through this mini-mall 'cuz that's a l-o-o-o-o-ong light up there—but you have to make sure the other kids don't steal her lunch. She won't say anything." We were somewhere in southeast San Diego, an area I didn't know at all, and I was scribbling his street directions into a notebook: Laine didn't provide route maps.

Roosevelt wove the little bus through the mostly empty parking lot and back into traffic. "Gotta get way over into the left lane *fast* here. Okay, left turn—" *Scribble scribble.* "—then a right down the alley in the second block. Don't go down the alley in first block, it's a dead end. Then another right, and Maria's house is the third on the right. And there she is. Her mom always waits with her."

Scribble.

It wasn't just that I wasn't going to be able to make any sense of the directions later; when I glanced down at them, I couldn't make any sense of them now. There was no way I was going to be able to do this the next day. Yet I was. Going to do it. But it was impossible. And it kept getting worse.

"Keep your eye on Katie," Roosevelt said as we pulled up to another house where a mousy girl, maybe 11, with a pinched face and tight smile, waited. "She likes to eat the floorboard. She's pretty sneaky about it, so you have to pay attention." I looked at the floor: old, black, filthy rubbery crap. Coming apart. Some pieces were missing. Katie's snacks?

Probably, because she hadn't been on board a minute before she leaned down, tore off a quarter-size chunk and crammed it into her mouth. I was sitting in the seat behind her. "Katie," I said. She took it out of her mouth and handed it back. I was wondering where to put it when her other hand went up to her mouth. "Katie," I said. She handed it back. I dropped the saliva-slick slabs and kicked them under the seat with my heel.

"Now, Toby," Roosevelt called out, "—hey, did you get that last left?"

Scribble.

"—Toby's not a problem as long as he's had his big black pill. But some days he just won't take it. Then, watch out." Toby stood on the sidewalk, staring straight ahead. "Can't tell," Roosevelt said, catching my eye in the rearview mirror. Toby stomped onto the bus and dropped into a seat. His gaze at the seat in front of him never wavered.

So it went for another 15 or 20 minutes. Four, five, six more pickups, my notes ever more illegible.

Suspicious-looking jaw movement. "Katie." She handed back more floor.

We're on the freeway, headed at last for school. Toby stands up. He takes a step forward, so that he's next to the boy in the seat in front of him. Toby makes a fist, draws back his arm, and hits the boy in the shoulder. Hard. He draws his arm back once more and now it's a piston, slamming into the boy's shoulder again and again and again. Toby's face remains impassive. The victim, unnervingly, just sits there and takes it. *Bam, bam, bam, bam!*

But he does begin to wail. *"Waaaaaaawaaaaaaawaaaaawaaaaaaa!"*

All this has happened very fast. I stand up. "Toby!" I yell. "Stop it!"

Roosevelt has picked up on the action in his rearview and calls to me: "Restrain him!"

Restrain him? What the hell does that mean? How do you restrain some-body? The CHP officer never mentioned anything like this. Toby's only about 12 but he's husky, maybe 140 pounds, and—not to put too blunt a point on it—fucking nuts.

So I stand behind him for a few seconds, wondering how to do this.

Bam, bam, bam!

"Waaaaaaawaaaaaaawaaaaa!"

I clasp Toby in a reverse bear hug, pinning his arms to his side. Now *he* begins to scream, an eerie, piercing *"Eeeeeeeeeeeeeee!"*

"Waaaaaaawaaaaaaawaaaaawaaaaaaa!" still coming from the other boy.

Toby, now confused and terrified, writhes as he screams, throwing his weight this way and that. Roosevelt brakes for something. Toby and I stumble forward. I pull back but overcompensate; we reach the tipping point and over we go. I manage to twist us so that we miss the jutting seats and land on my back in the aisle, Toby on top of me, my arms still around him. He's screaming *"Eeeeeeeeeeeeeee!"* into my left ear. I turn my head to get my ear away from him and see that Katie has taken the opportunity to rip out a strip of flooring the size of a Slim Jim. The poor, damaged girl has one end of it in her mouth and she's trying to tear off a piece, looking for all the sad world like a guy going after a good chaw of tobacco.

A few years later the Talking Heads would ask the question that I was at that moment asking myself: *How did I get here?*

Mary Williams

After Sweet Green Corn Ripens

I never knew that her given name was Maxine. Or that, as a girl, she dreamed of becoming a Rockette, and thus spent many evenings with her cousin Judith practicing those high kicks.

The very last time I saw Maggie, she was smooth-skinned, cheeky pink, and saucy. She wore a small brown pill cap on her head, which I thought looked smart and stylishly understated. Her explanation for it: "I'm having a bad-hair year."

I laughed. "Well, gorgeous, you sure know how to make that work for you!" I'd been having challenges along such lines myself, wearing decorative scarves to hide a thinning area just past my hairline. Her ornamentation reasons, of course, were entirely different than mine: she had been through several months of the "bone-crusher," aka the "soul-destroyer," her personal nicknames for che-motherapy.

What a far cry from when we first met—in the late 1980s, at a downtown San Diego protest against the Reagan administration's policy in Central America. I was there in creative-intellectual-rebel mode, on the verge of entering graduate school, espousing a hip cause popular with many of my twenty-something peers. She, on the other hand, had actually been to Central America, living there for many moons, witnessing suffering, reading widely among the works of the post-war Latin American poets, and writing gritty and gripping poetry in empathetic response to the political and social injustice she found.

So her objection in the poem "In The Distinguished Liberal," (written for the poet Claribel Alegria) came from a wholeheartedly different level of expe-rience than that of most who had gathered at that well-intentioned downtown demonstration. The title was simultaneously the first line of the poem, high-lighting an irony that I probably did not fully appreciate all those years ago:

In The Distinguished Liberal

Newspaper
I read of the Salvadoran poet,
now living in Nicaragua,
who came here to speak
of her country—Neruda's
delicate waist of America—
of the rich volcanic earth
of *corona de cristo* that blooms blood red
of executions in the dark…
The distinguished liberal
newspaper headlined its story
"Salvadoran Misery." Of course
severed heads are a misery.
Mutilated Indians are a misery.
Military escalations promoted
as humanitarian aid are a misery.
Yet *she* speaks of revolution
in San Salvadoran factories
in liberation churches
in pueblo-owned *milpas* after
sweet green corn ripens.

To her mind, it was the "distinguished liberals" who seemed disheartened and overly focused on bad news, unable to hear the yearning and the hope in these grassroots revolutions. It was also the "distinguished liberals" in academia who were often writing beautiful award-winning lyrical poetry, paying lip-service to justice-making and solidarity with the oppressed, yet remaining at an easy distance from it all—comfortable, complacent, tenure-tracked, safe.

Maggie's track was never tenured. Early on, some critics claimed her work needed more lyricism and form, that it flirted too much with bitterness and despair (and admittedly, I had moments when I agreed…), that it was overly political and time-specific in content. *Of course*, would be her retort. That was, in good part, the point. Mutilated Indians lacked a certain lyricism. Prisoners of South Africa's apartheid system danced with despair. Life in the world's war zones was invariably fraught with politics and the specifics of time and place.

When it came to poetry, perhaps, she tended to agree with Che Guevara. As her poem "Death of Che" attests, Che once said:

> … "I can't sleep
> on a mattress while my soldiers
> are shivering up there."

The poem continues:

> And he divided men into two groups:
> those who can sleep
> on a mattress
> while others suffer
> and those who won't.

That passage describes much of Maggie's poetry. It doesn't sleep on a mattress while prisoners are being tortured. It cries, rages, unveils, and refuses to cover its eyes.

> I step out of my car
> emptied of singing
> to work, to work
> Emptied by news of war
> the hungry, radiation…
>
> —*from "World of Dust" in* Seventh Circle *by Maggie Jaffe*

Yet Maggie herself was no mattress-rejecting ascetic. A luxurious bed was one of her most treasured indulgences during the final months of her life—along with cigarettes (she had quit a few times in her life, once for nearly fifteen years) and red meat (after losing too much weight after surgery and chemo, she enthusiastically renounced vegetarianism). She loved tasty food, good drink, exotic clothes, hefty books (her favorite: *Moby Dick*), opera, jazz, dangly earrings, thought-provoking films, liberation theologians, and left-wing activists. She had poetess-diva tendencies. Her cats—there were always one or two in her abode—were registered and pedigreed. Despite many rough patches, she dug in to life with great verve and relish.

◆ ◆ ◆

Maggie welcomed guests into her home with an effervescent hospitality. Once upon a time, she and her husband, also a professor, threw lavish end-of-semester parties for their students and friends, replete with wines, tamales, chocolates, Dadaism, and intoxicated sociocultural gabfests. I was a graduate teaching associate then, and I enjoyed most of those gatherings. But, introvert that I am, I loved more my solo visits with Maggie. An afternoon or evening with Maggie was always a step into a delicious, zestful Sabbath. Sometimes we'd go out for dinner and a movie—but more often she'd invite me over to her place and we'd stay in, noshing on Vietnamese take-out or some fabulous homemade delicacy, and watch rented films in her sumptuous bedroom-theater. This way we could get mildly, or perhaps deeply, buzzed without worrying about driving. Belly-full, wine glasses on night stand, and ashtray-ready, we'd prop thick pillows against the headboard of the king-sized bed. The windows to the room had these luxurious burgundy velvet drapes—which she would draw to block out any outside distractions. With the TV volume suitably adjusted and video forwarded to the film's beginning, she would dim the overhead room light to some deep shade of sangria, and we'd be ready to surrender ourselves to Kubrick or Almodovar or Lee or Wenders. We watched a variety of movies, from the obscure and ponderous to the popular and current: *El Norte*, *The Fringe Dwellers*, *A Dry White Season*, *Hiroshima Mon Amour*, *The Mission*. Sometimes we would "preview" films—that is, check out a flick we were considering showing in a class, and pedagogically chew the fat. I recall one evening when her husband, on his way out the door to teach a night class, crankily sneered at us as we started to preview the movie version of *Hair*. "You've got to be kidding me—*Hair*? Isn't that just *West Side Story* on acid?" That sealed my decision to show the rambunctious hippie musical during the final week of one of my English 100 classes, although for the life of me I cannot recall how I managed to connect that movie with written composition. Maggie's preference that semester was George Romero's *Night of the Living Dead*, which she saw as a smart and gritty critique of cold war politics and domestic racism.

> Liberate the lobsters!
> Expropriate the best sellers!
> Shoot the *New Yorker* in the kneecaps!
> Interrogate the whole damn magazine rack!
>
> —*from "At the Writers' Colony" in* Continuous Performance: The
>   Selected Poems of Maggie Jaffe

◆ ◆ ◆

Maggie loved exploring and teaching about portrayals of the oppressed in popular culture—particularly the working poor, prisoners, death row inmates, the "disappeared" in Central and South America, Native Americans, and the African diaspora. As an uprooted intellectual Woodstock-nation bard and secular Jew with a heart wide open to the cries of the downtrodden, Maggie staunchly refused to separate her hunger and thirst for justice from her writing and teaching.

Emily Dickinson

One of the few women
you can trust to keep
her mouth shut.
Dressed in virgin white,
married to Imagination.
Writing of ruby-throated
hummingbirds, Sir Death,
exquisite states of being.
Close by, Abolitionists thunder
out their oratory—
from the pulpit,
on street corners,
from the marriage bed,
from Frederick Douglass's
Prison House of Slavery—
even from her Papa's parlor.
But good girls won't disrupt
the class
for Lit profs who teach
the air-brushed canon:
15 [dead] white men & Emily.
Shoot the canon!

[for Deborah Small]

—*from* Continuous Performance: The Selected Poems of Maggie
Jaffe

Because of Maggie, I came across ideas and histories and cultural moments that I might not have encountered otherwise. We went to hear ex-CIA agent

Philip Agee when he gave a lecture at San Diego State, where we heard the horror stories about agents testing torture techniques on homeless people and crop-dusting viruses over American cities to see how well such biological invasions might disable a population. We went to the protests against CIA recruitment on campus, trying not to laugh as we chanted "The CIA is—you know—the U.S. version of the Ges-ta-po!" When some local neo-Nazis littered the campus with hate literature, Maggie invited the president of the local John Brown Anti Ku Klux Klan organization to speak in her classes. She gave me one of the dozens of T-shirts she'd bought as a kind of payment for his lecture— across the front was an image of a thick-booted skinhead—crossed out with an X—and large bright letters proclaiming, "No Nazis! No KKK! No Fascist USA!" I could not bring myself to wear this attention-attracting shirt in public, but she loved sporting it with her Indian earrings and beatnik beret.

Maggie lent me scads of books from her personal library: *Black Elk Speaks*, *Soledad Brother*, *Rules for Radicals*. One year for my birthday, she gave me a volume of artwork by the black collage artist Romare Bearden, a thoughtful and lovely gift. The first page of the book features a quotation of Bearden's: "The true artist feels there is only one art—and that it belongs to all mankind." Bearden's work—full of the specifics of biography, history, struggle, cultural ritual, and place—expressed a moral position that contrasted with the cynical detachment and disconnectedness reflected in the prevailing art of his day. Bearden rejected "art for art's sake," filling his collages with vivid images and tense energies that reflected the turbulence he experienced in the inner cities. As Mary Campbell noted in her accompanying essay, "In the urban scenes, on the city streets, there is a violence that is destructive, yet there is also a redemption and a transform-ing vision that allows hope." Bearden bore witness through his art, and when Maggie gifted me with a collection of his work, I sensed her encouragement for me to join her in creating "art for bearing witness' sake"—to find a way to do the same with my prose.

◆ ◆ ◆

Maggie generally scoffed at institutional religion (as did I back in those days), but she had a secret appreciation for the yearnings and values that had given birth to it. Once, she sheepishly admitted to me that she had taken to lighting candles for her father on the anniversaries of his death. She also confessed that she had "a thing" for Jesuits (Perhaps we had just watched the movie *The Mission*). Together Maggie and I saw the movie *Romero*, about the El Salvadoran archbishop assassinated in church because of his love and support of the poor in his country. I'm pretty sure it was through Maggie that I first heard about the liberation theologians Gustavo Gutierrez and Ernesto Cardenal and the Jesuit antiwar activist Daniel Berrigan.

Perhaps that is why she was the first of my academic friends that I "came out" to about my perplexing return to the Catholic church in the year 2000. By then, I had long since left academia and had moved away from the heart of the city where Maggie continued to teach and write. I had married; she had divorced. Our work lives had become busier and more stressful, and we both regretted that our visits had become fewer and further between. She took my re-embracing of my baptismal roots as a fine reason to invite me over for dinner and a bottle of red wine.

"You know, you are partly to blame for my stumbling back to church," I told Maggie, accusingly. "You and your Ernesto Cardenal. You and your *Dead Man Walking* and your *Romero*."

"Well, my personal theory is that with a name like Mary you're pretty much doomed to such a fate. You are what you are." She took a sip of wine.

"You are what you are?" I laughed and shook my head. "Holy Moses, Magalita! That's right out of the Hebrew scriptures: 'I am that I am.'"

"Well see, then, there ya go. Neither of us can keep away from this religious crap. I yam what I yam too, apparently. Like Popeye the Sailor Man."

Serendipitously, Bob Marley's *Exodus* album was on while we were eating. At the same instant, we both realized that the song "Jammin" was playing:

> we're jamming—
> to think that jammin was a thing of the past
> we're jammin
> and I hope this jam is gonna last

"Oh my God"—we raised our glasses for a toast, for this synchronicity was, well, truly jammin—and together, with Bob, we sang it: *"We're YAMMIN!"*

A decade later, things really were jamming for Maggie. She had won a grant from the National Endowment for the Arts that enabled her to take a sabbatical and finish her sixth book: *Flic(k)s*, a poetic exploration of "cinema and life's cinematic movements." She was in a relationship with a kind man who treated her like a queen. College lecturing continued to be hard (and underpaid and underappreciated) work, but more often than not, she was enjoying it.

♦ ♦ ♦

Then the crushing fatigue descended, along with a spate of urinary tract infections and various bugs that she initially chalked up to a weak immune system. "I tell those fuckers (her snarky-yet-affectionate nickname for 'students') to stay home when they're sick but somebody always shows up to cough in my face. I don't get it!"

"It's obviously a conspiracy," I joked. "If they can get you sick, they figure they can weasel out of a quiz or get you to drop a paper."

"Well, I do think that they *have* figured out that I give better grades when I'm high on Sudafed."

But the Sudafed and homeopathics and healthy eating did not stop what was ailing her. It turned out to be bladder cancer, advanced to such an extent that Maggie's entire bladder, along with her reproductive organs, had to be removed.

Maggie hoped initially that the surgeon would successfully scoop out all of the cancer. When post-surgical chemotherapy was suggested, she resisted it at first—dreading everything she'd heard about its side effects. Eventually she was persuaded to give it a go. It was, in a word, ruthless—and having to navigate the challenges of a urostomy and urine drainage bag compounded the long slog of exhaustion, nausea, and brain fog. Fairly soon after she finished her chemo sessions, however, she experienced an encouraging return of strength. For a few months, her scans showed no return of cancer. Plans were made for a second surgery—this time to construct a new bladder from a section of her intestine. She moved into a new, easier-to-manage apartment—a small place with a pool—and was looking forward to swimming again. We made tentative plans to share decadent "comfort meals" of rare steak, macaroni and cheese, and canned chocolate frosting. "And you know what?" she said to me one day on the phone. "This crap is getting me a whole two semesters off! In this world, the trick to getting a long paid sabbatical is: get seriously ill. Don't that fuck all?"

Her vim and spunk had returned. I hoped this jam was gonna last.

◆ ◆ ◆

One incision was as far as the surgical bladder-building team got with Maggie. They immediately stitched her back up, aborting the reconstruction after finding cancer inside her abdomen. The oncologist determined that it was inoperable and untreatable.

It was one of cancer treatment's horrible back-stabs—those false-negative scans, and the sensations of well-being and vigor that had invited hope and future plans. Maggie knew that there could be no guarantees in her situation, but she had been feeling healthy and had prepared well for another several months of post-surgical recuperation in her new abode, replete with her favorite legal pain-killers, tons of movies, and the possibility of being able to swim in a pool again by summer. Instead, she would have to procure new homes for her cats and experience the anticipatory grief of her family and loved ones.

At first she still wanted to do the decadent-eating thing, so we kept making plans to eat at DZ Akins (an outrageously yummy Jewish diner in La Mesa) and return to her place with the worst possible take-home dessert for us to savor as we watched schlocky movies together. But our plans were consistently interrupted: she had to contact lawyers; she needed to meet with a doctor about an experimental therapy; a painful tiredness would overcome her and make visiting impossible.

One night she called me up to apologize for having to cancel our plans yet again.

"No need to apologize, Maggie. We'll do it some other time. Whatever works for you. It's okay." I hated that she seemed to be feeling guilty about not being up for a visit.

"I can't believe how bad this sucks." Maggie's voice was a tense whisper. "Goddamned fucking cancer! I have so much to do, still. I hate it all. I hate everything."

As I mouthed some words attempting to express love and acknowledge the unimaginable suckiness of dealing with cancer, Maggie began to cry. Then to moan. Then to sob. And then to gulp for air between sobs. All I could do was listen and remain on the line, feeling absolutely, utterly helpless. The phone

grew hot in my hand; the sky above glittered horribly; the workdesk in front
of me exuded an awful woodenness. And for some reason, I could not cry at
that particular moment. The energy in Maggie's sobbing demanded all of the
emotive space—and all thirty-five miles of air—between us. There was nothing
to say or do. I listened as she sobbed, and I breathed in the thick darkness, wordlessly praying. My crying would come later.

This was not despair Maggie was experiencing—I think it was more like
a mournful anger. Despair usually lacks the energy that sobbing requires. It
dawned on me later (slow, I am) that whatever usually brings contentment or
happy anticipation—such as tasty food or a visit from a friend—might evoke
an angry or embittered grief in someone who is expecting to die soon. It's the
encounter with a naked existential unfairness—i.e. *the people and activities and
life I love are being ripped away from me; it hurts too much to enjoy them now*—
that enrages.

◆ ◆ ◆

Maggie and I never got together for that decadent meal. There were only two
more times we connected—both times by phone. One time it was to talk about
hospice. She had heard rumors that a residential hospice (rather than a hospital)
might be a good way to go: "they give you good drugs there, I hear." I shared
with her my only experience with hospice, which had occurred two years previously when another friend, Kathy D., was dying of cancer. I had been deeply
moved by the thoroughness and tenderness of the in-home hospice nurse's care
during Kathy's last days. I told Maggie I had heard wonderful things about San
Diego Hospice, which (at the time) offered a beautiful space for people to die.
She said she would check it out as her situation progressed.

◆ ◆ ◆

In the fall of 2010, Maggie and I had our final conversation.

I was thousands of miles away, visiting my hometown, Kansas City. I had
taken some time to myself in the afternoon to walk around the lake at Loose
Park. Maggie called me, still hoping that we could get together soon. She
sounded serene—even jovial—and told me that she managed to get herself in a
trial with an experimental anti-cancer drug. She was looking forward to trying

some other alternative therapies, because "what the fuck? Nothing ventured, nothing gained. Might be my final adventure."

She also wanted to talk with me about "spiritual things." "Seriously, Mary, I'm wondering about what life really means, if there is a great beyond, and shit like that! Can you believe it?"

"So then," I shot back. "You must have made it into the psilocybin trial? Or the ecstasy one?"

We both laughed hard. "I promise to save a little for you if I get some of the good shit," she said.

"Cool! So can we plan on shrooms and *Fantasia* for our next get-together?"

"Marking my calendar, girlfriend."

All joking aside, Maggie really did want to talk about spiritual things, and we continued to talk for nearly an hour. I had recently taken a course in spiritual direction, and she was hoping I had some juicy cosmic wisdom to proffer. In all honesty, I felt I had little to share in that moment that would not sound like some half-baked, paltry platitude. Furthermore, I am not much good at conversing via cell phone—communicating without eyes, gestures, facial expressions, and touch feels stilted and partial. And of course, a good friend's impending death is intimidating as hell. However, when Maggie asked for suggestions on "something spiritual" to read, a name did spring to mind.

"Check out the works of Rabbi Rami Shapiro," I said. "I've seen him speak at a few interfaith conferences. He writes a column for *Spirituality and Health* magazine. He's funny, wise, and deep. He has a more nondualist approach to religion and spirituality, and thinks of 'God' not as a Supreme Being, but Being itself. He translates YHVH as 'the One Who Is' rather than 'Lord.' I think you'd like him."

I had a paragraph from Shapiro's *The Hebrew Prophets* scribbled in my journal and I shared it with her: "When the prophet speaks to you in the voice of God, you are hearing the deepest truths of your own being echoed in their words. It is as if your greater self, the self aware of itself as one with God, were addressing your smaller self, the ego that, while also a manifestation of God, insists that it is other than God. It is the ego that sees the world as an arena of competing beings vying for the biggest piece of a fixed pie. It is the ego that shifts from self to selfishness, and engages in unjust, cruel, and exploitative behavior. It is the ego that needs to hear the prophetic challenge; it is the ego that needs to turn. And when it does, it turns toward its greater self and reconnects with God and engages creation justly, lovingly, and humbly...."

"Hunh." She paused to write his name down. "He sounds like he might be a *mensch*. Thanks for the suggestion."

◆ ◆ ◆

I want to take a moment to behold a couple of lovely ironies:

Through my years of exposure to Maggie's cultural and political tastes, I discovered elements and strains of Catholicism that I had not encountered previously in church or in Catholic school. And there, in our final conversation, I had offered Maggie a nugget from within her own inherited, albeit largely rejected, Jewish tradition. Our mutual loathing of institutional religion had been so strong when we first met, yet as our lives ripened, we each handed over—almost accidentally—something tasty and nourishing, like sweet green corn, from the others' rejected tradition.

The other irony is Maggie asking me about "things of the spirit," when the truth was that she had, in her own fashion, already *lived* the spirit through her writing and teaching and politics. Her work was inspired by and dedicated to all the beaten-down of this world—and like an incorrigible Hebrew prophet, her poetry and her life proclaimed : "Spare me the sound of your hymns, and let the music of your lutes fall silent; I am not listening. Rather let justice well up like water, let righteousness flow like a mighty stream" (Amos 5:24).

◆ ◆ ◆

My attempts to contact Maggie over the next three months were unsuccessful. I left her messages by phone, note, and e-mail but never heard back from her. One day, her answering machine was too full to receive any more messages. She had mentioned to me earlier that she might simply "let people go" at a certain point, and limit her contacts to a small circle of loved ones. Perhaps that is what she chose to do. Or—perhaps she intended to get in touch with people at some point, but was interrupted by death, the ultimate diva. She died at the San Diego Hospice on March 5, 2011, at age 62.

Several people among Maggie's larger circle of family and friends spoke at the memorial service. Maggie's sister recalled a favorite question they half-jokingly asked of each other over the years: *Oy, what happened to us? Where are all the Talmudic scholars in our family?* I shared humorous memories about the bad luck we both had with dentistry and our mutual idolatry of heavy, dangly earrings in the early 1990s—Maggie underwent surgery after ripping an ear lobe. Another friend and colleague mentioned that Maggie had actually felt rather well during her last two days—even "rallying" at one point to write a few lines and spontaneously hold a rambunctious poetry workshop for the hospice staff.

I love knowing that little detail about her final days. It still hurts that she is gone—and I am sad that I will not hear that particular *Noo-Yawk* accent again, the timbre of her voice with its unique mixture of sarcasm and concern and *chutzpah*—but I love knowing that she found her own way to stay in the flow as she was dying. That in her own fashion, she donned that mantle of Talmudic scholar—or, perhaps more accurately—of *chachamah* (wise woman)—teaching and subverting and loving well in her full, wild ripeness.

Gary Winters
Jihmye Collins' Anthem

man got himself set up on the San Diego stage
right shoulder slightly back—feet squared away
head tilted back a little—not too much
cocked and ready—he had something to say
the words rang out strong and clear—no miscue
I am Black—and we sat up—took notice
something in the way he said those three words
like a message from another region
far beyond international boundaries
or constraints of the illusion of time
these words came from a place of mystery
coming from a man who knew who he was
to let us know what a fine thing it is
I am Black—I am Black—what a fine thing

Chris Baron
Heavy Water

You tell me how much you love my body.
The soft, bottom lip kiss,
then hand in hand along Mission Bay,
and you are saying something else now.
I am just not listening
because now, near
the Fanuel Street playground,
children are running near the shoreline,
trunks, bikinis, splashing water,
golden and blue and alive.
One boy, falling behind,
his dark blue shirt cellophane-
wrapped to his oversized body
is edged to the outside
where the water is already silent.

I know this silence.

You push your body into mine,
and my skin remembers
how it longs for and hates to be touched,
the fear of the beach and bare skin,
every thought groping for comfort.

big-boned, born this way
wide, tall, big, broad-shouldered,
good-sized,
husky.

In eighth grade my mother
told me that she knew Dr. Atkins,

that she had once sold him
some of her paintings
in exchange for the miracle diet.
She sat me down, told me
we weren't going to eat pizza
anymore. Soon, I wouldn't
be ashamed to change for P.E.
We spent that summer at Stinson Beach.
I ate pork rinds and cheese rollups,
drank water and rejected bread.

chubby, butterball, tubby,
beanbag, roundy.

The boy drops to the water
in a sunlit heap. He can't keep up.
Sand falls through his fingers;
his body rolling into itself.
I want one of the girls to stop,
to turn around, to find him,
say anything to him.

slugboy, chubbypants, moon.

Lisa was my miracle,
my eighth grade friend.
In my mother's gallery
while sun burned art tourists
meandered through,
we listened to Def Leppard, imagined superheroes,
wrote stories about she-warriors named Elysium,
went to the beach. Me in corduroy Stubbies,
and she in a bikini that mattered.
Her frame far beyond her years,
the sweeping arc of her hips turned full grown men inside out
long before I could know what to do.

Fat boy.

Lisa did not see this part of me,
just lived with me in a treehouse life,

waves and sand pushing the sun away
until the carbohydrates and promises
became nothing more than walking
backward in my own footprints.

"Wow you look good!" "You lost so much weight?" "Haircut?"
"You have come into your own." "Did you stop eating?"
"Your face looks so thin."

It has to matter, doesn't it?
What other people think of you?
The names mean something
even when they wound.

The girl on my arm
will never discern
the whispers I hear.
My San Diego life
has buried them deep.
She will never know
how the nerves
stretched across my skin
in fragmenting isotopes
drowning in heavy water
memorized every name,
the arrangement of each word
and the vibration of syllables,
a thousand pins through the skin.

In the fall when Lisa disappeared
into her life, she hallowed
June, July, and August,
a bright beach, a deep pool,
an open field, a redwood soaring,
and the tender sense of her hand on my body,
me alive and unafraid for the first time.

The boy in the water
gathers in the sand,
forms it around his legs,

his hands over his eyes,
until in its own miracle of time
and story, the other kids
return in a twilight gesture
and bring him to life.
The moments before,
the tightness of clothes,
the tired legs, and the names,
float into the foam.

Marie Alfonsi
Eucalyptus

Perhaps home is not a place but simply an irrevocable condition.
—James Baldwin

It's late August and I'm headed home to visit family on a hot, Sunday afternoon. I lazily drive up the winding roads to my childhood hometown, a familiar heat wave welcoming me like it has so many times before. As I round Mt. Woodson and drop into Ramona along the only western entrance to the Valley of the Sun, the sudden merger of several lanes into one main street somehow feels constraining, an odd vestige signifying the difficulty of growing up as a lesbian in this small, country town. One-way in and one-way out can have a psychological effect. Coming home to this provincial town has never been easy and I brace myself for the day ahead as I maneuver my way along the single road. I pass a wide, gutted dirt road, with its famous row of charmingly crooked and dented mailboxes. I have seen countless photographers, myself included, pull over to capture these almost defunct remnants of another era. Their dented, tin boxes sit as crowns on stocky wood posts. They slant and bob if you face them head on, marked by numbers and the name of the street, "Hope."

Driving on, I count three liquor stores within half a mile and I note that the Chinese joint has gone out of business. I'm looking straight ahead but my view becomes interrupted by sudden shadows across my windshield. Out of nowhere appear symmetrical rows of towering eucalyptus trees that line the main entrance into this town, offering me temporary shade from the relentless sun. Long tree limbs reach out and above to greet those arriving from the west. A newcomer might be seduced by this first impression, perhaps given the illusion that these were guardians of something sacred up ahead, something magnificent that would appear at the end of this hallway of trees. I imagine tourists holding their breath in anticipation, but the observer quickly becomes disappointed when the giant trees recede and are replaced by a stretch of Main Street that starts with a Chevron and ends with a Sizzler.

As I drive down the main thoroughfare and pass through the trees, enjoying their shade and grandeur, I gently brace myself, letting memories trickle in as they always do. Even though I have taken this road a thousand times, I am once again momentarily transfixed by the trees' presence. A few moments pass, and inspired by the rural atmosphere, I crank up Johnny Cash and sing along, *Well I woke up Sunday morning with no way to hold my head that didn't hurt* and then crooning along with "Ring of Fire." At the next stoplight, an older guy, who looks like he just put in a hard day at work, pulls up beside me in an old pickup. He has on dirty Lee overalls and a trucker cap. With both hands on the wheel, he stares distractedly into space until he hears me singing. He turns his head and gives me a faded smile. I smile back. Like all good music, Cash's songs transcended the fact that we didn't know each other. Despite our probable differences, we might agree that Cash was a symbol of many things American. He was part cowboy, a rebel. The kind of artist that attracts rednecks and punks simultaneously.

Ramona. Cradled between Poway to the west and Santa Ysabel to the east. Inhabited and settled by so many, including my family. Forty-four years they have been here. They were from a different time—coming of age in the fifties— an idealistic era that emboldened them to leave their familial nests in search of greater adventures and a better way of life than in impoverished Detroit. Many older residents who had come here when Ramona was small could relate and that spirit and enthusiasm is what made up part of the original Ramona character.

But the town had grown over the years and now included misfits, drug addicts, Tea Party members, gun enthusiasts, yuppies, and suburban folk who were all mixed in together, creating a tension of the old and the new, the intolerant and the progressive. My family fit in perfectly with this tension as we had our own familial conflicts to navigate. For better or for worse, my parents settled their family business in one of the oldest buildings here and took pride in those roots. It was the dream of the open west, anything was possible in their eyes. Years later, I remember having read the blurred testimony of my father on my brother's adoption papers, something about wanting to raise his children in a more suitable environment than Los Angeles. And so he whisked us away to a farm in the middle of nowhere to grow up in the more "innocent" rural environment of his imagination.

Ramona. A name made popular by Helen Hunt Jackson's novel, which featured a half-Scottish/half-Native American orphan who was mistreated and whose plight represented the rights that were stripped of Mexicans and Natives as white settlers came into California. I wish I had better understood this complicated history as a teenager, before I fled the intolerance of this town. I would have held out my hand to others who felt similarly misaligned with mainstream culture that seemed dominated by a white, heterosexual, middle-class. The stories on the outside rarely get told and I think about the ones that I will never know, my own indifference, immaturity, and identity issues keeping me from understanding them.

I remember a Mexican girl, Arianna, who was my own age and would come to cash her paychecks at Sun Valley Market, the grocery store where I worked. She came every week—tired and quiet—and I longed to be her friend. I didn't see her in school, yet we were of a similar age. Her English was difficult to understand and I didn't speak any Spanish. In our exchange of check-to-money each week, I fumbled with my inadequacy to get to know her. Where was she from and what was her story? Why did she hand all of her money to her mother? Why didn't she go to a bank? Why did I have to call a manager to cash her check because she didn't have "proper" identification?

She seemed so burdened with the tasks of adulthood that she was too young to experience. Of course, I know some of the answers to these questions now, but the gap of not understanding then kept me from knowing her more. At that raw age, I craved the stories of people that seemed elusive, different. Arianna stood out to me because she wasn't from the U.S.... That fact alone made her *interesting.* But she also had a seriousness of purpose, intense and hard-working. And somehow my teenage brain hoped that the little queer girl inside of me would somehow connect to Arianna. Perhaps it was naive or ignorant to believe that, but at 15, I didn't know any better. Because even at that age I knew that different was not desirable, yet it was all I was ever interested in, a longing to know that place of splitting off from the mainstream. Perhaps if I could understand it, I thought, I wouldn't feel so alone.

Ramona. A town whose mascot used to be a fly. A FLY. As a kid, I remember gift shops that sold large fly ornaments as tokens of one's visit. I always mar-

veled, why would *anyone* want that? This town is a strange place. Although prejudice and intolerance could play out here, it was also a haven where strangers
were often kind to one another; there existed a deep mutual understanding that
the slower pace of life was a chosen luxury that allowed for pausing with one
another. You could count on slowness, a deliberate, maddening pace that often
rattled me as I came from the speed of the city.

Ramona. A name that also means protector. But the truth for many was not
a story of protection. Like the time a sixth grader, Natalie Jones, was called into
the principal's office and told her presentation on Harvey Milk would not be
allowed in the classroom because it violated a sex education policy. Homopho-
bia had seeped into the classrooms. Or when years later, I received the news that
my beloved choir teacher was dead from AIDS. No announcement that he was
sick, no funeral, and no goodbye, just an old pic and an announcement of his
passing on a Facebook memorial page *14 years after his death*. Or when I fled to
San Francisco because I couldn't handle the disappointment in my parents' faces
when I came out to them, revealing that I was not going to be the woman they
had imagined. Their silence swallowed me up, confirming what I was beginning
to believe about myself—that I had a strangeness that couldn't be shared and
shouldn't dare be "flaunted." The message I got was *hide who you are*, certainly
don't celebrate it. Many difficult years followed in which coming home to visit
was always a small torture. I was always quiet, praying no one would ask me
anything about myself. When I would get in my car and drive home, I left with
a stone in my belly, a knot in my gut. It would take days to recover, the same
pattern of rejection, isolation and reserve, following me around until it became
part of me.

Despite all this, I couldn't help but feel a baffling love for my hick town and
I suppose that's what home feels like for many, an inexplicable tenderness full of
contradictions. Ramona has its charms if you look deep enough. Even now as I
drive between the rows of fragrant eucalyptus trees—the smell transporting me
back—I remember all the sanctuaries I would seek out to dream about a larger
world outside of East County. I longed for solitude, a place for my restless mind
to feel some calm. Most days, I would ditch school for an hour and drive to the
soccer fields, a small refuge from school or parents. Many saw the experience of
growing up in the country as a lucky one. There was space, and I mean *a lot of it*,

a bucolic playground with so many fields to explore and get lost in, mountains to climb, remote areas where one could be mischievous.

If not for anything else, you could find the space and quiet to contemplate. The area around the soccer fields was my place. I'd sit under the shady oaks, smoking those long, slender, Capri cigarettes, and listening to K.D. Lang. *Constant craving. Has always been....* Teenage lesbian angst at its finest. I was very aware that this alt-country, gender-bender crooner wasn't cool to my peers, so before I would head back to school, I would crank up something more edgy, like the Pixies or Jane's Addiction. It was still angst, but a different kind. This was the late eighties, before coming out in high school was something visible. It was before Ellen announced to the world she was gay, before the camp of Gaga, and definitely before LGBT rights became a national discussion. Sweet young girls did not hold hands in school hallways like they do now. They were ostracized, sometimes assaulted, and rarely happy with themselves.

However, before the shame surfaced, before I had to fight to feel normal, there was a feeling inside of me that opened up to a larger—yet exciting—new world. Alone with my thoughts, I could fantasize about a world where my puppy crushes had a place. My first crush was on the Dutch exchange student. *Of course it was.* She was a safe bet because she would leave after a year, taking my crush with her. K.D. Lang's *Constant Craving* became the soundtrack to my unrequited feelings and my time alone at the empty soccer fields became a quiet landscape that reflected the longing and the loneliness I felt inside, yet I took great comfort in that stillness as I grappled with what it meant to be queer in a world that didn't represent my identity as an option.

With my former solitary afternoons at the soccer fields still on my mind, I continue to drive through the center of town and past the historical Town Hall, where I was in my first play, a story about summer camp and I was the lead, featured in the town newspaper. I was just a little kid, but I was so excited to be part of something creative and special. More importantly, I met a lifelong friend. Dawn was my first exposure to queerness, an 80s butch who rode a skateboard AND had the coolest bi-level haircut around. She wore boys' clothing and didn't give a shit about what people thought. Total badass. We became inseparable, leaning on each other throughout the years as each of us came out and dealt with all the challenges of sexuality, identity, and intolerance. It was especially difficult for her because she could not, nor did she want to, hide a gender expression that hinted at her sexuality and I watched her bravely navigate the prejudice and violence that would come her way.

I'll never forget the terror in her voice as she described an evening of harassment by some asshole teenagers. Coming upon Dawn and her girlfriend in an intimate moment, they taunted and surrounded them, threatening violence. For a while after this night, Dawn seemed less brazen about her open sexuality and I worried that this would leave a permanent scar. My sexuality was much easier to hide, but I withdrew into myself as I struggled with what it meant to desire women when there wasn't even language to bring that identity into form. Shame is a very powerful emotion because it disguises itself, taking shape in other forms that are damaging, but hard to identify. And when your family decides that the conversation of your sexuality is not one for the dinner table, or appropriate for any situation for that matter, the effect was a retreat from my family and myself that has taken years to come back from and is still a work in progress.

But friends like Dawn were always there to mitigate the loneliness. She became my savior of sorts, my one connection to a healthy attitude about identity. We were young and free, two restless teenagers on the brink of adulthood. She introduced me to another special sanctuary, "The Pond," a private body of water on acres and acres of uninhabited land. It would be *the* gathering place throughout my teenage years. There were wonderful, wild parties thrown there. It was a place to dream about the future and our places in it. Relationships began and ended there. Friendships were sealed for life. We just wanted adventure and couldn't wait to get the hell out of Ramona. Yet, I look back on this time, with these people, in this town, as some of the fondest memories I can recollect. These friends became my family when my own couldn't step up. We loved being in nature and exploring, endless space to play and learn and love.

Recently I was on a hike in the hills surrounding Ramona and noticed a sign at the trailhead that read, "Your safety in the backcountry is your responsibility." I was struck by how true this felt for me and most likely for countless others. For those who spent childhoods in rural areas, growing up in the country can feel like a wild frontier, for better or worse. It has been over twenty years since I moved away from this town, but each time I return, there is a familiar swell that starts deep in my belly and is usually in my throat by the time I hit Main Street. It seems I'm transported back to the spirit of a youthful heart's pain and longing. My body remembers and for whatever reason, it has chosen to hold onto a story of my hometown that is one of ambivalence: a woman longing to connect to her roots but also coming to terms with the shadows that still linger. And I can always count on stimuli that will transport me to an earlier time, when my simultaneous love and aversion for this wild place is evoked. Little reminders. Involuntary reflexes. Right now, on this day, it happens to be a positive one as the wafts of eucalyptus alert my senses and take me back. This smell will always be one connection with my childhood spent here in Ramona. And like the unexpected welcome of towering trees lining Main Street, Ramona is full of surprises and contradictions that continue to reveal themselves to me, links to a forgotten—but cherished—history.

I shake myself out of my trance as I continue to roll down Main Street, past monster trucks lifted beyond reason and new, pop-up strip malls that sell religion in cheap, temporary, stucco buildings—indistinguishable from all others of its kind—the temporary appearance a harbinger of impending closure, a fact that makes me feel sad rather than saved. I'm in "backcountry" all right, I muse, as I smile and continue down Main Street, eventually stopping at the building in the center of town where my parents are happily sitting on the bench outside watching the world go by. So many years later and I surprise myself at how little anger I can muster at the sight of them. I have managed to find my way, despite the years of silence surrounding my sexuality. In the end, this strength has come to be what I rely on most and, that, alone, will have to be what sees me through. As I pull into the driveway, they wave and smile and I get out of the car to greet them.

Sandra Alcosser

After Bathing

I melt into the air with a voluptuousness
so delicate I am content to be alone.
—John Keats

Aunt Ruth and I spent Saturday night
around a gray Formica table
eating hard-boiled eggs
Afterwards we'd read the Bible
I thought a girl might die from such a diet
but Aunt Ruth hit ninety, and I—
after hours of scented geraniums
a seacoast of motorcycles, painted
ducks, I bathe like John Keats
Saturday evening
freshly powdered in a dressing gown
I sit down
to the kitchen table alone near dusk—
a single egg, a dark cup.

Breeann Kyte
The Night Before Deployment

Jared crouches in the shower; water runs pink off his fists and legs. He wretches twice, but nothing comes up. The steady stream of water stabs staccato against his back.

◆ ◆ ◆

His sobs don't echo through the empty house. Wood, stone, concrete, and plaster; angles arranged just so. Jared likes things hard and angular. Beth would prefer something a bit softer but aims to please. Perfect lines from door jambs to the table to the curve of the overstuffed couch. No broken glass or powdered plaster lingers in the corners. No flung beer drips down the TV. The only things out of place are their three wedding pictures, hung now in a triangular configuration on the northwest wall. Arranged at Beth's height, corners at a 90 degree angle, the pictures form the head and shoulders of a ghost. The nail holes from their former placement in the hallway are already patched and painted, shiny.

Two green sea bags, stuffed and cinched, lean against each other near the front door. Inside are the necessities: underwear, socks, tee-shirts, soap, toothbrush, Xbox, Kindle, flask.

The granite kitchen counter absorbs the morning sun. The sink smells of Clorox as does the floor. There are no garbage bags gleaming white against the red wall; they are nested in the black bin outside, glass bottles making muffled clinks against each other as the bags settle. The recycling bin between the stove and refrigerator holds nothing except an empty bottle of cheap white wine. The kind Beth uses to get red wine, or blood, out of upholstery.

Their bed is a mess. Sheets tangled and stained. Duvet humped in a corner on the floor. The shades are drawn, checking the sunlight at the edge of open door, making the room seem darker than it really is in contrast. On a small table in the hallway, a set of neatly folded sheets sits ready.

On the dining table, a small vase props up a small card. Five yellow garden roses hang over the edge of the vase. They won't last the morning; they don't have enough water. The blinds drawn against the eastern glare variegates this arrangement. A lowercase "j" lilts across the card's envelope. Inside the envelope, the card's cover image is a tiny blue bird in a nest with a thermometer in its beak. The nest is formed of twigs that read in looped letters, "Get Well Soon." The card reads, "Last night was hard. I hope you feel better this morning. I will miss you. Be safe. Be happy. Love, Beth"

◆ ◆ ◆

Beth sits in the coffee shop, waiting for the daily drip to cool. It's a new coffee shop. Hidden in a canyon in a neighborhood none of her friends ever visit. She cups her hands over the steam but doesn't lean into the comforting heat. She sits upright, rigid, legs uncrossed. She is wearing her blue leather Mary Janes and grey drop waist dress. It's one of Jared's favorites. He likes to joke that the pleated skirt and turtleneck make her look like a school girl. "I like schoolgirls," he always adds, hand snaking up the back of her skirt, grabbing a fistful of flesh. Beth has styled her hair in a ponytail bump today. It isn't her usual style and took longer to do than she liked, hands shaking as she stared at her face in the bathroom mirror, willing the hairpins and spray to hold it all together.

Beth picks up her new book. Her friend said that it was one of the best books she'd read. Beth trusts her friend's judgment and is looking forward to starting the story. She just hasn't had the time with all the deployment preparations until today. As one hand braids the tendrils of steam rising from her cup, Beth opens to page one and spends the next thirty minutes enjoying her beverage as she reads. Her friend was right: it is a very good book.

Beth finishes her drink and looks at the woman at the table next to hers. "Will you watch my stuff while I go to bathroom?" She asks. In the bathroom, Beth winces as she lowers her underwear over bruised thighs. The pad she put on this morning is spotted with dark, clotted blood. Gingerly, she exchanges it for a new one, wrinkling her nose as she tosses the used one into the hygiene box. She counts to 120 as she washes her hands under steaming water. The soap smells like tomatoes.

Beth buys another coffee on her way back to the table; she places it on the gleaming surface as carefully as she settles into her chair. Beth thanks the lady who nods without missing a beat in the conversation she's having through her Bluetooth. The lady is telling her daughter to break up with her boyfriend because he doesn't appreciate her.

Jared appreciates Beth. He likes that she keeps the house clean. He is grateful that she manages their finances when he's in Iraq, Somalia, Afghanistan, or East Timor. She always puts extra money into savings even though she isn't working right now. He loves that she randomly sings throughout her day; he tells everyone that before they met, he heard her singing first. He raves about her talents in the kitchen. The first thing he does when he returns from deployment is to plan a camping trip just the two of them; he claims that Beth is the perfect companion: adventurous and joyful. He tells her often that he is so happy that she isn't like the rest of her no-good family. He says he doesn't know what he would do without her; that they are an unbeatable team. He is certain she'll make an excellent mother one day. Beth hasn't told Jared about the IUD she got during his last deployment.

Beth looks at her watch. It is a white Fossil, its hands inlaid with mother of pearl. Jared bought it for her so that she could manage her time better. Six hours, thirty-four minutes, and nineteen seconds, until the Carl Vinson leaves port. Jared should already be on board. She's glad she packed his bags yesterday. That way there wasn't any last minute scrambling this morning. She's also glad she cleaned the house before she left while Jared was still sleeping. She didn't want his last memories of their home to be a mess. Of course she couldn't make the bed, but at least she set the sheets out.

She looks up from her book at her empty cup, surprised that the time has passed so quickly: it really is a great story. Does she have time for a third? Beth decides that she does—but a decaf this time—and walks to the counter, shoulders back, head high, each step measured as if she has already gotten her refill and is balancing the full cup of steaming liquid on her head.

Una Nichols Hynum

I Can Never Go Where You Have Gone

A cold December sun just rising, the shadow
of a roof falls across my roof like your leg
over mine or the whole body before we drift
apart, one to start the coffee, the other to sit
at the breakfast table writing in a journal.
But you are called up, another deployment…
Afghanistan. And each time you go to war
less of you comes back. That lovely shadow
of you withdraws into itself leaving a gap
between us, an empty space
where it will never be filled the same again.

his and her chairs
in the backyard, a vine
growing between them

Ella deCastro Baron

Transubstantiation

for Jacob Emmanuel

Jacob, if this is what you choose, your mom will continue
to watch your skin bloom, newborn cries amplify
now exceptional lungs, your broken body mend
before our eyes, everything missing,
incarnate, rebuke medical prognosis
you are "incompatible with life."

In the fourth hour, your mom and dad left
the decision up to you and Jesus. You could stay
with him—face to face—they trust you both.
Or you could join them here, in this life.
Do Kingdom work together; meet the needs of widows
and orphans. You already surpassed
what doctors disclosed early on: he may not take
his first breath.

My Protestant aunt insists on this as heresy:
Catholics who dare declare transubstantiation;
bread and wine actually become blood
and flesh of our savior. *What entitlement,*
she resolves. Why would Jesus *literally* show up
when we need him most? We should live
in metaphors instead—incomplete
representations of what our deep spirit knows
as truth. If that were so, then all we do
to contend for your life are mere facsimiles:
sanctified sinners sing, pray and worship in dim rooms,
stand on scripture across continents, press
petitions into the Wailing Wall, fast (from food, water,
unbelief) make pilgrimages to healing rooms,

prophesy visions of you—a curly, dark-haired toddler,
words in white block letters, *This baby will live.*

Tribes converge at the hospital on Zion Street,
dedicate, petition, beg, war, shepherd, submit,
adore, flood your delivery room with *ten thousand
years, bright shining as the sun.* Your dad anoints
your head in oil, tears baptize soon after. Your mom
arrays you with the whole of her, wraps a prayer
quilt around your shoulders as you finish
the race, climb the ladder
towards your coronation.

You are sent to eternity with the profound sense of being
loved and wanted. Your parents know this best.

How could all this striving
be only symbolic? We neither
claim our blessing nor see goodness

in the land of the living? Everything in me says
it is not enough. We are made for more
than this. We are not *like* something

else. We *are* these clay jars,
filled and poured,
filling, pouring.

since your homecoming this prayer can't hold still isn't solid doesn't fill a
container like a liquid won't disperse into the atmosphere as a gas. somewhere
in between. a "both/and" state buckling and bowing. a plasma. maybe it will
assume
          the   shape   of   this   page
might slide slip wriggle yield from these stanzas. the pauses and periods. *Paga,* a
Hebrew word for prayer—"lightning." this—the violent part of intercession—
to strike and fall upon. to reach the mark. did you know that lightning is
plasma? other plasmas formed in earnest entreaty: the space between planets
between star systems between galaxies. a bit closer to home (in case faith
radiates terrestrial) there's aurora borealis where this substance pours back into
the atmosphere, just above true North, transubstantiated.

These are our prayers.
Unlike your transition, our wrestling
persists, hip sockets capitulate, feet
lose bearings. We find ourselves
prostrate on level ground. Eyes
stunned shut by stardust, our fingers
strain, perceive the risen
dough, the cup.
chew. sip.
swallow.

Nancy Farness Johnson

Walking and Working on the Boulevard

The high school I've worked at for the last 16 years has history in City Heights. Doors were opened September 2, 1930. The school was named Herbert Hoover, after the president who put people back to work after The Great Depression. A stone marker on the Der Wienerschnitzel side of the school announces that President Hoover's Civilian Conservation Corp (CCC) helped build the school. The student body was white, and the surrounding neighborhood of Talmadge was upper middle class. Movie theaters and family restaurants were on every corner, and mothers strolled through the neighborhoods with their children in tow.

Mothers still stroll the neighborhood with children in tow, but most don't live in Talmadge, and except for about 11%, they are not white. A report put out by La Maestra on Fairmount Avenue, calls City Heights the neighborhood of "New Americans." Forty-three percent of the City Heights population is foreign born. In the 70s they came from Vietnam, Cambodia, and Laos. In the 80s civil war brought refugees from Nicaragua, El Salvador, and Guatamala. In the 90s ethnic Albanians from Kosovo and Kurds from Iraq as well as East Africans fleeing border wars in Ethiopia and Eritrea arrived, followed by the Sudanese and Somalis.

Hoover reflects the ethnicities of City Heights: 70% Hispanic, 14% Asian, 12% African American, 2% White. Forty percent of the parents at Hoover did not graduate from their own high school experience. With or without an education, these parents emigrated from more than 60 countries and speak more than 30 languages and dialects. Their drive to become successful members of City Heights is admirable, but they must overcome numerous barriers including language and economics. They must fight for employment, often filling the lowest paid jobs.

In the last 16 years, I have read thousands of journals from these diverse immigrant students, reflecting the challenges of their individual stories. Students were given the option to fold pages in half if they didn't want me to read an entry. They knew before they ever turned in their first assignment that if I felt they were being hurt or abused in any way, or might hurt someone else or themselves, I must as a mandated reporter turn their story over to Child Protective Services (CPS). It still amazes me how many pages were not folded over, were just waiting to be read. It still amazes me the heartache and anxiety that can pour out of a teenage child's fingertips.

One young girl wrote about the fear she experienced when her mother went off to work at the 24-hour Mexican restaurant on 22nd and University Avenue, from 6 p.m. to 2 a.m. She was left with her father for the evening. He drank his first Taurino Cerveza when he walked in the door after working all day shoveling someone else's dirt or loading up someone else's discards. He frequented Del Cerro, Hillcrest, and North Park in his dilapidated truck because those neighborhoods had the money. Their rejects kept him comfortable while he made his way through a twelve-pack before the evening was done. The light would creep into this young girl's room when the door to her bedroom was pushed ajar. She would pray and feign sleep. But it didn't matter what she said to Jesus or what she did to try and fool her drunken father; he would overpower her delicate body time and time again.

I asked her to stay after class the next day, and shared with her my obligation to the County of San Diego. More importantly, I shared with her my concern for her safety and well-being. I shared how much I cared for her and told her that no daughter should have to protect her body from her own father. She furiously screamed, "You have no business ruining my life! You have no idea what will happen to me!" She cried and pleaded with me not to tell.

Teachers never know what happens after we file CPS reports, and a student will rarely give up the details to an informant. The student never spoke to me again, and didn't make it through the school year. A year later, she showed up in my classroom after school one day. The second I made eye contact with her, she began to cry. She walked across the room into my arms, and by the time she reached me, I was crying too. She said, "You saved my life. I just wanted you to know."

Another 16-year-old girl wrote about her boyfriend and how much he loved her. He had scoped out the canyon behind Hoover, directly across the street from those fancy Talmadge homes, and found a cozy place where the two of them could have sex, a different period every day so no one would catch on. Sometimes the school narcs would check the canyon, so he would have to choose a secluded alley off Highland or the romantic spot underneath the stairwell of the 200 building. Her story didn't stop with the great sex. It went on to say that sometimes he would slap her, punch her, or give her a shiner...but he promised to stop. I didn't have to wonder if her facts were true; I could see the evidence myself.

CPS informed me there was already a report on file, confirming that the other teachers knew as well. I tried talking to her, especially after a fresh beating when she was open to hearing my facts about red flags and the cycles of abuse. I printed out articles for her and begged her not to stay with him, but the bottom line was she would do anything for him.

A journal entry written in pink ink with hearts on top of every "i" was written by a 14-year-old student who was a mother and didn't really understand how she had become one. A San Diego County health teacher had come in to teach a mandatory course on male and female anatomy, stages of dating and intimacy, venereal diseases, and contraceptives. This naïve mother wrote about how embarrassing it was to see all the pictures, and drew a pink penis next to a girl and a cartoon speech bubble, saying "penis, penis, penis." Inside was her rendition of a giggling emoji. She wrote about a party she went to in someone's garage on Chamoune Street just six blocks from school. No parents around. An advanced-level game of spin the "Two Buck Chuck" bottle left her as the winner. She was taken into a dark corner behind the dilapidated couch, barely slipping down her pants for the insertion of something that she had never seen before, during, or after the birth of her child.

If you were to read my journal entry from my Mt. Miguel High School English class, four decades before these young women, it would tell you that when my boyfriend pressured me to have sex, I broke up with him. He smashed in the passenger door of his new car with his fist to prove his love for me. He bought me a dozen red roses and asked me to forgive him. I did. A few months later, he manipulated me with a tearful confession about a failed sexual encounter with a previous girlfriend. "Do you think something is wrong with me? If

I just knew I could do it, I'd be okay with waiting." My entire life, I had been taught to wait, but my concern over a possible threat to my boyfriend's manhood changed everything. I didn't wait. And after that first manipulation, I got more red roses every time he lied, slipped into another woman behind my back, or punched one more hole in the wall.

So, is my story any different than my students' stories? Has the culture of San Diego high schools changed in 40 years? We should have known then to change archaic belief systems about girls and rights and safety, but we should certainly know now after nearly half a century. Society has always seen what it wants to see, and forgotten what it wants to forget. Even though my story is not that different than my students' stories, I don't want to see the truth. I don't want to imagine that my students are being hurt, manipulated, or forced into sexual encounters that they didn't choose for themselves. Being a mandated reporter, I have never had the luxury of refusing to see what was right in front of me.

These girls in my high school classroom didn't have the luxury of…well, they didn't have any luxuries. Many of my students can't be involved in healthy extracurricular activities like those students memorialized in the History Room of the Bookie Clark Media Center at Hoover. Unfortunately, most City Heights students can't live the San Diego billboard life, taking the Number 7 to surf in the afternoons (nevermind the beach is at least two transfers and an hour and a half away), studying at the Weingart Library in the evenings (their parents don't allow them out after dark), and catching a late flick at the AMC Mission Valley 20 (Oh, that's right, my mom works nights, my dad's been deported again, and I have to watch my little brothers and sisters).

What we don't want to know is that yearly hundreds of San Diego high school girls, who may have started out being abused in their own homes or by their own boyfriends or simply by a stranger at a party, become victims of sex trafficking in San Diego. We don't want to understand that victims of sexual abuse may continue to be sexually abused if they are manipulated with promises of love and money and possibility. Even after my personal experiences of abuse, and even after intellectually knowing the truth about abuse and who it happens to, I held onto my own archaic understanding that such terrible things only happen in poverty, in the seedier parts of City Heights, Barrio Logan, or Encanto, parts of San Diego that I don't have to frequent if I don't want to. Such atrocities could never happen in my own neighborhood or in my own classrooms. I held on to an archaic understanding that those involved in sex crimes were involved by their own choice.

What saved those of us who went to high school at Hoover or Mount Miguel or San Diego High in the pre-1980 years? What was different? Why were over 300,000 girls forced into sexual trafficking last year? Were the young girls of my generation that different than the young girls of today? I don't think so. There have always been dark things going on behind doors, in dimly-lit garages, in shadowy alleys. We have always chosen not to see them. We've gotten away with it for a long, long time. But the statistics are too shocking now. The means by which a boy can manipulate a young girl have increased exponentially with technology. And to young girls, he's just a cute boy on Facebook or Instagram or in the cool car cruising El Cajon Boulevard. Many of these fine boys have found a lucrative diversion from their own difficult home situations by becoming pimps.

The Hoover of the 21st century does a pretty incredible job of seeing what tourists, politicians, and business mongers choose not to see. They have an amazing Health Center that serves hundreds of students a year. They bring student advocates, psychologists, counselors, and yes, even CPS workers onto campus to address the real issues facing our teenage girls and boys. There is an active parent center and even legal help available for students and families. Through one of the many programs at Hoover, I met a detective who handles sex trafficking cases in San Diego County. He confirmed that many of my own students had been propositioned, threatened, or were already working the streets. For every story I shared with the detective, he had hundreds of similar stories. His unit operates stings where young girls are caught prostituting and later put in safe houses where they are protected and given life skills to change their destiny. Once they feel safe, their testimony is used to identify leaders of sex trafficking rings across the United States.

How did girls comparable to my own students end up as prostitutes? Maybe they were being abused at home and decided to get the hell away from the very people that were supposed to be protecting them. Maybe their sexual exploitations started off innocently at a party where the spinning bottle stopped and a blow job or worse was required instead of the obligatory kiss. Sometimes the girls were blackmailed after the first act that went too far, and threatened with exposure to their parents. Sometimes the perpetrator threatened to hurt a younger sibling if the girl didn't sleep with someone the boy set her up with.

Rarely in these high school dramas did a young girl wake up one day and want to be sexually exploited, or dream in their princess dresses of growing up to be prostitutes. Recently, the detective who talked to me about sex trafficking in San Diego put me in contact with a sex trafficking victim who wanted to tell her story, hoping she could help girls who faced the same atrocities she had. The victim was a young woman who had been sexually exploited for the past 15 years.

Amy sits across from me at The Tin Fish restaurant a few blocks north of Market Street and within walking distance of Father Joe's Village on E Street where she is living. It's on the edge of the Gaslamp, maybe too much character for some tourists, but loved by locals for its fish tacos, fried fish and chips, and frosty beers. The patrons lucky enough to be enjoying this beautiful weekday morning at 11 a.m. would never know that eight months ago Amy's testimony helped in the arrest of four major players in the San Diego sex trafficking ring. We settle on a table removed from the fray, and Amy nonchalantly, but incessantly scans her environment. Amy has stunning, piercing, golden eyes. She is eight months pregnant with her eighth child. She is wearing blue jeans and a yellow v-necked top that shows a tattoo across her chest. Down her arms, there are three other small tattoos, the last right above her wrist. She shows me the scars on her wrists, mangled one on top of another, where she has tried to take her life. Her short brown hair is covered with a blue and purple scarf pulled over her forehead and tied in the back. From her backpack she brings out a pack of cigarettes, a Ho-Ho, a Butterfinger, and a small recorder that memorializes her voice reading poetry that she wrote while in jail.

Amy: No date, but it's important.

> Fuck the world in which I live.
> I'm tired of being pushed, shoved,
> abused and used after all that I give.
> These men are scoundrels, piss ants,
> and poor hustlin' asshole fools.
> I won't take their mistreatment or bull.
> As a prostitute, call girl, drug dealer, student,
> I don't have time to be played like a fool.
> That's why I started way back when I was just ten years old,
> using my body, not as a treasure, but as a tool

to get around all the dumb ass male fools.

And I'll die living by that rule.

Nancy: Ten years old. Wow. You were obviously super intelligent. Have you finished all your schooling?

Amy: Uh-huh. I'm a certified information technologist, certified production assistant, certified food handler, can type 65 words a minute. I have my diploma.

Nancy: Man, girl. There's a lot for you to do out here.

Amy: As a girl now, it's kind of weird staying in a homeless shelter. I'm creating a life for the little baby inside my stomach, not knowing whether someone is going to come try to take her, or whether somebody is going to shoot me or kill me once the baby is born. I've had this pimp's family chase me around town saying, "Oh, wait until that baby's born. I'm going to kill you, shoot you dead. She'll live on without you." It's just....

Nancy: Terrifying.

Amy: Yeah. And if it weren't for me being able to call the detective and the girls from BSCC, I wouldn't know who to turn to, you know? Other than God himself.

Amy then talks about the threats against her life and the pimps she has helped to imprison.

Amy: At the time when I was busted, I was taken to a safe hotel by BSCC from the Bilateral Safety Corridor Coalition here in San Diego County. What they do is they bust us working girls, us escorts. They send an undercover officer to our room to get us. Once they have us in custody, then they interrogate us until they break us down...and it's not hard to break us down...although it took them 13½ hours to get me to break.

Amy shares her attempt to take her life, fearing what would happen to her if she testified. Afterward she was put in a safehouse until trial.

Nancy: Can you go way back to your earliest memory of family or street life?

Amy: I was taken from my mother when I was nine, and for the longest time I didn't understand why I was taken from my mom. But then things started piecing together. My mother was a crack-addicted prostitute. She didn't give a damn. Her drug addiction meant more to her than I did. Men meant more to her than I did. Because of that, I became a runaway. I ran away from 29 foster homes, and about 16 group homes. Two families wanted to adopt me. I took off from them. This is in the process of age nine to 18. I accumulated 149 points on my juvenile record. I was considered for adult prison by the time I was 15 due to some trafficking charges, that I was trafficking for my oldest son's father, my son who is now 19. I got pregnant when I was ten by a dealer who my mom owed ten dollars to, had my son at eleven.

Amy shares later that the money was owed for a $10 piece of rock cocaine. She goes on to talk about her pregnancy.

Nancy: Were you in a foster home at that time?

Amy: No. I ran away and I was gone the entire time that I was pregnant with my oldest son. I didn't go to pre-natal care, stayed at home, was locked in a room by myself the whole time. I had home delivery.

Nancy: Were you back at your mom's during your delivery or were you in foster care?

Amy: With the baby's father, the drug dealer. He wouldn't let me go nowhere. Every time I tried to go outside, he would block me. I was already smokin' crack at the time so…I started usin' crack when I was 14, but I was snortin' cocaine when I was 10, 11 years old. Smokin' pot, drinkin', hangin' out late at night. I started trickin' out my body when I was 13 to a dude named…to different dudes…mostly my mom's tricks or johns.

We spent another hour talking about her father and brother, her children, and her eight pregnancies. Only two children survived. Amy ends the interview by reading a poem she wrote to her own mother:

> Mother, oh mother, why did you leave me?
> Now I'm alone to deal with the guilt and shame.
> Mother, oh mother, you introduced me to the drugs.
> Now I'm crawling around picking at the rugs.
> Mother oh mother, do you know
> that I wouldn't have turned to prostitution and drugs
> if you would have given me more love and hugs?
> Mother, oh mother, did you know
> I attempted suicide because of the way you died?
> Mother, oh mother, please try to understand me.
> You created this monster in me,
> but I forgive you as the Lord has forgiven me.

According to a January 2014 FBI report, a San Diego-based investigation, much like the one Amy was involved in, recovered 60 female sex trafficking victims, including 11 minors. In its press release, the FBI reported that "twenty-four alleged North Park gang members and associates [were] charged in an indictment...the racketeering conspiracy involved cross-country sex trafficking of underage girls and women, plus murder, kidnapping robbery, and drug-related crimes." Those charged managed prostitutes, forcefully coerced women into prostitution, maintaining their obedience and loyalty through acts of violence, and grew their business through advertising and booking motels where acts of prostitution could take place.

There is hope. Programs like San Diego Youth Services (SDYS), just ten minutes from City Heights, provides emergency services, safe houses, transportation, food, education, and much more for young women that end up on the street for a multiplicity of reasons. One of the programs under the umbrella of SDYS is called STARS, and is coordinated by Laura McLean, who I met at a STARS fundraiser held at the Joan Kroc Center on University Avenue. McLean explained to the crowd, "STARS provides services for teen girls between the ages of 13 and 17 who have experienced commercial sexual exploitation" (sdyouthservices.org/STARS). McLean works tirelessly to encourage the public to stop using the word "prostitution" to refer to our young girls who are being sexually exploited. She says, "Being a victim of human trafficking isn't a choice, and we should use the best descriptive words for these victims of human trafficking."

A lot has changed at Hoover and in San Diego since 1930. We have more immigrants coming into San Diego from Mexico and Central America, but recently also from many war-torn, terror-striken countries in Africa, Iraq, and Albania. Unfortunately, what hasn't changed outside of Hoover—through the affluent, political, critical lens of outsiders—is the tendency to see what we want to see and believe what we want to believe about what we choose to see. The beauty of the changes at Hoover is in the diversity and tenacity of the student body. Students are learning to see what is before them, call out the demons of the dark, and insist on protection, dignity, and the right to walk proudly in the light. Hopefully, the outside world will catch the reflection of the City Heights kaleidoscope that is the next powerful generation of change.

Justine Bryanna

Confessions of a Runaway

Tonight was the night.

I didn't sleep. I was tossing and turning like a tadpole growing legs, panicking and clutching my stuffed lion tight. Tears flowed silently down my face and I choked on them, washing away the pain of an only child, too long neglected. I was alone. I was ready for anything the world had to offer. I was twelve years old. The weight of the world was on my small, bruised shoulders.

I crept quietly into my parent's bedroom, holding my breath as I waited to see if it was safe. I stood above them, clutching my fists so hard that my nails dug into my palms. They both looked so innocent, so peaceful. Their dreams could be sweet. My mom's mouth was hanging open, and her husband, my stepfather, had a furrowed brow. I wished I could smash his face with a hammer, and let the blood wash over my hands, cleansing me of his sins. A child should not feel these things.

Most people look innocent when they are resting, and even the darkest evils can be hidden behind the mask of sleep. The only difference between good people and evil people is what they dream about when they are sleeping. Evil people have to face their demons every night, and here I was, facing mine in consciousness. I didn't want to be a living demon; I didn't want to be evil. I knew if I stuck around I would become like him, or become a drunken pushover like my Mom.

I loved my mother, but I knew I couldn't rely on her. In between her first and second marriage I became her caretaker—I was her only friend. She loved me so deeply and told me I could do anything…she never failed to make me think I was invincible. But she could never be there for me, and for many years I fostered resentment against her. I was angry that she didn't save me from my stepfather. I forgave her because I knew that she could not fight my demons when she could not even escape her own. I forgave her when she divorced that monster. I never forgave him.

This was my only chance for freedom. If I didn't leave now, I felt that the entire world would cave in on me. I would end myself somehow; I would self-destruct. Or, more accurately, I felt my stepfather would end me, and I was determined to beat him to it. I make the decisions about my life, not a man who hardly knew me and didn't care about my wellbeing. Since my mother was no consolation, it was all up to me. I was my own savior; my saving grace was my self-esteem.

Back in my bedroom, I quietly shuffled for my favorite dress, clean underwear, and socks. Pants would be better, but the doctrines put forth by my religious step-grandparents forbid me from wearing anything but feminine attire. I only owned school uniforms and Sunday clothes. A dress is an awful thing to run away in—it makes you look weak. I seemed so innocent, so fragile, but inside I was a tiny warrior, fighting to be free of the oppression I felt in my body, mind, and soul. I lithely pulled the lacey pink dress over my pounding head, which was twanging like a broken cuckoo clock…sore and stressed, but I was ready.

I would have to change clothes as soon as I got a chance. And my hair, too. I would change my name; I could be another person the moment I walked out that door. I had to kill my former self, a child that got straight A's, a girl who had friends and played Barbies and painted her nails. That girl was now dead, I smeared warpaint on her face and she was reborn as a phoenix, flying out of a burning building. I had been training myself for this moment, knowing it would be the scariest thing I would ever have to do. I could jump fences. I could run fast, even in a dress. I could steal. I knew how to hotwire a car, even though I didn't know how to drive. I could talk my way out of any situation by batting my eyelashes.

I grabbed my toothbrush, toothpaste, and a hairbrush to tame my long, wild locks. It's best to look presentable in all situations. I put them all in my backpack, and closed the zipper in slow motion so as to not make a sound. My backpack had a piece of plastic on the front that could be written on, generally reserved for immature ramblings. I scribbled FREE across the back and pulled my arms through the straps.

Mustering up the most grace and stealth I had ever known, I crept down the stairs, avoiding the step that creaks like you avoid hot lava, or cracks in hopscotch. All the lights were off in the living room, so I followed the wall with my hand, careful not to bump into anything. I traced the picture frames, bitter memories of synthetic smiles and forced happiness. I saw my cat, peacefully sleeping in his bed, and I said a silent prayer that he would be safe without my presence, and that no harm would come of him. I would have taken him, but even at my young age I knew he would be a burden to my survival. There would be no more cats to lap up my tears at night, where I was going. If my parents awoke, I was still going to run like my life depended on it. I would run into the hills of City Heights and never look back. I would be found years later, with the media in awe of how I survived among a pack of feral dogs, my hair matted and tangled, unrecognizable even to my mother. I had lots of fantasies of how my adventure would end. My life did depend on this moment.

Just hours ago, I had been thrown across the same living room, then stripped naked by my stepfather. He flung me around like an old flag in a storm, ripping this way and that until only rags remained. I was ordered to stand at attention and recite a letter from his superior officer that praised his duty in the military...wearing rags. His greatness was artificial; he was a coward, a bully and a liar. The letter was really about his superior ass kissing skills. Although my mother half-heartedly tried to fight him off, it became too clear that I could no longer stay here. She was too drunk to help, still drowning her own childhood away. I should have been more upset with her, but she taught me how to punch, and how to respect myself when no one else does.

I had fought him that time. That's why he ripped my clothes to shreds. It's tough to say what I did wrong that time—when the punishment is more severe than the crime, you get lost in the suffering. He wrestled me to the ground, and I pretended I was hurt, crying and holding my knees and rolling on my back as a scared child does. All he wanted was for me to read the letter, and I refused to the point of being attacked. My leg was spring loaded, and as he stood over me, thinking himself powerful and mighty, I cracked my leg out as hard as I could, and my mary jane heel hit him perfectly, precisely and squarely in the balls. Thanks for the tip, Mom. Men had a weak spot that I otherwise would not have known about. As he doubled over, I felt a power I had never felt before, and I regret that I did not kick him again, when he was down. I was going to pay for it either way, as these things often go. The blood rushed to my face and I screamed as loud as I could. I wanted to whole world to know that I had just kicked my evil stepfather. Justice is a dish best served with a swift foot to the nuts.

Just days before I had celebrated my 12th birthday party. My friends from school came over, and my Mom made vegan carrot cake that nobody could tell was vegan. Even then, it was obvious to my friends that things weren't right in my home. As word got around, I was able to sleep over with other families on the weekends, but that still wasn't enough of an escape from the cruelties I experienced. Knowing what a regular, loving, functional family is like makes your situation seem that much worse. But the kindness I experienced from strangers was also what kept my hopes alive. The world is full of good and evil people, and the only way to tell the difference is in how they treat those who are weaker and worse off than them. My descent from one reality to another led me to believe that it was time to liberate myself from tyranny. It was time to run...so I plotted my escape.

After saying a final goodbye, I locked the door behind me. The air was frigid, and sliced right through my thin, pink dress. I shivered from the moisture, I shivered from my fear, and I shivered from the adrenaline pumping through my ice-cold veins. I was in shock for the first few steps, waiting to hear the clambering of footsteps, the screaming of my name, or the sudden flash of lights in the upstairs window...but nothing happened. It was as silent as a horror movie before the first person gets killed, the suspense could stop my heart from beating.

Each step felt entirely new: I was learning how to walk again. As I started putting one foot in front of the other, I realized that this stupefied pace would get me nowhere. It was then that I resolved to run, and I didn't stop running for many years. I ran to the gate, and I let it slam as I ran across the road like an animal before it becomes road kill. My footsteps beat the pavement like a marching band belting out a victory song. I could feel the beat vibrating in my head. I ran up a hill, sweating and panting and vomiting out everything that had made me such a victim before. I ran from my troubles, from the police, and I ran from my Mom. I ran to survive the hand that fate had given me. But most importantly, I ran for myself.

Nancy Cary
Parrots, Bullets and Dreads Flying

Our lives were different now. I'd built myself back up, slept with the phone turned off, and took ocean swims. My husband and I traveled.

We'd made it through a long, dark passage. My son was 25 and on his own. His late teens and early twenties were years of drug arrests, homelessness, and sickness. Now he was alive and healthy.

A community college graduate, he had a studio on 30th and C Street and had just transferred from City College to UC San Diego. Once in a while, he'd call midday to see if I would mind taking his dog out. I'd enter his studio and practice not looking around. No more vigilance, just be mom walking his pit bull around the block.

I was thinking of *this* on one of those hotter-than-summer, back-to-school afternoons. People's Market in OB wasn't the usual cart-bumping scene—just some locals moseying. But I was in a big hurry. My dogs were in the car, windows down, with those goofy dog-smiles they get when they smell Dog Beach. They barked at a flurry of cross-country runners in maroon track shorts. I had my Garden Salad in hand and was deciding between the homemade Green Goddess or Tahini Dressing, half listening to a produce guy with sandy dreads, ragging on the Padres pitching staff. *That's* when I heard firecrackers pop off. I didn't think much of it—Labor Day had just passed, and hey, it's OB—until maybe ten seconds later someone ran into the store screaming, "It's a shooter."

The produce guy's eyes were hazel, like my son's. He looked stupefied, "What the hell?" For several seconds no one moved.

Then everyone scrambled. I heard someone ask, "Where? In the store?" I remember seeing bright sun streaming in through the stock room backdoor. I'll run out that way. Wait. I'll get in trouble. I don't work here.

More shots cracked the air. "Shut the fuck up, listen!" Someone yelled from over the aisles, where I imagined others lying on the floor. At least I had the pyramids of oranges and the tomato counter.

I should ditch my purse. That didn't make sense. They can take my purse, my money and cards. My hands shook as I pulled apart my wallet. From the plastic protector, I grabbed the photo of my son when he was ten and a creased photo of my husband when he was the same age. I stuffed them in my bra. I wanted to survive.

"I hope someone's calling 911," a guy mouthed off. People's Grocery was one of the first to have a gentle suggestion of *No cell phones on in the store.* I'd left mine in the car.

Crying people were streaming into the store now. I scanned the front for the friendly, young cashiers, praying they were OK. More shots. They sounded louder, closer. I could hear the green parrots, outside along Voltaire, squawking the way they do when jets scream close over OB. Some of the cashiers were starting to stand up—elbows crooked and ducking again as they dashed for the back. They looked big-eyed and scared shitless.

I was nervous, mouth dry as a rag. I'll grab a juice and pay them later. Why was everything happening outside? Maybe it was a carjacking gone wrong. Maybe there's more than one robber, like a bank heist.

Fucking movies.

A woman crawled in from around the apple stands, slipping on her long gauzy skirt caught under her knees. She sobbed, "Someone's been shot. Please bring him a blanket. Bring him a blanket. Cover him." Then more people still crouching, crowded into the store. It was a swarm. I overheard conversations. I wanted to hear them, to know what could be known.

A guy said he counted fifteen shots. A woman said she saw at least one guy on the ground, really bleeding. She said he didn't look that old.

No gunfire for maybe five minutes. Those of us in the store could look out the long vertical windows and see clumps of people standing around, some shoppers with cloth bags, runners. People were in shock.

Someone said, "No one leaves until the cops come." Still, a few people slinked away on foot. I waited in the store.

Then I remembered. My dogs. Gawd, they're still out there. I tried to see if I could spot them in the backseat, maybe sitting up. Nothing. The car was maybe fifteen feet from the entrance where now a body lay under a blanket. When the police and investigators arrived, we were told that the area was being secured. Some of us were asked to give statements. A cop led me to my car. My dogs popped up. I was shaky and couldn't help but stare at the person beneath the blanket, the maroon track shorts.

One of his teammates screamed, "His fucking father killed him." I heard people say they'd seen the dad step forward and fire three more shots into his son's head.

A cop directed us to the alley—the driveway entrance wrapped in yellow tape. Loose gravel and dips in the asphalt jangled me. Feeling like some new, unsure driver, I hesitated trying to make a right into rush hour traffic on Ebers. Driving was too much. I remember being afraid I'd hit someone. Skaters. Surfers on bikes, boards tucked under arms. I noticed kids, piled into SUVs, parents driving them home for dinner.

It was all so normal.

I wanted home. I wanted my husband. I wanted to call my son.

My husband had the news on. Not knowing where I'd been, he was watching a SWAT team standoff with *that* man, holed up in a townhouse a couple miles away. Helicopters gave the bird's-eye view of the surrounded street and angled cop cars.

Don held me. Then he got up to take care of the dogs and find something for dinner. I was OK. But I wanted to be alone. I kept the TV on and channel surfed between local news coverage. I learned that the boy's name was Evan Nash. He was 14 years old, a tall, pimply teen with braces. He'd just started high school that week.

A couple of things ran through my head before I called my son. I wanted to be careful not to dump the whole thing on him, all that I could have said about how happy I was that he was back in my life.

I might be a wailing mess on the phone, crying and unable to just share what I'd been through. Seeing that boy dead, on the ground had hit me in the gut, not just for the loss of his young life, not just because I'd been lucky and not hurt, but because my son had gotten his life back. And because earning a life back doesn't mean it couldn't randomly be snuffed out.

I dialed. He was driving home from school. He listened. He told me he loved me. That's what I remember.

Over the weekend I continued to stay glued to the story. I watched for coverage on the news. I bought the local paper and poured over accounts online. I read that during the stand-off with the SWAT squad, Hoffine left a message on a friend's answering machine: "I have murdered Evan. I am going to kill myself. I'm so sorry that I had to do this."

I learned that late into the stand-off night, police had tried to keep negotiations going with the father. Finally they fired tear gas and flash bang grenades into the townhouse. Police broke in the townhouse and found Hoffine dead. No suicide note.

Sad, complicated details of parental disputes over child custody and child support unfolded in local and national news sources. I wanted to know about this young teen. I searched for interviews with people who knew Evan or his parents. I read that friends, teachers and others remembered Evan as an "intelligent youth with a sunny disposition." He had been a leader in a program to curb youth violence. While he had been in the local middle school, he helped found a chapter of the Tariq Khamisa Foundation, a local organization—named for a 20-year-old killed during a pizza delivery robbery—dedicated to antiviolence. I had been near Normal Heights—always a name that struck me as ironic and hard to live up to—in San Diego when the murder took place. I remember feeling shocked by the random violence and realized that pizza delivery boy had forever lost its innocent ring. The death of one son and the incarceration of another son left two fathers in anguish. The two men met and supported each other in establishing the foundation. Out of their grief, they found a way to move forward. To have hope.

Even though Evan and his father had spent father-son time together—camping trips and doing math homework—as Evan grew up, it was learned that Evan had mostly been living with his mom. By late August family relationships deteriorated to the point that Evan's mom initiated getting a restraining order. Less than 24 hours after being served with a protective order, Evan Nash's father killed him. At that time in California a person served with a protective order had 72 hours to show proof to a court that they either sold or surrendered their firearms.

At the time of his death, it was reported that Evan Nash had been gunned down by a large caliber pistol.

Later, police investigators recovered a .357 Magnum, a .380 caliber pistol, and a .45 caliber handgun from the dead father's possessions.

What did Evan Nash's mom, Lucy Nash, do with her grief? At the time I only learned that she had been a school employee and had been raising her son alone for many years. At the time of his death she had cried, "All my hopes and dreams are gone."

Eventually though, like the grieving fathers who founded Tariq Khamisi's Foundation, Lucy Nash would turn her grief into a way to survive, by dedicating herself to gaining local and state support to get additional protection for people seeking protective orders under the Family Code. Within three years, due to Nash's pressure and the legislative support of local San Diego Senator Christine Kehoe, then Governor Schwarzenegger signed Senate Bill 585. "This law is dedicated to the memory of Evan Nash, the San Diego teen who tragically lost his life while under the protection of a family court protective order. His mother, Lucy Nash, fought to change the law to further protect victims of domestic violence," said Senator Kehoe.

Senate Bill 585 adds provisions to the Family Code to allow law enforcement to consider seeking the immediate surrender of a firearm from a person served with a protective order; it reduces from 72 hours to 48 hours the time frame by which a person served with a protective order must show proof to a court that they either sold or surrendered their firearms; and it requires that application forms for protective orders ask what types of firearms are in the possession of the respondent. In the *California Chronicle* Senator Kehoe explained, "[I]n some cases the issuance of a protective order is followed by an assault or even murder. In certain circumstances, it is important to remove the guns as quickly as possible after a protective order has been served to help increase public safety." I kept thinking about the fact that Evan's father had mowed him down in less than 24 hours after being served with the restraining order.

For the time being, during that weekend I shifted between news articles and my own memories and thoughts about what I'd seen and felt. I searched for a way to calm down, regain myself. I knew that I needed to be able to keep my heart open and stand before my students again on Monday morning. I wanted to go back to People's. I needed to go back there that weekend, but I didn't know what I'd say. I felt like I wanted to find someone who had been through the experience that day. My husband and friends listened to me, but I still felt restless, irritable and lost.

I remember being kind of pissed off at People's. Why couldn't they have reached out to us more? I thought, "Why didn't they take our names and phone numbers? Maybe some of us trapped in their store were going to have some issues after experiencing the horror that happened right on the sidewalk and driveway of their store. They could have called us, asked how we were feeling. Maybe they could have had a meeting with a crisis counseling team in the so-called Community Room; after all, part of the mission and vision of People's was to serve the community and foster a healthy, caring spirit. At the moment, I didn't feel healthy. I must have wanted more caring, too, I guess. I knew some of my expectations were silly. Besides, People's management wasn't expecting to get caught up in something like that murder: how do you plan for violence?

I drove over. I spotted the sandy, dreadlocks produce guy and asked him how he was doing. I told him my name and asked his. He seemed kind of embarrassed and looked around. Said the whole thing had been really rough.

There was no sense to be made. I walked over to a memorial gathering of candles, flowers, and stuffed animals. It seemed small, kind of pushed over to the side so that it wouldn't block the entrance to the store. That Monday I drove by, and the whole memorial outside People's was gone. Snuffed.

Francisco J. Bustos

San Ysidro Blues: 30 Years After the Massacre

I remember playing on the kitchen floor when the shots started firing.
I remember my cousin and I running outside the apartment, like many others did.
The sound of bullets instantly changed everybody's eyes and nobody could
  explain it.

We lived on Sunset Lane, just a couple blocks, *de aquel Mac Donals*, 30 years ago.
We jumped outside at the sound of more bullets,
if we could make it to the corner, we could catch a glimpse of our San Ysidro
  Boulevard.

I don't know why we tried running to that corner. Something pushed us.
With every step that we took, more shots sliced the air,
and more shots and more shots, again and again and again.
Our eyes and ears, between each bullet sound, squeezed tight, very tight,
if only we could catch a glimpse of our San Ysidro Boulevard.

We never made it to the corner. It was impossible.
We were children and we were not able to save anybody.

Running back home, more bullet sounds ripped the air,
sirens started, one helicopter, maybe more, maybe a hundred.
The TV news flashed images of waves and waves of police cars and police men
while the real time bullet sounds from outside our apartments kept cutting through.
We locked our doors and we closed our windows, and still, the bullet sounds
  kept cutting in,
if only we could catch a glimpse of our San Ysidro Boulevard.

And that's when it happened
Nuestro San Ysidro pulsó y se congeló y nada sería igual después.
Nuestro San Ysidro pulsó y se congeló y nada sería igual después.

Silence squeezed tight between each bullet sound
if only we could catch a glimpse of our San Ysidro Boulevard.

Until, until, until, they finally stopped the man with the rifles and the guns,
finally, *por fin*.

But we must have kept hearing the shots, even after we went back to Sunset School
and some children did not make it back, and we knew why they weren't with us,
and when those children, our neighbors, didn't get back, we kept on hearing
    the shots
and we never forgot their faces and we never forgot their smiles.

We remembered walking to the cafeteria with them,
we remembered walking to the library with them,
and we remembered sharing the playground with them.

We must have kept hearing the shots, even after some of their moms
kept going back to our school as volunteers.
Those moms didn't leave us, and we never forgot them.
Those moms kept coming back to our playgrounds and cafeterias
and that somehow helped us heal,
and eventually we protested together and we demanded together
que el lugar ese del Mac Donals had to close for good
on that massacred, San Ysidro piece of land.
That spot was no longer theirs.
It belonged to the lost faces and smiles.
It belonged to those who lost their hearts and broke down on the boulevard.

We were just children and we couldn't save anyone,
but we marched with candles and with moms and dads who were broken
and we kept marching and we demanded a memorial park,
and eventually, we got it.

We got it because we refused to forget those bullet sounds and those lost faces
    and smiles.
We got it because of broken moms and dads, together, healing, marching and
    chanting.

30 years later,
the wind along our borderlands

still carries echoes of those endless bullet sounds,
still carries San Ysidro playground laughs of lost neighbors,
every one of them, forming *llorona* like border beats and chants in the middle
   of the night,

memories pulsating through our San Ysidro boulevard and beyond.

The Last Telephone Booths | *Kelly Mayhew*

IV. THROUGH A LENS DARKLY

Jim Miller

Excavating San Diego Noir: A Jumping-Off Place

In Mike Davis's seminal discussion of *noir* in *City of Quartz* he defines the genre as "a fantastic convergence of American 'tough-guy' realism, Weimar expressionism, and existentialized Marxism—all focused on unmasking a 'bright, guilty place.'" Born in the minds of the "Depression-crazed middle classes" of southern California, the "nightmare anti-myth of *noir*" trafficked in alienation and a distrust of the morality of capitalism. More specifically, Davis notes how "*noir* everywhere insinuated contempt for a depraved business culture while it simultaneously searched for a critical mode of writing or filmmaking within it." Thus in the "through-the-glass-darkly" novels of this new genre, early *noir* writers created "a regional fiction obsessively concerned with puncturing the bloated image of Southern California as the golden land of opportunity and the fresh start." In so doing, they transformed "each charming ingredient of the booster's arcadia into a sinister equivalent."

Davis then goes on to do a historical survey of Los Angeles *noir* in the broadest sense, starting with James M. Cain's *The Postman Always Rings Twice* and ending up with *Blade Runner*, along the way touching on the work of Raymond Chandler, Nathaniel West, black *noir* writers, *noir*-influenced science fiction, as well as contemporary crime writers. He ends his discussion of the evolution of *noir* by citing Thomas Pynchon's vision of "the Disneyfication" of it in his novel *Vineland* where the characters visit "the Noir Center" and shop in stores like "Bubble Indemnity" and the "Mall Tease Flacon." Perhaps, Davis fears, postmodern *noir* is heading toward a vanilla commercialization, full steam ahead.

San Diego Noir (2011), an anthology of local writing put together for the Akashic Books "Noir" series, has a few pieces that fit into the "nightmare anti-myth" tradition of Southern California, but (sadly) most of the pieces fall into the "Disneyfied noir" category. Indeed, in her introduction to the anthology, editor Maryelizabeth Hart notes that "through the stories in this volume, readers can visit many of the popular local sites," clearly indicating that the volume is intended to be a kind of airport book for tourists rather than a "through-the-glass-darkly" debunking of San Diego's frequently feeble boosterism.

The pieces that Hart writes "could occur in any city—but are colored with the particular scents and sounds of San Diego" indeed read like they could be set anywhere, and are consequently largely generic tales with San Diego props tossed in here and there. And, unfortunately, even some of the other stories that try to be more deeply embedded in the landscapes of the city lack enough convincing thick description to evoke any kind of "thereness." Throwaway references to the weather, the beach and the zoo confirm rather than defy the tourist stereotypes of San Diego. Indeed as the *Library Journal* review of the book notes, it is "[p]erfect for adventurous book groups and for travelers seeking the less rosy side of the cities they are planning to visit."

Perhaps this is to be expected as the *Union-Tribune* observed in its article on *San Diego Noir*: "When it comes to the literary genre known as noir—that dark terrain of desire and desperation, of passion and paranoia—certain cities come immediately to mind. Los Angeles. San Francisco. New York. Not San Diego." Well, not exactly.

While San Diego does not have as rich a literary and/or filmic history as Los Angeles, it too has some *noir* in its past. In the 1890s, Thomas and Anna Fitch saw Coronado as a suitable location for testing a doomsday weapon in *Better Days: Or, A Millionaire of To-morrow*. Then famously, in 1932, Edmund Wilson labeled San Diego the "The Jumping-Off Place" as a result of its nation-leading suicide rate. The city, it appeared to Wilson, promised liberation but could only deliver a chimera of false hope for the sick and economically devastated. Three years after Wilson's seminal essay, the narrator in Max Miller's novel *The Man on the Barge*, noting the "march of pain" of desperately ill sun worshippers, dryly commented on the unspoken alienation under the azure sky by saying, "Nothing often happened here except the sun." And who could forget the perfect San

Diego *noir* swan song of Raymond Chandler who drank himself to death in La Jolla, a place he described as "nothing but a climate," in 1959?

Jim Thompson's 1942 novel *Now and On Earth* is arguably San Diego's greatest classic *noir* work. While not a crime novel, it captures wartime San Diego through the glass darkly indeed. In his essay in *Sunshine/Noir: Writing from San Diego and Tijuana*, local historian Matt Bokovoy gives some background for Thompson's vision of San Diego:

> *Now and On Earth*, a wartime novel of socialist realism, captures the bleak landscape of downtown San Diego under racial violence, anti-communism, wartime housing shortages, and social dislocation. *Now and on Earth* is a story about a failed "hack writer" and aircraft industry clerk caught in a web of graft whose radical past puts him in double jeopardy. In the summer of 1940, Thompson and his family traveled from Pampa, Texas to San Diego in the Oklahoma Communist Party automobile, a gigantic four-door Plymouth donated by Woody Guthrie. Recently fired as director of the Oklahoma Federal Writer's Project for his communist politics, he took a job at Ryan Aeronautical scraping paint off the floor, and he ultimately became an inventory clerk. He later worked as a timekeeper for Solar Aircraft. The Thompsons lived in a small Spanish mission duplex in Middletown at 2130 Second Avenue, a hilly neighborhood wedged between downtown San Diego and Balboa Park. It also had commanding views of San Diego Bay and the Pacific Ocean. Despite the natural beauty of the city, San Diego's diversity and cultural fusion fascinated Thompson under the stress of wartime competition and scarcity.
>
> Often prone to periodic drinking binges in the San Diego Rialto, Thompson described the alienation and the broken dreams of war workers found in places like Eddie's Bar, the Bomber Café at 849 Broadway, and other downtown jazz clubs, dance halls, and juke joints. With the city filled with sailors at all hours, downtown was a 24/7 environment of cafes, restaurants, and entertainments. Many of the dance halls were fronts for prostitutes and drug dealers, who made their living from the meager wages of young servicemen. For Thompson, the difference between work in the war industry and the leisure found downtown had eroded, offering only new forms of degradation and exploitation. Portuguese and ethnic Mexicans

stand as the only redeemable characters in the novel, generous and
non-materialistic to a fault. In the end, *Now And On Earth* [argues
that] ordinary people deserved social democracy in their own lifetime due to the human indignities caused by a country at war.

And of course, San Diego native, the late (and great) Oakley Hall, author of over
two-dozen books, dished up some *noir* of his own in *So Many Doors*, *Mardios
Beach*, and others. And while *The Corpus of Joe Bailey* has been praised for its
mixture of "dread and wonder," his last book, *Love and War in California* looks
back at San Diego during World War II with precisely the kind of *noir* perspective Mike Davis discusses. In my 2007 *Union-Tribune* review of that novel
I wrote admiringly of Hall's vision of the San Diego of his youth and how his
main character comes to disdain the "bullshit" of American life:

> In *Love and War in California*, Oakley Hall takes us back to war-
> time San Diego and paints a much fuller portrait of the lost city of
> old than does his first San Diego based novel. It too is filled with
> wonder, dread, love, and longing but what makes the book note-
> worthy is its keen eye toward history.... The novel begins in the
> cafeteria of San Diego State College on December 8, 1941 where
> we meet the novel's protagonist, Payton Daltrey, an aspiring writer
> struggling to find his way in the world. A child of divorce, Payton
> is the son of a Republican businessman who lost everything in the
> Depression (and never quite lost his bitterness) and a working-
> woman who bounces from boyfriend to boyfriend and, like her
> mother, is a New Deal liberal. Payton's brother, the favorite son,
> went to USC, where he played football and busted Okies' heads
> as a strikebreaker. After college, Richie works in Hollywood and
> dates Elizabeth Fletcher, an aspiring starlet and the daughter of the
> prominent San Diego family, before joining the Navy as a pilot.
> Payton is the younger, idealistic, "slacker" son who works delivering
> groceries as well as for *the brand* a local left-wing newspaper where
> he sometimes writes articles about child molestation cases designed
> to draws readers who might then absorb some of the paper's social
> commentary.
>   It is at *the brand*, that Payton's boss Tully, one of his mother's
> ex-boyfriends, advises him that, "to understand Social Reality one
> must be inside it." The young writer is not a "commie" himself and

dismisses Tully as "all talk," but ends up taking his advice nonetheless.... It is in San Diego where Payton is subject to red baiting for
working at *the brand*, tailed by the American Legion, and forsaken
by his fraternity brothers. He sees ugly racism and anti-Semitism at
his father's house and is shocked when his Japanese football buddy
from San Diego High is sent to the relocation camp at Manzanar.
His other football pal, Calvin King, is a black man who works as
a pimp "south of Broadway" and whom Payton helps rescue from
marauding sailors when the Los Angeles Zoot Suit riots travel
south. Payton comes to befriend one of Calvin's "girls," a prostitute
named Dessy who ends up jumping out of her hotel window. He is
haunted by this as well as the visage of "a kitten-faced girl" of fourteen who he sees working in a donkey show at the Molino Rojo in
Tijuana where he has gone to research an illegal abortion clinic for
his sweetheart who is hoping to terminate an unwanted pregnancy,
the result of Bonny's pity for the father, who died in the war after
he left her knocked up at home.

All of this leads Payton to cultivate a profound sense of out-
rage at the exploitation of the weak by the strong. Whether it is
the abuse he takes from fussy rich customers while working as a
delivery boy in Mission Hills or the abuse he sees the world dish-
ing out to the powerless, Payton yearns to understand the nature
of injustice. At one point, in an outburst to Bonny, he rants, "the
rest of the stuff in *the brand* is about molesteds, too. Strikebreak-
ers, Okies, and Japs, and bad judges, and money more important
than people, and power used to make people miserable. AJAs in a
concentration camp, women and children and kids four years old.
Because they have epicanthic folds in their eyes! And what's going
to happen to Calvin King in the Army because he's colored! And
those fourteen-year old girl prostitutes in Tijuana with syphilis. I
mean, it's all connected." Payton comes to add an explanation of
war as "the ultimate molestation of the young" to his theory of
exploitation. And when he is driven to enlist early after his brother
is killed in action and he inexplicably loses Bonny's affection, he
gets to see "their fucking war" first hand.... Hall, the war veteran,
gives us a masterfully stark view of the war, full of irony and devoid
of patriotic bombast. The result is a portrait of a grunt, full of mis-
givings, that makes you admire the sacrifices of the many men who
defeated Fascism during an era when it was everyone's obligation to

fight, like it or not. It is during his stay in Paris when Payton decides
to leave his French lover and not desert, that he has an epiphany: "I
thought I could be a writer from the outside looking in spectatorly
on the bourgeois bullshit of Amurrucun life. But I would have to
write about the bullshit from inside Social Reality, condemned to
being just what I had hoped to rebel against."

Amen. Rest in peace, Oakley.

Richard Gleaves
Foot Tunnels

Old Town

With tunnels fear is a given.

Mission Valley

The standard solutions—the security esthetic of gates, intercoms, and billboard-intensity signage, or the distraction esthetic of band-aid public art—only make things worse.

Silver Strand

For these reasons, foot tunnels are a rarity in San Diego.*
Most were closed decades ago, and city policy now favors
bridges.

*The exception, of course, being the border.

Stephen-Paul Martin

More Dangerous

Gabe repeats the magic words: "The laws of history are obscured by the accidents of history." He's not sure where he first came across this line, and he's not even sure he understands it. But he likes the way it sounds, and he assumes that others will too, especially if he can deliver it with confidence, with the tone and facial expression of someone who knows what he's talking about. He imagines himself at work or on a date or at a party or bar, having what seems like a normal conversation, then tossing off the line like it's the kind of thing he says all the time, like it just popped into his head and hasn't been carefully prepared. He's eager to see the expressions on people's faces, the obvious respect the line will command.

He isn't quite ready. He hasn't been able to memorize it yet, so he takes it on a yellow post-it everywhere he goes. Now he's got it between his legs on the seat of his car as he drives to work. He reads it, looks at the road, reads it again, looks at the road, reads it again, pauses a minute, then says it out loud, "The accidents of history are obscured by the laws of history." It doesn't sound right. He looks between his legs and makes the correction, "The *laws* of history are obscured by the *accidents* of history." He knows he can't afford to make a mistake like that when he finally delivers the line. What would people think? He imagines looks of contempt, blunt ridicule, amused questions. Or maybe no one would notice. Maybe the line would work even if he messed it up. After all, he lives in San Diego, where tanning seems to be more important than thinking.

He comes to an intersection of two-lane roads. He knows that there's never much traffic here, so he doesn't come to a full stop. Out of the corner of his eye he sees a car approaching on his right. He decides to keep going, turning left onto the intersecting road, figuring that the other driver has plenty of time to slow down and let him go first. He's confident that there won't be a collision. After all, the laws of history aren't obscured by accidents on the road.

But the other driver hits his horn, roars out into the oncoming lane, passing and cutting back and stopping suddenly, forcing Gabe to slam on the brakes, narrowly avoiding a collision. The driver jumps out of his red Corvette, gives Gabe the finger, shouting obscenities. Gabe wants to shout back, but he can see that the guy is powerfully built and has a dark tan, as if his muscles were made of San Diego sunlight. Gabe lacks physical confidence. He's pale and flabby and spends too much time reading books he doesn't understand. So he stays buckled into his black Honda Civic and takes the verbal abuse, terrified that he might get yanked out and beaten up. He's so freaked out that he doesn't think of using his iPhone to call the police, or securing the power windows and doors and driving away. Instead, he stares at the digital clock on the dashboard, worried that he might pee in his pants or start crying. Finally the guy stops yelling, smirks and gets back into his car, revs the engine several times and roars away, leaving rubber.

At first, Gabe is relieved, glad that he didn't get his teeth knocked out. But then he wants to kill. He feels pathetic, like the wimpy guy who got sand kicked in his face in the Charles Atlas ads that appeared in sports magazines he read in his early teens, back when he used to memorize baseball statistics. The guy in the ads transformed himself, became muscular and self-assured and sexy. But Gabe knows he'll never become the new Charles Atlas. He's too lazy, too undisciplined, and eats too much junk food. He feels helpless, so disgusted with himself that he calls in sick and goes home and makes himself a bowl of buttered popcorn.

He's always done his best thinking on popcorn, and he's only halfway through the bowl when he gets an idea. He can still remember the driver's vanity license plate, HOTCAR, and he uses it in an Internet search, finding out that the driver's name is Duke Archer, a personal trainer who lives only five blocks away. Soon Gabe is taking time each day to follow HOTCAR through the city, learning that early on weekday mornings Duke travels to a gym on a dead-end road near Lindbergh Airport, a neighborhood of abandoned factory buildings. He unlocks the place, turns on the lights, inspects the equipment, then does paper work at the front desk. He opens the doors an hour later, when a few early birds arrive to work out. But in that first hour, when Duke is there alone, Gabe never sees anyone on the road to the gym. The situation is perfect for what he has in mind. His anger is filling him with a determination he's never felt before.

He buys a gun and goes to a firing range five nights a week, imagining Duke Archer's face in place of the target, the faces of guys who pushed him around in the past. Five weeks later he tells himself he's ready.

He waits at an intersection about a mile from the gym, watching the sun come up behind the dark industrial buildings. When Duke's Corvette approaches, Gabe pulls out in front of him. Duke does exactly what Gabe expects, passing and cutting him off and braking suddenly, jumping out and firing off the same insults he used before. Gabe watches him for a minute, amused by the performance. Then he steps calmly out of his car and returns exactly the same offensive language. Duke throws off his sweat shirt, showing off his big muscles, advancing firmly. He looks like Charles Atlas.

Gabe pulls out his gun. Duke freezes, then flashes a tough guy smile and keeps moving forward. Gabe puts a bullet in Duke's right foot, knocking him down onto the blacktop. Gabe pauses to enjoy his work, fully taking in the shock in Duke's contorted face, then orders him to get up and take off his clothes. Duke is writhing in pain, unable to respond at first, but when Gabe puts the gun to his head, Duke staggers up and takes everything off. Gabe has memorized a string of clever insults he found on the Internet. He presents them in the clinical tone of a scientist giving a paper at a conference, informing Duke that his birth certificate is a letter of apology from the condom factory, that he's so ugly it looks like his face was on fire and someone tried to put it out with a fork. Then he tells Duke to get down and beg. When he hesitates, Gabe puts a bullet in his left foot, and Duke is quickly on his knees, pleading through tears and clenched teeth.

Gabe thoroughly enjoys Duke's pain and desperation. If he weren't so busy holding his gun with both hands like they do in the movies, he'd be filming the scene with his phone. He looks quickly back down the road to make sure no cars are approaching. The coast is clear. But the San Diego skyline in the background, the sunlight flashing off the cluster of tall glass buildings, briefly leads him to question what he's doing: Shouldn't someone who enjoys the privilege of living in America's finest city behave in a more dignified way? Shouldn't the sunny skies have made him mellow enough to come up with kinder gentler ways of resolving his problems? Gabe knows the obvious answers, but he's never liked the predictably cheerful weather, the oppressively polite people smiling and telling him to have a nice day. He turns back to Duke and says: Repeat after me—The laws of history are obscured by the accidents of history. Duke gives him a strange look, so Gabe slams the gun across his face, drawing blood from his nose and mouth. Gabe smiles and snaps: Look me in the eye, motherfucker! Repeat after me—the accidents of history are obscured by the laws of history.

Duke looks Gabe in the eye and timidly asks: Which way do you want it, the first way or the second?

Gabe snarls: Both ways at the same fucking time, dumbass!

Gabe wants to prolong his enjoyment of Duke's panic and pain. But he thinks that the last thing he said sounded lame, that he failed to pronounce the words *fucking* and *dumbass* with the necessary sting. He thinks he can see contempt beneath the terror in Duke's eyes, and he almost loses control. He grabs Duke's curly black hair and yanks his head back, jams the gun into his mouth and prepares to pull the trigger.

For a second or two, the only sound is the music booming from the open door of Duke's idling car. A song ends, another one starts. It's one of Gabe's all-time favorites. He pulls the gun out of Duke's mouth and says: Is that your music, or just something on the radio?

Duke says: It's from a CD I made of my favorite songs. It's Steely Dan's "Don't Take Me Alive," though at this point I'm kind of hoping you'll ignore the lyrics and take me alive.

Duke sounds smarter than Gabe expected him to. His enjoyment of a clever band like Steely Dan tells Gabe that Duke might deserve to live, even with his offensively stupid license plate. Gabe can't keep himself from smiling. Duke sees the change in Gabe's attitude and quickly says: Look, I'm really sorry I jumped out of the car and started cursing you out. It's a bad habit I'm trying to break. I've even signed up for an anger management class. It starts next week. If you want, I can text you the information, and—

Gabe says: Text *me* the information? Why would *I* want the information?

Duke tries to smile: I mean, you know, just in case you wanted to take the class too?

Gabe snaps: Take the class? Why would I want to do something like that? *You're* the one with the problem, douchebag! You flipped out on me once before, a few weeks ago. But you probably do it so often that you don't even remember me—or any of your other victims, for that matter.

Duke says: Listen, if you put away your gun, I promise I won't press charges about the bullets in my feet. I'll even let you sleep with my girlfriend Susan. She's tanned and blond and utterly gorgeous, the perfect San Diego girl. She's damn good in bed and—

Gabe says: I can't stand beach bimbos. I hate how aggressively dense they always are. There's no way—

Duke says: No! Listen! Susan hates the beach! She's really smart. She's got advanced degrees in history from Stanford. She's even got published articles. You can look her up on the Internet.

Gabe laughs: If she's really so smart, what's she doing with a dumb fuck like you?

Duke says: I met her at the gym. I was her personal trainer for a while, and I got her a free membership. We're good between the sheets.

Gabe hates it when people claim that they've got a good sex life. He imagines them with deep tans, tight abs and perfect teeth, covered with designer sweat, making all the right moves and all the good sounds. He can't picture himself being anywhere near as telegenic in bed. But he has to admit that Susan sounds amazing: a San Diego blond with brains! Someone who might be impressed by the line he's trying to learn! He says: She'd really sleep with me to save your life?

Duke says: I'll call her right now and explain the situation, and you can listen to the whole conversation on speakerphone.

Gabe takes a step back but keeps the gun pointed at Duke's head. He says: Okay, dial. But don't try anything funny. Make sure to tell her you'll be dead meat if she calls the police. I'd hate to shoot a fellow Steely Dan fan, but I don't like it when people make me feel like shit.

Duke quickly nods, pulls out his phone and speed dials Susan's number, switching to speakerphone.

Susan isn't really his girlfriend. She's just been using him for sex. Duke Archer isn't the type of guy she usually dates. She plans to drop him as soon as she can find a more sensitive man, someone who's not so desperate to seem tough and decisive. Right now she's five miles away, in Pacific Beach, rushing out of a small glass office building. She's excited because she's finally worked up the nerve to quit her job, pleased that she took her boss by surprise, interrupting his early morning coffee, making a fierce and well-rehearsed speech and then storming out of his office, slamming the door behind her.

She feels her smart phone vibrating in her pocket. She pulls it out to check the number, but she's not watching where she's going and bumps into someone.

Her phone gets knocked onto the sidewalk, where a man accidentally steps on it with the sound of a snail getting squashed. He quickly apologizes, bending to gather up the shattered pieces, handing them back, a short young man wearing an old three-piece suit and a black fedora. She starts to tell him there's no need to apologize, but something about him prevents her from getting the words out. It's not just that he looks like he's been clipped out of an old black and white magazine and pasted onto a postcard version of a clear San Diego morning. It's also that he's looking at her like he doesn't know how to look at a human face, as if she had no face and he was just pretending to see her.

She finally says: It's no problem. I hate smart phones anyway.

He says: Smart phones?

She shrugs: I don't know why I've even got one. I almost never use it. All the special features make me crazy.

He says: A smart phone? How is it different from a stupid phone?

She laughs: I'm starting to think all phones are stupid. But everyone here in San Diego is totally in love with them.

He says: The thing I just broke is called a smart phone?

She laughs again, more tensely this time: You don't know what a smart phone is? An iPhone?

He shrugs: It looks like a mechanical device. How can it be smart—or stupid, for that matter? Isn't it just a thing you can use to get something done?

She looks at him like he's got to be joking, but there's no humor in his eye, just quiet confusion. She tells him to have a nice day and turns to leave, but he says: Excuse me, I know you're probably busy, but can you take me to the beach? I've heard it's a nice place to go.

She's been brought up to be a nice girl, so she turns back to him and says: The beach is just a few blocks away. She points toward the ocean, which is visible at the end of Grand Avenue.

He says: But it would be nice if you came with me, in case there are things that need to be explained.

She says: Things that need to be explained? There's nothing at the beach to explain. It's just a bunch of idiots lying on the sand.

He says: But surely they're enjoying the sound of the waves crashing on the shore.

She says: They're not even listening to it. They've all got pods in their ears. The only reason they're there is to work on their tans.

He looks puzzled: Work on their tans? Is a tan something you can work on?

She laughs: The idiots in this town seem to think so.

He says: But you have a tan, and you don't seem to be an idiot.

Susan smiles: I go to a tanning salon. That way I don't have to bother with the sun.

He still looks puzzled: But you're always bothering with the sun here, aren't you? I've only been here a short time, but I keep hearing people praising the weather, how wonderful it is that it's sunny all the time. It sounds like they're boasting about it, like it's something they've accomplished. But I don't think I would want to live in a place where the weather is so predictable. I think it would get boring.

She says: It's worse than boring. It's deadening. It makes people dumber and dumber the longer they stay here. I'm a good example. Ten years ago, I would have laughed at people who went to tanning salons.

Susan can hardly believe that she's having a negative conversation about the San Diego weather. It's the first one she's ever had or even heard. She feels like she's violating a sacred understanding, saying subversive things that she might get punished for, especially if this weird little man turns out to be more danger-ous than he seems, and his awkward behavior is just a cover-up, a way of conceal-ing sinister connections. Normally, she wouldn't talk to a stranger, but he seems so misplaced, so out of context, that she can't just walk away. She's fascinated by his slightly mechanical way of talking, as if the words were being projected through his mouth from a remote location, or perhaps from a place that doesn't exist anymore. She says: Why don't we get out of the sun? There's a nice café right around the corner. What did you say your name was?

He says: I didn't say my name. Do you want me to say it?

She nods and smiles: Sure, why not? By the way, I'm Susan.

He nods and comes close to smiling, but happiness doesn't seem to be part of his facial routine. It's like he's afraid to show his teeth, afraid to reveal the dark-ness in his mouth. He finally says: Hello, Susan. My name is Gavrilo.

Susan starts to smile with all her teeth, but stops herself and says: Gavrilo? Like Gavrilo Princip? The guy who shot the Archduke in Sarajevo a hundred years ago? The guy who set off the chain reaction that ended in World War I, the war to end all wars?

He looks disturbed: That's my full name—Gavrilo Princip.

She smiles: In a more intelligent city, having a name like Gavrilo Princip might be a problem. But here in San Diego, no one knows anything about the past. It's like the people here assume that only what's happening right now makes any difference, like history is something that happened long ago and far away. Especially here in Pacific Beach, you'd have trouble finding ten people who would know that you've got the same name as a famous assassin.

He looks even more disturbed, then says: If my full name makes you feel strange, you can call me Gavro.

She says: Is that what your friends call you?

He says: I don't have any friends. They all died a long time ago.

She says: Oh, sorry.

He says: There's no need to apologize. They did what they had to do, and after that there was no need to continue.

Susan isn't sure what to say. Though she knows it would be weird to say *cool* or *awesome*, the words so many San Diegans use when they don't know what to say, she also feels that it's her turn to talk, that saying nothing would impolite. But when she hears herself say *wow* she feels like an idiot. It's another sign that she's been in San Diego far too long.

Gavro tilts his head and says: Wow?

She says: I mean, that's really impressive—that your friends had what it takes to do what had to be done.

He shrugs: I suppose it was better than the cowardly alternatives.

She starts to say *wow* again, then starts to say *cool*, then catches herself and takes a deep breath and says: Okay, so I mentioned a nice café right around corner. Let's get ourselves out of the sun and drink something cool.

Gavro nods, and they walk in silence to a small café surrounded by palm trees. On the flagstone patio, sleeveless men and women sit at plastic tables, typing and reading text messages and nursing caffeine drinks with Italian names. Inside it's dark, with three round wooden tables beneath slowly turning fans. There's a small wooden bar on one side, a unisex bathroom on the other, and a back door opening onto a street, where a celebration of some kind is in progress, or perhaps a reenactment, since everyone is wearing outfits that went out of date a long time ago, in some other part of the world. Susan is surprised that the door is open. She's never seen it open before, and she's always assumed that it faced an alley with garbage cans, not a tree-lined boulevard lined with old buildings.

They sit by the back door. The waiter comes and she orders two Bloody Marys. She winks at Gavro and says: It's my treat. It's not every day that you get to have drinks with a famous assassin.

Gavro says: That's very nice of you, Susan. But can you buy me a sandwich instead? I'm terribly hungry, and I don't have any money.

She nods and tells the waiter to bring only one Bloody Mary, and a glass of water for Gavro. The waiter gives Gavro a puzzled look, like he's looking at a celebrity whose name he can't remember. Gavro returns the same look, and for less than a second Susan thinks they've traded faces, or that they're twins, even though the waiter is tall and tanned with long blond hair and a tropical shirt, the typical San Diego surfer look. She thinks of Gavro riding the waves in his old black suit and fedora. She wants to laugh, but she knows that it would look like she's laughing at nothing, and people have always told her that she looks weird laughing at nothing. She's learned to keep it under control, though the impulse is hard to avoid in San Diego, where she often finds things ridiculous without knowing why. For now she decides to act like things are normal. She looks at her watch and covers her mouth and starts coughing. The waiter finally manages the smile his job requires, says that he'll be right back and goes to get their drinks. Susan asks Gavro what he wants, pointing to the list of sandwiches on the blackboard behind the bar.

Gavro stares, creasing his brow, as if the menu were a list of coded instructions. He finally shrugs and says: I'm not sure what I want.

Susan looks at him carefully, wondering why she's spending time with such a strange man. In the past, she never had trouble walking away from people who made her uneasy, but with Gavro she feels like she's under a spell, an impression that's more embarrassing than disturbing, since the concept of being under a spell would have seemed silly to her five minutes ago. With most of the men she sleeps with, like Duke Archer from her gym, she's firm and assertive, but with Gavro she feels like she's been taken from the place where she's lived for the past ten years and dropped into a place she doesn't know, a substitute San Diego that exists for the sole purpose of replacing the real San Diego, though Susan knows she would never use the word *real* to describe San Diego.

The waiter puts their drinks on the table, and Susan tells him to bring a grilled cheese sandwich. Then she looks at Gavro expecting him to speak, to at least say thank you. But he's looking intently out the back door, like he's expecting something or someone. He reaches into his pocket and pulls out an old gold watch, studies it for a second or two, then slams it facedown on the table, breaking the crystal. He looks surprised at what he's done. He picks up the watch with his thumb and index finger, treating it like a squashed insect that might still be alive and try to bite him, carefully placing it face up on his napkin. The numbers peel themselves off the face of the watch and stagger out onto the table, looking around as if trying to get their bearings. Then they collapse and dissolve into the dark stained wood beside Susan's Bloody Mary. She blinks and grabs her purse and starts to get up, but again something stops her, the strong sense that something important is waiting to happen outside, carefully assembling itself in the carnival atmosphere, something that won't properly take place unless she's observing it. The sunlight from the back door plays on the broken bits of crystal on the table, taking her back to her freshman year at Stanford, an angry social science professor from somewhere in Eastern Europe—no one seemed to know exactly where, though there were rumors that long ago he'd written a manifesto calling for ethnic cleansing in the Balkans, and Susan often wondered why such a sinister person was teaching at a great American university. But what comes back most forcefully now is a phrase he kept repeating like a mantra throughout the semester: The laws of history are obscured by the accidents of history—a line from Tolstoy, or maybe Trotsky, he kept getting them confused, as if the famous names of the past were nothing more than a deck of cards to shuffle.

The waiter brings the sandwich and asks if he can get them anything else, but before Susan can shake her head and smile and say no thanks, Gavro is biting fiercely into the toasted bread, quickly chewing and swallowing, then taking another big bite. In less than a minute the sandwich is gone. He leans back in his chair, resting his back against the exposed brick wall, and something close to a smile settles into his face, like he's just had really good sex. He closes his eyes and says: Thank you, Susan. That was truly wonderful.

Suddenly there's a loud noise from the back door. He looks up and squints into the light. Susan can see a grand and beautifully kept old car with its top down trying to back up, a man and a woman in the back seat wearing elaborate old costumes looking confused, someone dressed in what might be a Halloween general's uniform shouting at the driver, who keeps shaking his head and grinding the gears. Gavro gets up from his chair, pulls a revolver out of his inside jacket pocket, steps quickly out the back door without even a glance in Susan's direction.

She sits with her Bloody Mary, not sure what to do next. There's a pause that feels like a hundred flashbulbs punching the sunlight out of the room, turning the moment into a black and white photograph framed in a dusty museum, a place that will soon be closed because no one goes there anymore. Then she hears two gunshots, screams and shouts bursting in through the door. History feels more dangerous than it ever did before.

Josh Baxt
June Gloom

It's late spring, you can tell by the low clouds and chilly breeze, and Jeff has escaped to the small wall outside the office to avoid the sullen preparations. Sybil joins him, which is awkward for no apparent reason. He has never actually met Sybil, but often sees her out of the corner of his eye. She is the Human Resources version of the Grim Reaper and has been busy lately, visiting with severance checks and outplacement packets. When she enters the suite of offices where Jeff works, people recoil in dread.

Sybil pulls out a cigarette and eyes him defiantly. She's not supposed to smoke on the wall. She's supposed to smoke in the corner of the parking lot by the dumpsters and the emergency generator. She silently dares Jeff to confront her, but that isn't going to happen. It doesn't pay to piss off HR. He may need one of those packages.

Jeff recently discovered spirit animals, the symbolic creatures Native Americans invoke as emotional guides. They provide endless entertainment as he assigns them to people around him. So not really spirit animals at all but just people animals—making the practice little more than an excuse to mock.

Sybil's spirit animal is a lab mouse; one of those wizened critters the grad students name because nothing can kill it. She smokes Marlboro Lights and unwittingly places her fingers over the tiny holes they add by the filter to reduce the tar.

Good job Sybil.

Each pull on the cigarette is a measure of her devotion to smoking: long, fervid draws and slow, deliberate exhales. Her cheeks go reverse Dizzy Gillespie on each inhale. She gets her money's worth.

During the most recent brush fires, Sybil and her smoking buddies—strangely absent now—braved the sepia air and falling ash to get their collective fix. Jeff was grossed out but compelled by their sheer dedication. It's a trait he lacks.

"You're in fundraising aren't you?" she says. It's a rhetorical question. Sybil knows who he is, what he does. She knows about the time he got his left nut ultra-sounded to make sure that little lump was nothing dangerous, which it wasn't. Okay, kidding, Sybil doesn't really know that. But she could if she wanted to.

"Jeff Ashby," he tells her. Yeah, that Jeff Ashby. Divorced, 38, five foot eleven and three-quarters, 175 pounds. Brown hair, hazel eyes, a large mole on the small of his back, of no significance whatsoever. If you saw him, you'd recognize him. Or rather, you'd recognize someone else in him and be disappointed (or relieved) that it isn't the person you thought it was. He blends in but not well enough.

Sybil nods and looks down, as if pairing the face to the name. Not reassuring. "Sybil," she says, and then, "a lot going on down there." She has a Brooklyn accent. Jeff thinks it's Brooklyn. Maybe it's the Bronx or Boston. East Coast something or another. Anyway, it makes her cragginess almost loveable.

"We live in interesting times," says Jeff. He thinks he's made a clever joke, but Sybil doesn't even smile.

"So what do you do down there, anyway?"

"Next to nothing."

Sybil laughs this time, and it's only by the grace of God that it doesn't devolve into a wicked cough.

"That's good, you won't mess anything up that way." She pauses. "This weather sure sucks."

Oh yeah, the weather. You have to talk about the weather in San Diego, by law. The entire city is like an insecure lover: lack of enthusiasm = hatred. Pretty days require obeisance. A spate of rain generates malignant commiserations at the grocery checkout.

Spring has its own pathology. Clouds blanket the coast most days in May and June—coastal layer, changing ocean temperatures, you know, meteorological crap. An opaque, gray dome of moist air, one continuous cloud from horizon to horizon, without even the catharsis of rain. Fleshy tourists glare at the sky and wonder where they went wrong.

"June gloom," Jeff says and she nods knowingly. Yes there's a name for it. May gray, too. See if you can find that in a visitor's guide.

Jeff likes the clouds. They keep the world cozy, subdue the harsh angles on buildings and people, muffle traffic noise, keep planes in the air; provide a roof, shelter, security. The sun makes him feel exposed, like a rabbit in a parking lot.

"What time is it?" he asks.

"Straight up two."

"I have to go," he says and feels the need to explain. "There's a going-away party."

"Another one?"

"Yeah, they come in sixes."

She laughs again, and it lifts his spirits. "Nice to meet you, Jack." Jeff starts to correct her but shrugs it off. "Let her call me Jack," he thinks. "I kind of like being Jack."

The party is being held in the ACA (Administrative Conference Area), a small room with a big table. Jeff is late, but so is George and that makes it okay. George despises tardiness in everyone but himself. No one is mixing. People file in, find a chair and take root. There is a wide flat Costco cake, white icing, *Good Luck* inscribed in industrial cursive. There are open seats but Jeff prefers to stand near the door.

Carol, one of the few cynics left, stops in the doorway and looks knowingly at Jeff. Carol maintains her own personal conspiracy database. Recently, she's been wondering out loud if they aren't housed in a sick building. On the face of things, the two deaths in the previous ten months might bolster her argument. But Len died from an aortic aneurysm and Kyle succumbed to pancreatic cancer. Still, she points to the ulcers, the migraines, the fibromyalgia. Carol wants the guys in hazmat suits to burst in and do a clean sweep.

"Is there any hope?" she asks.

"Hope comes on a sliding scale," says Jeff. Carol eyes him quizzically and grabs a seat. She's a gerbil, and won't come out of her little plastic tunnel until assured, and reassured, that it's safe.

It's early Friday afternoon, Memorial Day weekend, and people are literally counting the minutes until they can go home. Paula, the paranoid office manager, has been scrolling through her ancient Blackberry and suddenly stands, amazed at a new revelation. "I just want everyone to know that George is going to be a few minutes late."

This mystifies the group as George, George McClellan acting director, is already a few minutes late. Paula certainly believes she is providing a great service but receives only grunts of derision for her trouble. She starts to sit down but someone audibly clicks their tongue, causing Paula to pause and scan the room in an oddly theatrical half-seated, half-turn. Paula maintains a tight orbit around George and must fight with those who would displace her. The battle fierce; the stakes low. Her animal is the owl and not the cute endangered kind but the big bruisers that snatch house cats and drop them from great heights.

Paula's primary competition is Suzan—Suzan with a Z, as Daniel used to say before he was asked to leave. Suzan has mastered the art of seeming peeved and chipper at the same time. High probability it was her tongue click, though it could have been anyone. Could have been Jeff. They all grasp at these passive-aggressive moments as a means to rescue their humanity.

Suzan is tall and, with all the sun damage, of indeterminate age—could be 40, could be 60. She has short stylish, blonde hair and worships a cosmetic surgeon a reasonable person would sue. Her boob job is out of proportion to her frame and the nipples don't match, one pointing almost due east, like a wandering eye. She once caught Jeff staring and preened awkwardly in response. She didn't realize his attention was clinical rather than sexual: examining the deformity the way he might fixate on a dwarf with a goiter. She thinks she's a lynx but she's actually a pound dog missing a leg. "Please, please, somebody take me home or at least stop and stroke my matted fur."

The staff is noticeably restless. Some manically finger their smart phones; others join conversations or stare into space. Someone suggests, on the condition of anonymity, that maybe the group should move forward without George. After all, he isn't the only one with things to do. It's bad enough the staff has to drop everything to mourn another fallen colleague, but to have to wait for the acting director to make an appearance—that's just bad time management. Everyone listens attentively and nods, but no one takes the logical next step of proceeding.

"I'm sorry I'm late," says George rolling in like a gutter ball. Canula Group is a non-profit devoted to complementary medicine and healthful living, but no one seems a bit concerned that George looks like he's downed 30 Big Macs in quick succession. Len, by contrast, was fit as an Olympian. He was only 56, and Jeff hates the fucker for being dead.

George's spirit animal is a giant ball of twine. Don't ask what it means, these things are organic.

Jeff flattens himself against the wall as George passes and assumes his most pensive stance: slightly hunched, arms folded, head down. He's aiming for deep thought, worry and eagerness to proceed. The head down is a special touch; it gives the appearance he is concentrating intently. Anthropologists might recognize an ancient Mayan posture to ward off evil spirits, though he's simply trying to avoid unnecessary eye contact.

Across the room, Tom and Jerry (their real names) radiate team-playerness. They want George to know they're in it to win it, regardless of the consequences. They are foible-ridden men, as is Jeff. Jerry has nuclear breath, and Tom has chronic underwear-in-butt-crack syndrome. His right hand is irresistibly drawn to the problem. Sometimes he chases himself around the office to extricate the offending cloth.

"Thank you all for coming today," says George. Jeff marvels at his geometric roundness. He is like an outtake from Lewis Carroll: squat, round, slimy, his pants hiked to his armpits, his tie tucked into his pants—a creature made entirely of oatmeal and bacon grease.

This is the fifth going-away party in as many weeks. Those are only the voluntary departures; the forced ones get no fanfare. The staff has acquired a viral case of post-traumatic stress. There's little elective talking. People start sentences too political to complete. They walk around sheepishly, afraid to communicate. Weight change is endemic. Some respond by porking out. Others lose their appetites. No one has the strength to buy new clothes.

Even George has grown queasy. He was merely a consultant, imposed from above, when Len died. McDermott, the CEO, installed him as ACTING VP and never refers to him without the A-word attached. McDermott wears boots—alpha wolf—and stands so erect people fear he might fall over backwards. He keeps George's balls in a leather satchel attached to his waist and pulls them out occasionally to stroke them roughly.

George's deepest fear is that McDermott might notice the exodus and think ill of his management. George is known for two things: his ability to manage-up and his deeply held paranoia. He suspects that this thing, this series of departures, this statistical aberration, is a clever conspiracy to circumvent his control, to send a coded message through the chain of command. He suspects the staff is using Human Resources the way a crafty kidnap victim might jiggle the brake lights from the car trunk to send an S.O.S. to other motorists.

He needn't worry. McDermott knows the drill. People leave. *You gotta break some eggs.* But George is a victim of low self-esteem and it drives him to overkill. He has developed a network of informants to keep the lid on. Jeff's friend Daniel was overheard making critical comments in a restaurant. Daniel is no longer with the organization.

Jeff used to enjoy the work, but now he thrives on the chaos. He literally does not know what might happen on any given day. Sometimes he imagines he's in an espionage thriller, thus the experimentation with stealthy postures. He uses code words in conversation and replies by phone to contentious e-mails to short-circuit the paper trail. With so many people gone, and so few replaced, the system breaks down on a daily basis. "Now that X has left, who's responsible for Y?" echoes through the halls. It's like having a front row seat for Armageddon but without all the annoying dead bodies.

The going-away parties are a special time to taste the fear. Reactions break on generational lines. Tom and Jerry are in their late fifties. They have mediocre achievements and questionable hygiene. Who knows where they'd end up if George streeted them. They'd lose salary, but what's more important, they'd lose benefits. Early retirement is almost within their grasp. The young ones have a different view. They leave on their own and share resume tips, sotto voce, in the hall. Ginny, today's honoree, seems relieved, her peers, envious.

Sometimes Jeff ranks the parties. How is the turn-out? Are there yummy snacks? Is the pathos quality? This one has streamers, a nice touch. He sees it as the breakpoint between the morbid sadness and self-pity that characterized the earlier events to a more transcendent appreciation of someone making their escape. The next phase might recall the American Embassy in Saigon, 1975. People will claw, climb and scratch to gain the final perch on the last helicopter out of the war zone. Give me your new job. Please, please give me your new job.

"I don't have a lot to say," says George. "Candace has been with us for some time." There is an audible sigh from the group. First Jack, now Candace, what the fuck?

George is not an attention-to-detail guy, so getting Ginny's name wrong is not a big surprise. But there is an actual Candace and she's sitting uncomfortably in the room being told she's leaving, which is probably her deepest fear. Is it a Freudian slip? Does George have a list of future deportees in his pocket with her name on top?

Oblivious to his fidgety subordinates, George continues. "She has been stalwart, through good times and bad, and has always gone the extra mile...."

◆ ◆ ◆

Jeff wants to intervene, but he promised his former boss Richard, who got disappeared himself two months ago, that he would take a vow of silence—security through obscurity. No one knew Richard was leaving until he was gone. There had been no warning. No memo. His office had been emptied, as if the desk, chair and bookshelf had been quarantined.

On the day after Richard's last day, his phone and computer sat lonely on the office floor, huddled for protection, the keyboard leaning precariously against the monitor. Richard's former colleagues stood, empty, in his empty office and felt the ripples of his departure or pondered the phone and computer, like tombstones. The red voice mail indicator was lit and no one knew Richard's password. They wondered if it was an important call.

"I can honestly say that Candace—"

"Excuse me, George," says Tom, tepidly raising his extraction hand. Jeff knows what's going to happen, and it fills his heart with love.

George is annoyed. "Yes, Tom?"

"Um, I believe the woman's name. Um, in other words, the name of the woman who we are currently, you know, sending off. Um. I believe her name is Ginny."

The room exhales in unison and a few people nod approvingly at Tom who, surprisingly, took one for the underlings.

"Ginny?" George looks squarely at Tom, as if he doubts him. Ginny intervenes.

"Ginny," she says, waving. She is evidently a microscopic organism and hardly rates the cake.

"What did I say?"

Tom hesitates, as if he expects someone else to pick up the mantle. "You said Candace, George."

"Well that's ridiculous. Candace is staying, aren't you Candace?"

"As far as I know," she says, putting on her bravest face. Candace, you are an ant. Sure you get stomped on daily, but there are millions of you.

George clears his throat. "Very good." He gestures towards the cake and they need no further encouragement. Free sweets are one of their few remaining perks.

◆ ◆ ◆

The parking lot faces downhill, towards the highway, which is moving intermittently. Fridays are ugly. Holiday weekends even worse. Sybil darts by.

"Goodnight, Jack."

Jeff waves halfheartedly, and is about to get into his Civic when Tom appears out of nowhere.

"Some meeting today," he says. More awkwardness. Jeff's shoulders slump as he encounters this one last obstacle.

"Yeah it was. Thanks for setting the record straight." Jeff has beeped his locks open but Tom is in his way and appears unmovable. Tom is tall and big from left to right. Jeff could probably feint to the side and reach the door handle, but a hip check would hurt like hell.

"That was weird."

"It was." Jeff nods, unsure what he's agreeing to. He has a reputation for being agreeable, but what started as an amiable character trait has been reduced to a defense mechanism. Being agreeable is the quickest way to get out of these conversations.

"But you thought I did okay?" Oh, right, the meeting. The name, the correction, the weird look George gave him. Jeff gets it now. Jesus man, you're almost sixty fucking years old. Grow a pair.

"Yes," Jeff says, with definition. "You did great." Though his admiration is now being tested.

When Jeff wasn't let go, the rumors/conspiracy theories had him in some kind of Faustian deal with George. *Keep your job in return for a little intel on your colleagues.* Does Tom believe it? Hard to say, but he sure likes to hedge his bets.

"I've been here ten years, you know. I mean, I was here before Len. The guy right before Len, his name was Tony; he used to pick his nose in staff meetings. He lasted about six weeks. And the guy before that...."

"Traffic looks pretty bad," says Jeff. The Civic's lock mechanism has timed out and the doors make an audible click. Jeff feels good about cutting him off. Who knows how far he'd go down the memory hole before pausing for breath? Tom needs approval, even from Jeff, and it makes him hesitant to get to the point. Hard to get shot down if you're talking nonsense.

"It's just that, what I want to say is. You know, we could do a lot worse than George."

Jeff has an answer on his lips: *No, we couldn't.* But it never sees the light of day. Is he getting wise as he pushes 40, or is it just that agreeable thing again? But he does need to respond, so he nods his head, freakishly.

"You know Tom, you're probably right," Jeff says with the back-slapping conviction of a long-lost fraternity brother. "But I've got to go."

"Oh yeah, sure. See you on Tuesday?"

"Yes Tom, of course, Tuesday."

Andy Koopmans
The Pot Run

"Why don't you take Sebastian," Victor says. The words hang in the air and I feel my heart hit pause.

"You ain't coming?" says Koa.

"Nah, man. I'm good. It's your connect, you handle it." Victor squints and rubs his bare, lean midriff, tanned from beach running, which peeks out of his open shirt. "I'm gonna stay right here. You guys go."

He's sitting on the end of the futon couch in his apartment, king of all he surveys, which at present includes a 60" TV playing *La Notte* through with the sound down for the second time that afternoon, two massive six-foot ribbon speakers standing on either side of it blaring Stevie Wonder's *Musiquarium* album, a half-dozen Ikea bookcases full to groaning, and a flea market coffee table holding several empty beer bottles, a bong, and an ashtray piled to overflowing with Victor's American Spirit butts.

About a half hour ago Victor opened the cigar box where he keeps his weed in crinkled baggies, the strains neatly marked in Sharpee on the front of each. He looked through them with increasing agitation, finding them all cashed except for tiny bits of shake, which he gathered onto the front of *Musiquarium* and added the tarry bong resin, which he scraped out of the bowl with a pocket knife. He loaded the tiny resultant pile into the bong, fired it up, and it was gone in two burbling hits, which he didn't share. "That's all folks," he said.

Victor's weed guy was out of town, so Koa took his cell outside and called around until he found someone. When he returned he looked pissed. "Everybody's on fucking vacation or some shit," he said. "My boy KK's got a 'z of Purple Kush but I'd have to haul all the way out to I.B."

"I.B.?" I asked.

"Imperial Beach," said Victor.

"Is it far?"

Koa snorted. "Where you from anyway, white boy?"

"Michigan."

"Detroit?" Koa asked, and I almost tried to lie, but shook my head.

"Ann Arbor."

I could sense Koa's opinion about me slip one further notch down.

"Yeah, I.B. is pretty fucking far," Koa said.

I considered offering to drive because unlike the rest of them, I was sober. I hadn't inhaled any of the pot, instead pulling the smoke into the bong's chamber and then leaving it there and passing it off. Nobody was paying me much attention, so they didn't notice. I used to get stoned with friends in high school, but eventually I noticed people stopped inviting me. I get unaccountably morose when stoned and frequently cry at some point, and that wasn't the impression I wanted to make the first time hanging out with Victor and Audra. But I realized I couldn't offer to drive because I'd been saying things like, "Oh wow, I'm so stoned," and laughing too hard along with Victor and Koa at private jokes I didn't get, not wanting to feel left out. Telling them I'd been faking would've been too embarrassing.

"Dude, be the party hero," Victor says, digging into his surf shorts and coming up with a wad of crumpled $20s. "Drive down, pick it up for us. Half a 'z should do it. Here, I'll even get the weed and throw in for gas."

Koa doesn't look pleased. He's sitting in a large vinyl bean bag chair that from my angle is barely visible around his bulk. Victor says he's Hawaiian, Samoan on his mother's side. They went to school together as kids. Now he works as a bouncer in a couple of clubs around town, and I'm fairly sure he could tear off my arms with no problem whatsoever. Koa jerks his planet-sized head in my direction without actually looking at me. "Okay, but what do I need him for?"

I choose not to be insulted. Going on a drug run with a terrifying guy who doesn't like me isn't exactly the afternoon I'd hoped for either.

"Well, you know, man, a little privacy for a while might be nice," Victor says, his hand drifting over to caress one of Audra's bare legs, which are tucked under her as she stares at the TV. "Come on, guys. You know how it is."

"That's nice," Audra sighs in a dreamy voice that makes my stomach flip. I can almost feel her warm, smooth skin beneath my own palm.

Audra took many generous hits from the bong right off and over the past couple of hours went from talking manically about how much she loved getting high to lapsing into a hypnotic trance of the profoundly baked, watching every movement of Marcello Mastroianni on screen as he passed through the landscape of Milan. The video belongs to her. She's doing an article on Antonioni whom she says was one of the best filmmakers of all time. Every twenty minutes or so she snorts or sighs at something in the film then looks around at us with a beatific smile to see if she's alone in witnessing the minor miracle on the screen. I've been sure to meet her eye every time and nod and smile, drinking in the dreamy look on her face.

Koa sighs, resigned. "Alright, I guess I'm Stepin Fetchit and the babysitter." He looks at me for maybe the third time that day. "Fuck it, let's go, white boy," he says, then takes several rocking lunges before overcoming gravity and rising out of the bean bag. When Koa gets to his feet, he towers over the rest of us, filling the room. Acres of stiff, new denim hangs low around his waist, bunched at the cuffs over size 15 Timberlands, the suede pristine and brushed, the laces untied and loose. His torso is tented in a black LA Raiders jersey with a big white 80 across the front, and several heavy gold chains hang down to his chest from where his neck should be. A bunch of indistinct blue-black tattoos litter his knuckles spelling out something I can't make out.

I look over to Victor and Audra, hoping to catch Victor's eye, let him see that I really don't want to go on this errand, but he's already leaning in, pecking kisses down Audra's bare shoulder, moving aside the bikini strap of her top. My heart starts racing and I know I have to get out of there before I explode with jealousy.

I get up to go and just then Audra says, "Sebastian!" I know it's ridiculous, but I think for a second that she wants me to stay, that she's calling after me because she's realized that I'm what she really needs. She laughed at my jokes earlier. She even asked why I didn't have a girlfriend. Maybe, I think, maybe she—

"Don't hurry!" she says and finger waves at me across the room, her body now unfolding as Victor's stretches over her.

In the few rapid paces it takes to leave the apartment and cross the driveway, my mind races. I decide to tell Koa, not untruthfully, that I have a paper for my narrative theory class to write by Monday, then I'll get into my shitty little car, drive home, and masturbate bitterly before studying. It's a solid plan, but Koa is waiting at the curb, holding open the passenger door to his black Monte Carlo SS as if waiting for his prom date. I try to talk but find my tongue won't work. I hesitate long enough for Koa to get irritated. "Well? You fucking getting in or what?"

I get in. Koa slams the door after me as soon as my ass touches the seat and the edge of it nearly catches my shoe. He walks around the long nose of the sedan, brow knitted, lips moving while he mumbles what I'm pretty sure are obscenities about me. Or maybe Victor. Doesn't look like he's happy about being the errand boy. When he gets in, the shocks sink and groan, tilting the car so drastically to port that I have to make an effort not to slide down the bench into his lap.

Koa slams his own door and settles in behind the wheel. It's a tight fit for him even though it feels to me like we're sitting in the trunk. The dash is so far away I can't touch it with my arms extended.

"Put your seat belt on," Koa says, and I waste no time following the order. Then he brings his own belt over his shoulder and rests the buckle on his massive lap.

I look over at the belt and then up at him and he says. "Just for show. We get hit, I'm not going nowhere, know what I'm saying?"

Koa grunts as he leans forward to turn the ignition. The engine is four times the size of my Civic's and it lunges powerfully under the hood, like a team of horses pulling impatiently at the reins, eager to run. Before shifting into Drive, Koa squints into the rear view at his bloodshot eyes. "Gonna have to go the gangsta route."

"The gangsta route?"

"Stay away from the po-po," he says.

My expression apparently betrays my ignorance.

"The fucking police, white boy," he says, shaking his head and stomping on the accelerator.

A couple of weeks ago, Professor Llewellyn assigned me to critique one of Victor's short stories for our fiction seminar. I've always been kind of shy and introverted, and even after speaking in front of people a bunch of times during my undergrad program at U of M, the idea of standing up in front of class and reading a critique was bad enough, but having to critique Victor scared the crap out of me. Victor is by far the best writer I've run into in the program, or in school generally. Everything he's turned in this semester reads like it came out of an already published book.

By rights, Victor shouldn't even be in a lower-level creative writing class, but Llewellyn is his thesis adviser and Victor's been sitting in on all of his classes to generate enough work to finish a collection of long stories and graduate. They've been working together for years, and Victor and Llewellyn seem really tight— like friends or colleagues rather than professor and student. So when Llewellyn made a point of assigning me, one of the youngest and most inexperienced writers in the class, to critique Victor, I could only see it as an act of generic academic sadism, but I wasn't about to give anyone the satisfaction of flinching. I decided to write the best goddamn critique of my life.

Like a lot of the creative writing classes, the seminar meets for two and a half hours a week, all on one night, so I had seven days to agonize over the critique. Even so, I wasted no time getting started. I went home and read the entire 40 pages of Victor's manuscript in one sitting. It was dense and intelligent but also artful and moving. If you didn't know Victor from class, you wouldn't believe his writing came from the mind housed in the head of the surfer-dude in the cut offs, flip flops, and skater shirts who always arrived late for class reeking of pot. But Victor speaks often in class and is effortlessly smart and funny and insightful. He's always making references to things like post-structural theory, political movements, history, eastern philosophy and a bunch of other stuff. It's like Jeff Spiccoli swallowed Noam Chomsky. In class, we all listen when Victor has anything to say.

I spent every non-committed moment over that week on the critique. I reread the manuscript three more times through, making notes in the margins, Googling references I didn't understand, and then working with careful reverence on the writing, struggling clumsily with the language. The first few drafts gushed too much and I didn't want to come across as fawning, so I made a point of finding two things in the manuscript that I thought could be better. Both comments were about fleshing out the one female character in the story. She seemed a little flat, except for her breasts, which were described several times in the manuscript with imaginative synonyms for "large" and "jiggling."

When it came time to deliver my critique, Llewellyn called me to the front of the classroom where I stood, head down, eyes locked to the page, which shook between my hands. I'd practiced a dozen times or more in my apartment in front of the bathroom mirror but all that went to hell. I sprinted through the critique in a terrified monotone, ignoring the careful punctuation I'd agonized over like a poet, and just as the last word escaped my mouth I raced back to my seat, my pulse goosh gooshing in my eardrums and sweat cascading down my back.

I sat there with my eyes down as Llewellyn spent the next ten minutes critiquing my critique, restating my points at a more human and leisurely pace. When he was done, he said, "A well-considered reading, Mr. Ross. Good critique, in concept at least. In presentation, well, that will come with time."

My face felt like it was on fire. I could feel everyone look at me, but I didn't look up until the class was dismissed, when I bolted towards the door. Before I got there, Victor called out to me from across the room. "Hey, Sebastian, c'mere a sec!"

I turned and crossed the floor to Victor's desk. He offered his hand and I shook it, which at 23 still made me feel like I was a kid trying to play grownup. I knew, but wasn't sure that he did, that this was the first time we'd spoken all semester, one on one. I'd fantasized about how this would go. I hoped my hand wasn't too clammy.

"Hey, man, really appreciated the words about my text," Victor said. I managed to meet his glance. His eyes were sea blue circles filled with large dark pupils, the corneas webbed with bloodshot capillaries. "It seems like you gave it a lot of thought. I'm impressed, sincerely."

"Ah, no big deal," I said, just as Audra appeared by Victor's shoulder, her left hand snaking up around his neck and combing long fingers into his sun-bleached hair.

"It *is* a big deal," she said, her large green eyes and light auburn hair almost making me lose my breath. From the first week of class, I've watched her whenever I can get away without anyone noticing. "Not enough people really get Victor's writing. And you're right, he doesn't write women very well."

"I didn't say that!" I said, feeling my scalp start to sweat and itch. "I just said that I thought she should be developed a little bit more. I mean, I'm probably wrong, but, you know, I thought...."

"It's cool man," Victor said, nodding. "I heard that. It's a good note. I'll definitely think about it. Most definitely."

"He thinks characterization in women all comes down to nipple size," Audra said and then craned her neck around Victor and stood on her toes to kiss him on the lips. When they broke, they smiled at each other, eyes connecting deeply like no one else was around. It made my stomach hurt.

"Well, see you guys later!" I said, starting to flee.

"Wait up!" Victor put his hand on my shoulder and I froze. I spent most of my public school life as a bookish, lame gazelle trying to hide from the predators on the school yard Serengeti, and a hand locked on my shoulder rarely meant anything good. But Victor was still smiling when I looked back. "Do you want to get some beers at Monty's with us?" he asked.

I shook my head. "Sorry. I can't. I've gotta get to work."

"A working man! Look at that, America isn't completely on the skids after all," Victor said. "I haven't earned an honest dollar in over a year. Been living on grants and loans, but soon as I get this thesis done—well, shit, hey, I'm having a procrastination party on Saturday at the crib. You should come."

I shrugged. This was a coveted invitation, but I couldn't imagine accepting. That would mean having actual conversations with him and possibly Audra, and I was sure they'd find out I was a fraud. An imposter hack writer among real artists. "Thanks, but I'm not sure I'll have time. I have a bunch of studying."

"Take it from me," he said giving me a wink, "studying can always be put off. Look, it's not a lot of people. Just me and Audra and maybe a couple others. We'll hang out and talk about writing and shit. You should come, seriously."

Audra nodded and smiled. "You should!"

Friday night, I stayed up late making potato salad from scratch in my postage stamp–sized kitchen. I listened to podcasts of *This American Life* while peeling and boiling potatoes, dressed only in my underwear because the steam turned the apartment into a sauna and the one window on that side of the apartment is painted shut.

My mind drifted to Audra repeatedly. She's not only beautiful, she's only a couple of years older than me and already has a CV crammed full of accomplishments, including a publication in *Cineaste*. She writes dense, taut short stories populated with figures borrowed from pop culture, especially movies. She recently turned in a story retelling Jean-Luc Godard's *Contempt* told from the point of view of the Brigitte Bardot character that caused a huge class debate about the male gaze.

She and Victor are like the Kennedys of the department, but I noticed early on that even though they always arrive late to class together, she never sits next to him and almost never makes comments about his work. Same goes for him, so maybe they have an arrangement to be a couple only outside of class. Whatever their arrangement, I have a crush on both of them the way I did on Mulder and Scully on the *X-Files* when I was a kid: I want to be him, I want to have her.

This morning before the party, I dressed in my favorite vintage Pixies concert T-shirt and a pair of shorts and slip-on Converse sneakers. I tried on just about every item of clothing I owned before deciding to err on the side of casual—I've learned that underdressing is far more acceptable than overdressing in San Diego. When my parents came out to help me find a place at the beginning of the fall semester, they took me out to a fancy restaurant in Horton Plaza and even at $30 a plate almost everyone but the wait staff were wearing shorts, T-shirts, and flip flops.

When I arrived at Victor's apartment in Normal Heights carrying the potato salad and a six pack of beer, I was more pleased than I had a right to be to see Audra sitting out front in a lawn chair next to Victor. On the other side of her was the human mountain called Koa.

Koa guides the Monte Carlo east on El Cajon Blvd. and then turns south and drives us through neighborhoods I don't know at all. I spend most of my time either in the college area or at the beach, which, along with the sunshine was my main motivation for choosing San Diego State for my MFA. Twenty-three Michigan winters were enough to last me a lifetime, thanks very much.

The economics of the neighborhoods rise and fall but mostly fall as we head south, the prosperity or lack thereof marked in abundance or scarcity of green space. The further we travel, the more concrete dominates, but under the sunshine, even the poorer neighborhoods look inviting to me.

Koa ignores me in silence for about fifteen minutes until he suddenly he jabs me hard in the arm with his elbow and points out his window toward a sprawling complex of buildings surrounded with chain link. "That's Gompers, where Vic and me went to school together."

"Victor went to school down here?" I say, immediately regretting the tone of disbelief in my voice.

"What, you think this hood ain't fit? This is where I'm from, white boy. Look around, this is the real San Diego—not fucking Sea World or Horton Plaza or that tourist bullshit. This is where real life goes down."

"No, I just thought he's, you know, such a surfer, he probably went to school near the beach or something more...."

"White?"

"No, just, you know, different."

"Uh-huh. Yeah, well, Vic was a brain so his Moms got him sent down here because it was a like a magnet school and shit. They had all these special science and arts programs for kids like him. Vic, man, he was always too fuckin' smart."

"Yeah," I say, nodding, happy to be able to agree with him about something. A minute later he jabs me again and looks at me sideways with a little smile on his face. "You like that girl, huh? I can tell."

"Who? Audra? Nah! No way! We're just in class together!" I realize I'm completely unconvincing. I've never been able to lie.

"Bullshit, it's written all over you, way you look at her. You think Vic didn't see it?"

"You serious?" My heart crashes against my ribcage. I feel exposed and small and hot.

"Hard to miss, man," he says, then closes the case by reaching over to the stereo and turning it on for the first time. A subwoofer in the trunk blasts low frequency waves which pummel my body like fists through the seat. I clasp the door handle to fight the urge to clap my hands over my ears to save them from annihilation. The speakers in the car doors shake and rattle with every beat as we ride further south. People on the street turn to watch us pass. Koa's face is expressionless and hard, his eyes squinting, his beefy left forearm resting on the edge of the window. I try to imitate his look and fail. I feel every pair of eyes on me as we pass, all asking the same question in Koa's voice: What the hell are you doing here, white boy?

We drive alongside the concrete snake of the 805 freeway 100 feet overhead and then pass under it. We end up on a street called Highland which we follow for several miles past markets with Spanish names, liquor stores, notary publics, used car lots, and check cashing shops amidst the familiar global franchises for fast food, auto parts, and gas. After a while I realize that I'm the only white person I've seen for a long time and feel strangely comforted to be riding with Koa.

We keep driving south, south, south in the afternoon heat until I start to drift. I don't ask Koa how much longer we have to go. I can only think of every mile we travel having to be retraced on the way back. I look at my wristwatch. We've been driving almost an hour and I have so much work to do before Monday that I start getting another stomach ache. I try to think of something else and end up with a vision of Audra and Victor back on the futon, athletically, beautifully fucking while I'm here on the endless road of strip malls in the burgery odor of road sweat emanating off Koa, having the hair cells inside my ears carpet-bombed by Public Enemy.

We get on Palm Avenue and head west again, and the sun is in my eyes. I'm beginning to lose faith that we will ever make it to our destination when we pass by a mosaic sign of a sailboat. It reads *Imperial Beach The Most Southwesterly City in the Continental U.S.*

After another 20 minutes or so in heavy traffic, Koa turns onto a street lined with tall palm trees and old but well-kept houses with large lawns and long driveways. He reaches over and turns the volume down on the stereo. The relief makes me giddy and I say too loudly, "Nice neighborhood!"

"Yeah, KK does alright. Crib right near the beach."

"How long has he been your... you know, dealer?" I realize as soon as the words are out of my mouth that I shouldn't be asking.

He turns and scowls. "What the fuck you want to know for?"

"Just making conversation. Sorry. Didn't mean to make you mad," I say.

A beat passes and then Koa says, "I know KK from Calipatria."

"Calipatria?"

"Calipatria State Prison."

"Oh," I say.

Koa grunts as he Y-parks the Monte Carlo along the street and we walk a few houses down the block, my legs happy to be moving again. Koa turns up the driveway to a large white stucco place with a Spanish tile roof, set far back from the road. A yellow Hummer 2 and three expensive-looking racing motorcycles are parked out front.

"Nice bikes," I offer, not knowing anything about motorcycles.

"Yeah, KK collects them."

"They're all his?"

"Think so. Hey, now listen white boy, just let me do the talking here, okay? F'real, KK can be kinda high strung."

At the door, Koa stands in front of me and rings the doorbell. The house explodes in barking noises and then heavy, rasping scratches flail at the other side of the door. Footsteps approach and a raw voice yells, "Dino! Cut! Down you fucker!" But the barking and claws don't stop until I hear the meaty sound of flesh on flesh and a surprised yelp. "I said cut, goddammit! Bad dog!"

The door swings inward revealing a skinny white guy in jeans and a tight wifebeater that shows off a jungle of wrist-to-shoulder tattoos. He leans back, pulling hard on a metal choke collar against the weight of a large brown and black Rottweiler. The dog barks again and rears on its hind legs, wheezing and choking as sinewy muscles swim beneath the skin, working to break free and get to the porch, presumably to eat us alive. At least Koa is in front of me, I think. Maybe the dog will get full before it gets to me.

"Sup K?" Koa says.

"Dude, where the fuck you been?" KK says, then shoot me a sidelong glance. He jerks his chin at me. "Who's the fuck is this?"

"Nobody. Just a friend of a friend," Koa says and I produce a tight thin smile to confirm that I am, in fact, nobody. It has never before seemed so true to me as today.

KK jerks his head. "Alright. C'mon," he says, walking backward, pulling the dog with him. Koa eclipses my view as he passes through the front door, and I follow them inside.

"Close that fuckin' door after you!" hollers KK as he pulls the dog down the passage and across the living room toward a glass door emptying into the back yard. The dog sees where he's going and drops his body weight into the collar to be less cooperative, scraping his nails across the hardwood floors. KK's arms strain, hard as cord wood, as he finishes expelling the dog.

The living room is filled with expensive consumer electronics, several Gibson and Fender electric guitars on stands, and dozens of colorful custom skateboard decks mounted on the walls like abstract artworks. Despite the size of the house and its expensive furnishings, it has the same dank, close odors of Victor's tiny place—pot, stale food, and B.O.

KK brushes the dog hair from his shirt and takes another look at me, which seems to confirm that he doesn't need to acknowledge me. "So what the fuck took you so long? I've been waiting around," he says to Koa.

"Took white boy here the scenic route," Koa says. "Can't catch another DUI anyway."

"Alright. Well, fuck it, let's sample the product," KK says.

"Tight!" says Koa clapping his massive hands together.

I turn sideways and lean in towards Koa. "Look, do you think maybe we should get back? I mean, I've got to do a bunch of work and besides, won't Victor wonder where we are?"

"Relax, white boy. Don't be so uptight," says Koa, and I realize I've lost another hour or so.

Koa and KK sit down on the long leather couch facing the big screen. KK lifts a 3-foot purple double-chambered bong from the floor and puts it on the coffee table next to a box of Ziploc bags and a digital scale. He reaches under again and brings up a large freezer bag filled with green. "So, you want the whole 'z or what?"

I watch KK load the bong, take his hit and trap the remaining smoke in the upper chamber. He hands it off to Koa, who clears the smoke and fires again. He leaves some smoke for me and tries to hand off but I shake my head. "Nah, I'm good."

"What's up with that shit?" says KK. "You a narc or something?" His eyes are small and dark and mean. I've seen them in the faces of dozens or hundreds like him and I just want to go. I start thinking about calling a cab and charging it to my dad's credit card but it would probably cost a hundred bucks to get back from here.

Koa says, "He's not a fucking narc," and for a moment I feel a wave of affection for him.

"I'm just not feeling great," I say to KK. "Would it be alright if I were to use your facilities?"

"'Would it be alright if I were to use your facilities?' KK parrots, mocking me. "Dig this guy. Yeah, the shitter's off the kitchen. Go crazy," he says nodding toward the back of the house.

They watch me walk away and then say something that makes them both laugh as soon as I'm out of the room. I don't care. I'm tired, hot, fed up, and fucking used to it. I didn't think I'd still be putting up with it in graduate school, but I'm starting to realize that there are bullies and assholes of every age.

The bathroom is squalid and smells of mold and urine. I pee into a toilet that's not been cleaned in some time. There's a ring around the water line and dark streaks near the drain marking a recent shit. When I flush, the water threatens to back up over the rim before receding.

I go back into the kitchen and quietly open the refrigerator since Mr. Manners hasn't offered a beverage. There are about forty bottles of Miller High Life, a few bottles of condiments in the door, and a Domino's box containing a very old looking slice of pepperoni pie. I remove a beer and pop the cap with a magnetic church key stuck on the door, then pound it down. I usually hate watery beer but it tastes good and slakes my thirst. I stifle a belch into my fist and then look around for a recycling bin with no luck.

I open a door into the garage and feel around until I hit the light switch. Two fixtures of bare fluorescent bulbs flicker weakly overhead and cast the space in a flat white light. It's a big two-car garage but there's nothing but a large empty square of cement. The only garage in California not filled with crap, I think, but then I hear something odd coming from around the corner of the near wall—a combination of whirring and jingling and thumping.

When I crane my neck around to see what it is, I feel like a fist has hit me low and I physically recoil, taking a step back before looking again.

A treadmill in the corner is running and a stocky pit-bull mix dog is on the deck, trotting quickly on his short bowed legs to keep up with the conveyor's pace. The dog's face is partly obscured by a wire cage fitted over his short snout, and long streams of bloody saliva ooze from it, dripping onto the deck. A choke collar is fitted tightly around the dog's thick neck and tied off with a leather leash to the front of the treadmill so that the dog has to keep moving or fall and get choked. The dog's breathing is fast, shallow, and wet, and I can tell by its loose, stumbling gait that it's exhausted.

Without thinking, I rush toward the machine, a huge WTF? the only thing in my brain. Is this some sort of bizarre health thing? Is this a weight loss program for the dog? No. I know without knowing. The air is hot and close, humming with flies and permeated with the odor of old cigarettes and sour animal sweat. I can almost smell molecules of pain floating in it.

The dog sees me and, even in its condition, dips its head at me and growls a little. The muzzle is on too tightly for the dog to bark, and I can see it's digging into the animal's snout, rubbing raw black-bloody spots around sides of its face.

I walk slowly in a wide arc around the side of the treadmill. The dog is a male, judging by the enormous, full scrotum swinging between his rear legs, and he tries to turn his head to watch me, but the leash is too tight and the pace of the treadmill too relentless.

My eyes trace the power cord from the treadmill to an outlet high on the opposite wall. I grab the cord and yank hard, making the plug spark as it jerks free and the cord to lash back like a snake, narrowly missing clipping my shins.

The treadmill quickly slows to a stop and the dog drops to his belly, a high-note relieved whine seeping out of him as he pants. Meanwhile, the lights almost double in brightness and I really see the room for the first time: heavy bags and pads are scattered in the corners, covered in silver duck tape patches, a half-dozen small plastic animal crates are stacked nearby next to a mound of burlap bags stained with blood, and a half-obliterated circle about ten feet across is chalked on the floor. Within its circumference, faded coppery stains are visible on the concrete.

I feel dizzy, like the beer and the heat are going to my head. The garage begins to close in around me, narrowing the aperture of my vision. I squat and breathe until it passes, but in my head I know what I've seen and it's making me want to leave the house, my body, the planet. In my life I've never seen a dog fighting pit, but I know without a doubt that is what this is. I can feel the press of men standing there in the hot nights with the doors closed for privacy, the din of their shouting loud but not enough to obscure the tearing, gnashing growling horrorshow noise of two dogs tearing each other apart. I turn and wretch up some of the beer in my belly onto the floor.

The dog raises his head with effort to look at me. He looks like he doesn't know whether I'm a threat or not. I creep forward on my haunches and a low, steady growl builds in his barrel chest. In the better light I can see bare marks along the dog's hindquarters: several circular scars tightly grouped. I see the cigarette embers held there, hear the confused, anguished yelps. Furious tears sting my eyes, and I wipe them away with the back of my hand. I want to go back into the house, grab one of those skate decks off the wall and beat KK to death with it. I want it with all my heart. My pulse is racing with adrenaline.

How long before they come to look for me, I wonder.

"Hey buddy, how ya doin'? You okay?" I say to the dog. I try to make myself smaller. I've had dogs and cats around me all my life until moving away from home, and I've always gotten along better with them than any two-legged beasts. I know the dog can probably smell the fear on me like bad cologne, and I know that a dog in a weakened position can be dangerous. Cornered, starved, fucking tortured, a dog will turn on his master let alone a stranger.

Still squatting, I move slowly and deliberately to the front of the treadmill, watching the dog peripherally, careful not to look directly into his eyes. The dog's heavy square jaw frames his sharp yellowed teeth, which he bares beneath the muzzle as I reach very slowly toward the leash and untie it from the treadmill.

Another growl, lower, a little stronger.

"It's okay, pal," I say with a high and light singsong. "I'm just gonna get you out of here and…."

And what, asshole? You're about a million miles from home in the house of a drug dealing dog-fighting sociopath. I consider the obvious—call the police. But I'm one of the only people on Earth who doesn't own a cell phone because I can't afford it. Besides, getting KK busted right now would mean getting Koa busted, and while I don't have any love for Koa, I don't want him arrested. Particularly because he and Victor are so tight. After chasing my mind in circles looking for a plan, the only thing I can decide on for sure is that I'm getting this dog out of here.

I stand up and in response the dog jumps to his feet, but his rear legs collapse under him. He loses his balance tumbles off the treadmill onto the pavement, making an unsettling noise as his shoulder bone connects. He whimpers.

I leave the end of the leash on the ground and go back into the house, quietly shutting the garage door behind me. I can hear the roar of fake race car engines blaring from the next room as KK and Koa play video games. The acrid odor of the pot is strong. They're smoking out heavy and apparently haven't wondered where I went yet. But they will soon, I'm sure of it. I look by the fridge where I remember seeing a water pan on the floor and pick it up. I take it over to the sink and slowly run cold water into it until it's full then take it back out into the garage.

The dog hasn't gotten up. He's lying on his belly on the cool concrete, still breathing heavily. His head jerks around when he hears me coming and he makes another low growl, but he sees the bowl in my hands and the growl turns into the high whine again as I put it down a couple of feet in front of him. He tries to get up but I make it easier by sliding the bowl toward him with the toe of my Converse.

He dunks his nose and the muzzle into the bowl, clanking and scraping against the bottom as his long pink tongue snakes out through the cage and greedily scoops water into his mouth.

I feel tension coiled in my belly so tightly that I can barely think. I keep hearing voices in the kitchen, so I go to the door, press my ear to it. I hear nothing but the ambient noise from the game in the next room.

I hold my breath and press the garage door opener. When I do, the twin doors rise in unison, letting a widening swath of yellow sunlight inside and leaving behind a line of sawdust and cigarette butts where they were. I'm sure it's been ages since they've been opened. They aren't quiet, and I am now almost panicking, but I look down and see the dog has stopped drinking. His eyes are half closed against the sunshine and a sense of calm seems to come over him as it spreads across his skin and the cool sea breeze wafts in, chasing off the close, dankness of the garage.

"Okay, buddy, let's move," I say quietly, approaching to pick up the end of the leash. He looks up at me and with his thirst slaked, his eyes look better. "That's right, buddy, I'm your friend. Let's go now. Let's go! C'mon, boy!"

The dog tilts his head when I speak, but then he moves and seems to remember the pain, and his head dips again.

"It's okay, buddy. I'm not going to hurt you," I say, and my voice catches a little. I can't imagine how long he's been here. What that fucker has done to him. "It's okay," I say, "I promise. It's okay. C'mon. I'm not going to let anyone else hurt you."

Whether the dog understands or not, he rises to his feet and his legs move beneath him as I lead him out of the garage. I check behind me again, sure that I hear KK and Koa as we walk out. I lead him down the drive keeping the Hummer between us and the front of the house until we're to the sidewalk. I try to get my bearings. The sun is about ten degrees above the horizon at the end of the street. I start walking toward it, checking the house behind me and then looking down. The dog's gait is still loose, but he sniffs enthusiastically at the ground and pauses to lift his leg at a telephone pole before resuming his quest to smell the entire world.

"Okay," I say to him, "I know you're tired, but we need to go faster. C'mon, let's go!" I start a slow jog down the sidewalk, happy to be putting distance between us and the house. With effort the dog picks up his pace and catches up with me.

"What a good boy! Let's go! Not too far!" I say, realizing I have no clear idea where we're going, "C'mon! Not too far!"

David Lemmo

Gruesome Sideshow

My name is Richard Valentine, I'm a private investigator, and I am also an addict. I'm not a drunk, drug fiend, gambler, sex nut or anything like that. I was unaware of my addiction until I was working a case looking for a missing woman. The trail led past something having nothing to do with my search, but a lot to do with me.

There was a bar in the Chollas View area of San Diego that I had to check out the next evening, and I wanted to walk through the area to get the feel of it, check out the nearby side streets and alleys. Maybe I'd have a peek at the inside of the bar, Jaycee's, without making anyone suspicious or paranoid; I'd even dressed in worn jeans and a long-sleeved sweat shirt in order to fit in, more. When I got there it looked like the place was closed, boarded up. It wasn't. Jaycee's was a chipped and cracked red-brick hunk with a tacked-on looking wooden door. A one-story abomination on 47th Street near Market.

A noise came up from behind and I turned. A white woman in a jagged grey sweater, stained pants and dirty tennis shoes toiled at a metal cart full of clothes, plastic bags full of things and a well-worn sleeping bag. Her Anglo face, layered with the grime of the streets, looked my way as she approached; greying brown hair was tied back with a blue scarf.

The resigned green eyes went wide at the sight of me. She stopped. A dirty right hand clawed into a front pocket, rummaging around. Her face screwed up tightly; her eyes screamed at me from within—frantic-mumbled words entreated. She yelped as her hand withdrew and held up a crumpled photo-graph.

I took this as her desire for me to inspect it, and reached out—she thrust the photo into my hand. The woman swallowed hard, took a deep breath and let go of the cart with her left hand. She raised her arms overhead like a worshiper in supplication to a god. I noticed that both of the elbow areas of her filthy sweater were worn through showing a green undergarment.

I looked at the photo. An infant. I turned it over. According to a penciled inscription I could barely make out, the photo was ten years old.

The woman now wrung her hands, bleating like a lost animal and nodding toward the photo.

Pity nudged me. I shook my head and handed her the photo. "Maybe I can help you," I said. "Could you use some money?"

She slowly pushed the photo back into her pocket.

"Do you understand me?" I asked.

The woman's green eyes lost all hope again.

Her left hand took hold of the cart's handle. Her whole body lurched in the effort of pulling the cart into motion again. She moved down the street slowly, broken-down, aging by the second and probably better off dead. Did she know she would never find that baby?

I took a deep breath, tried ignoring my feelings of pity and then turned back to Jaycee's. Against my better judgment, because I didn't want attention which could get back to the later, night crowd, I entered.

The music was surprisingly pleasant, Ray Charles, and a few older black guys at the bar were talking and drinking. Not the usual nighttime crowd that had been described to me. The bartender was a burly light-skinned black man with a chef's apron over his clothing. Before he looked at me I pushed my way back through the door into sunlight. Nothing was happening inside. There weren't enough people in there for me to get a little nosy without drawing someone's interest and suspicions.

I checked out the area near the bar for several blocks around, walking among the usual panhandling homeless. I found mostly liquor stores, convenience stores, pawn shops, crappy motels, down-and-out hotels, hair salons, and a few struggling markets. There were many other people walking the streets, mostly black, and after almost an hour of checking the area out I had the hustlers spotted. These people were out of any mainstream way of making a living but were not eating-out-of-garbage-cans homeless. They made their livings by the streets and the streets alone. Theft, prostitution, drug dealing, mugging, pick-pocketing, one hustle or another, take your pick.

It all went back into the mainstream economy, in the end, anyway.

There were many unoccupied boarded-up buildings waiting for the demolition crew to wipe out their existence. Until then, people could still occupy
them for the night. Others, squatters, really knew how to hustle for a living but
couldn't quite afford to rent a cramped, filthy room in the projects or a shitty
hotel. Not if they wanted to eat regularly. They lived among the homeless in
abandoned buildings, usually aligned with a few friends so that someone was
always around to protect their belongings.

I snaked my way through filthy alleys and dead ends, and climbed fences,
scaring a cat, interrupting a blow-job that was going down, and was offered a
bag of meth by a young Mexican kid before coming upon Jaycee's, from behind.
I had to climb over the chain-link fence of a great apartment complex to get to
the back door. The one-story chipped and cracked brick shack had graffiti over
graffiti covering graffiti on the wall.

I stuck an ear up against the door and listened. Nothing. I stepped back,
listening again. More nothing. A car horn blasted in the distance and then
another. I grasped the doorknob. It was locked. I twisted and heaved, and then
let go. I could tell from my test of the door that I could kick it in easily. There
was no real need for anything like that. Now. As Jaycee's was set flush between
two other buildings, there were only two windows, both barred.

I turned around facing the chain-link fence and the giant apartment building. To the left an alleyway led to another metal fence which ended at the ten-
foot taller fence of the apartment complex. There was a tree on the other side of
the shorter fence.

To the right, a long alley ran into a two-story stucco building. Instead of
going back the way I had come, I turned left and walked down that alley. I had
the fence and the five-story apartment complex on one side, and different one-
and two-story buildings on the other. I climbed over the shorter fence near the
juncture of both, and stood there a moment listening to a jet scream overhead. I
kept my eyes on my surroundings.

There were four large ugly stinking garbage containers in an area behind the
one- and two-story buildings. The ground was decorated with broken glass,
fast food wrappers, general trash, feces and other examples of our progress as
humans. The three guys standing by the tree had probably been startled still at
my appearance and were watching me.

One was a tall sour-faced black guy in soiled worn fatigues. Above the bill of his cap the words *Cosmo Man* were stenciled in black. The other two were white. An inbred blond with a pendulous bottom lip and an attempt at a beard wore layers of filthy jeans and long-sleeved shirts. The short chunky darker guy in last century's polyester pants and a shredded-stained brown leather jacket was putting something into his back pocket.

None of this was any of my business. There was every reason for me to be on my way. Something made me want to find out what was going on. I began walking toward them. The black guy fidgeted. The blond looked at the black guy. The short one in the leather jacket glanced about the area. His wide brown eyes told me something was wrong. I halted four feet from them. I waited a few seconds. The black guy's face was grizzled as a warthog's. He nodded his head at two of the nearby trash containers.

I looked back at him, and then ran my eyes around the containers again. There it was. Something stashed on the ground between both of them. I walked over to it feeling the three behind me being very still. I halted. Jammed between two stinking containers was a worn, grey and brown figure. It looked like a woman. The brown pants had been pulled down to the ankles. The grey sweater was torn, revealing a soiled green undergarment. I stared at the blue scarf lying at my feet, near hers.

I turned and looked at the trio. They stood there trying not to register emotion. The inbred guy smiled a second, his blue eyes looked befuddled. I turned back to the probably-dead body of the baby-seeker. It had only been an hour since I'd met her. I got on my haunches and had a closer look. Breathing shallowly because of the garbage stench and to slow my pounding heart, I looked at the scratches and abrasions over the exposed bottom half of her grime-encrusted body.

Her neck was at an odd angle because it had been broken.

A line of sweat appeared above my forehead. I wiped it away and wiped that hand on my jeans. I stood, wondering about her metal cart. I opened one of the dumpsters and looked inside. Just the usual accumulated filth of civilization. I closed the lid, and then stepped over to the other dumpster. I lifted this lid. There was the metal cart emptied of its contents, which were neatly spread out. Even the ragged sleeping bag had been rejected.

I closed the lid and turned around. The two white guys were gone but the black guy was still there. His creased face looked as curious about me as I was about him. I walked slowly over to him.

He watched with slitted eyes as I stopped four feet away.

"Who were those two guys?" I asked. I could smell the whiskey in him.

Cosmo Man said, "Ah came here on my way somewhere and they was fuckin' with the woman. They claim they was trying to wake her."

He looked at me and nodded, saying, "Wake her—they was actin' strange, scared, so Ah 'trad to ask them questions by pulling out a joint to make them stay around." His eyebrows raised and he scratched along his jaw. "Ah was about to light up when you appeared."

"Ever seen her before?"

"Seen her?" His black face broke into a brief grim smile. "We all know her around here. She was harmless." A breath forced its way out of him. His brown eyes, touched by tears, misted. He shook his head, tugged at the brim of his cap and said, "She like to drink beer and watch football at the bar down the street."

I smiled and nodded.

Cosmo Man waved down the alley beyond the tree. "With that cart she always had, she had to come here this way."

We backtracked the way the baby-seeker could have gotten into that corner of the streets. Cosmo Man and I eventually had to squeeze, single file, through a narrow alley formed by two multistoried, rotting buildings. The stench was sickening, and I looked for anything remotely resembling a clue as we scuttled along like rats, stepping through puddles of rank water, broken glass, trash, urine, and over feces. We finally found ourselves on 47th Street three blocks from Jaycee's.

The building that had been on our left was a shabby three-story hotel. The one on our right a closed-down boarded-up food market. We stood in the foyer of the abandoned market. Dusk was sneaking around the next corner and a slight breeze felt good for a few moments.

Cosmo Man told me, "Ah never seen them two guys around here."

I nodded. He had to be thinking that he'd never seen me here, either.

Cosmo Man nodded as if in reaction to my thoughts. "Ah go and ask around. Find out where they are." He nodded curtly, turned, and bopped off down the street as if to the beat of music.

I walked away from the direction of Jaycee's and at the first phone station I came upon called the San Diego Police Department. Disguising my voice and speech patterns, I quickly told them what was what, where it was, and described the two white guys. I hung up, and then walked away and got my car.

The baby-seeker's fate played like a movie in my mind as my subconscious drove me toward Lemon Grove, where I was expected for dinner with my family.

At my first encounter with the homeless woman I'd thought that she would have been *better off dead*. Now she was. I felt…weird about myself. It was like I'd made a judgment that had come to pass. In a horrible form. I felt dirty, sweaty and there was something deep inside me gnawing away.…

By the time I was in Lemon Grove I needed to pull over to the first bar I saw. I needed a shower. A bath. I got out of the car and went into the bar not noticing anything about the place. I ordered a beer, paid for it and went into the men's room. I took my shirt off, and washed myself at the sink.

Richard Valentine, private detective, trying to clean the streets off him.

Scrubbing myself with water, I thought about how someone finding the dead baby-seeker might not want to get involved by reporting it to the police. I dried myself using half of the paper cloths in a dispenser. Had I not anonymously reported the murder from a phone station, the baby-seeker could have ended up lying there for days until the weekly garbage pickup, the stench, or dogs and cats feeding forced someone into reporting the decomposing body.

Putting the shirt back on, I looked at myself in the mirror over the sink. I didn't like what I saw. I also didn't know what it was about what I saw that I didn't like. The door opened and someone entered the rest room. I heard him step over to the urinals; the stench of a chemical deodorant wafted about a few moments.

I ran some water through my hair, and made myself as presentable as I could. I looked better than I felt. I left the bar without touching the beer, got into my car and drove six blocks to my parents' home on Buena Vista Avenue near Broadway.

Through dinner my father, as usual, did most of the talking and Mom had to intrude questions at my sister, Michelle. This left me able to settle myself down. I couldn't stop thinking about the doomed baby-seeker and how she was a gruesome sideshow of this missing woman case.

Or, was it that she was really a gruesome sideshow of *my* life?

"Richard," Michelle interrupted my thoughts. "Come back. You're on the streets, again."

I suddenly knew what it was that I didn't like about myself.

While washing up in the rest room of that bar, just before arriving here, I had looked into the mirror and didn't like what I saw. What I saw was that I fit into the fabric of the streets... how I was part of it. Filth, crime, dead bodies—it was all no big deal. Business as usual. I had to take a deep breath to keep myself from shouting in disgust.

I looked at Michelle, hearing her voice, in my head, saying, "You're addicted to the streets."

Dead Apartments | *Kelly Mayhew*

Sydney Brown

mi corazon / el cajon

what a guzzler—this eucalyptus
never belonged in my chest

my valves are shrimp-eyed,
jellied in the valley of a jail

my civic center busted—there's
no commerce in its chambers,

just a metallic taste
a drip a drip a drip

in the throat of my goat

on a daily basis
a mean-ass hummingbird
with machinegun wings
assaults my fluid

& there's an uncontrolled burn
in my inferior vena cava

(alas, my love for the fireman is unrequited)

my parks are not played
on Taco Tuesdays; the kids
are in homes huffing Dust-Off
& pharming Skittles

baseball players, motocross racers,
and NASCAR champions thicken
my walls; I have millions

of unpublished poems for jimmies
in my drawers

but no art in my arteries

still, the steady blub
in my one spongy lung
& that pinkish-orange
slam-dunk of the sun

will need to be reconciled
on someone's
bloody ledger, the valves

hardly open for—
whatever

—there's no pump
in my fist pump!

& that black velvet Elvis
with red kingy wings—

the veins,
they just don't giggle no more

Mel Freilicher

Mystery at the Ski Dump

Mangled Minks

"BRR-R, it's cold!"

Nancy Drew shivered and pulled the collar of her coat higher against the driving snow.

"Well, shut the window, silly Jilly," sang out Hannah Gruen affectionately. Hannah Gruen had been with the family ever since Mrs. Drew had died way before Nancy was ever born.

Bess Marvin, and her cousin George Fayne, the female invert, arrived at eight o'clock. Clad in boots and ski pants, they were pretty high.

"How about blowing up the old steeple," George giggled, "or some old people."

"Well, I'd rather stay inside," said Bess, blond and pretty. "Maybe we can make some 'fudge,'" she added hopefully. Bess lived on sweets, and worried little about her weight.

"No can do," cooed Nancy. "We gotta go outside and get mistakenly arrested for traversing in young minks."

Just as they got into George's red red roadster, Bess' eyes suddenly grew wild with fear. "Girls! Look at those two men across the street! They're staring at us as if we'd just escaped from jail."

As the girls watched, the two men slowly jerked off. Then a big, sticky hand pulled open the door beside Bess.

"Which one of you is Nancy Drew?" he demanded in a deep voice. "You're wanted for shoplifting. I place you under arrest!"

Suddenly the side door was flung open by a distinguished looking gentleman, plucked like a clucking hen.

"Judge Hoffman! Am I ever glad to see you!" Nancy cried, pushing forward to greet her father's old college friend who happened to be the asshole currently conducting the trial of the Chicago 7. After the cops rioted outside the 1968 Democratic Party convention in Chicago, beating many protestors senseless, the 7 were charged with: conspiracy to incite a riot, crossing state lines to start a riot, obstructing police officers during civil disorder, and intending to create incendiary devices to use during a riot.

Soon Judge Hoffman cleared up the whole mess about stolen young minks: after all, everyone knew that the Drews were a distinguished family who possessed only *old* minks. The next day, Judge Hoffman took Nancy to court with him so she could admire his verisimilitude.

Curious Dealings

In the gallery, Nancy and her posse witnessed the first of a multitude of bizarre conversations between the pompous Judge and William Kunstler, distinguished radical lawyer for the defense, to whom Hoffman had already doled out a 5-year sentence for contempt of court. Judge Hoffman had also sentenced the other defense attorney Leonard Weinglass (whom the Judge insisted on calling either Feinglass, Feinruss or Weinstein), and every one of the defendants, for contempt: lengthy sentences which would all be reversed, and greatly ridiculed, later.

> **Mr. Kunstler:** You cannot even consider the Government's motion here without at least hearing strenuous arguments on the Spock issue....

> **Hoffman:** It would be better for your nervous system if you don't argue strenuously. You are fond of describing your efforts as strenuous argument.

> **Kunstler:** We all have our own idiosyncrasies.

"A good one!" announced Nancy, punching Bess in the arm, firmly enough.

> **Hoffman:** Ordinary argument is good enough for me.

> **Kunstler:** No, your honor. This case deserved better than an ordinary argument. It's not good enough for me essentially, and I think that I have to present it in the way I think its worth merits.

> **Hoffman:** This is about the first time in 22 years serving on state and federal benches that anybody has complained about my voice. And it is

amusing—you know, *I'm* not forbidden to read the newspaper. I haven't forbidden myself, that is (*guffaw*), but I'd see even press friends of mine refer to my voice as being rasping. Then, on the other hand, I heard it being referred to by your associate—what is the name of the actor—

Kunstler: Orson Welles, your honor.

Hoffman: —as Orson Welles who has a magnificent resonant voice, now take your choice. It is either rasping or it is as resonant as Orson Welles'.

Kunstler: Well, I don't want to characterize the voice of the Court, however—

Hoffman: I do my best to use the vocal facilities that the lord has endowed me with.

"Quel windbag!" declared Nancy to Bess who was chomping on a tootsie roll grande. "And I used to find him so distingué."

"I don't get it, sugar, what's this trial thing even about?" ventured a benign Bess.

"Yeah," George drunkenly drawled, "all the kids—even my jock frat boy buddies—know that the cops rioted on that bloody eve in Chicago."

"I think it's about Judge Julius Hoffman wanting to punish Abbie Hoffman for having the same last name," Nancy opined judiciously. "You know the judge is an old friend of dad's. They were at Northwestern together, and both were Mu's—well Mu Nu Pi Epsilon Theta Zeta Eta Omicron, really."

"But Abbie Hoffman's so compellingly anarchic—"

"He *is* rather handsome," murmured Nancy, only slightly demurely.

"And Judge Hoffman is such an old fart," George finished flatly.

"And Jerry Rubin's positively an edible pixie," Bess parried pertly. "I think he practically winked at me!"

As Ned and the others skied over to congratulate Chuck, Nancy scanned the crowd of spectators. Curiously, Mitzi Gaynor did not seem to be either present or absent.

The Hidden Cabin

Once Nancy and the girls got to the ski dump, they discovered that even more young minks were missing, so they decided to attend a play at a nearby regional theater. There, at a typical backstage brawl, Nancy was gratified to meet the original Narrator from the Broadway production of *Our Town* who appeared to be concealing some clues about where Mitzi Gaynor might be breeding the illegal yet lucrative animals.

(Two arched trellises, covered with vines and flowers, are pushed on stage.)

> *Our Town* **Narrator:** There's some scenery for people who think they have to have scenery.

> **Nancy Drew:** You know, dawg, you should catch some of this Chicago 7 trial. Abbie Hoffman was such a cutup the other day! He and Jerry Rubin came in dressed in judicial robes; when asked to remove them, they complied, and were wearing Chicago police uniforms underneath. Abbie Hoffman blew kisses at Judge Hoffman. Then he said, "You would have served Hitler better, your idea of justice is the only obscenity in the room."

> *Our Town* **Narrator:** Did they ask if the word "motherfucker" got them hot, like they did at Lenny Bruce's trials?—over one of which the honorable Hoffman also presided.

> **Bess:** Pepperoni pizza, pals! Prurient pertinence, please!

> *Our Town* **Narrator:** But before I do, I want you to try and remember what it was like to have been very young.

> **Bess:** But we *are* young!

> *Our Town* **Narrator** (ignoring her): And particularly the days when you were first in love; when you were like a person sleepwalking, and you didn't quite see the street you were in and didn't quite hear everything that was said to you.

> **George** (eyeing Nancy nervously): And you're just a little bit crazy? And as jumpy as a flea on a hot griddle?

> *Our Town* **Narrator:** Yes! Yes!

> **Nancy Drew:** I never felt that way. I *did* once feel like a young mink (who) was trying to wriggle into *my own* griddle!

> *Our Town* **Narrator** (rolling eyes): Well, as I said, it's about dawn. Or about 9:30 at night. The day's run down like a ragged frock. Most of the

lights are out. There's Constable Warren cracking open the heads of a few protestors who are still lollygagging about the streets.

Nancy Drew: But I simply *must* tell you more about hoary old Judge Hoffman. Turns out he had refused to permit defense attorneys to screen prospective jurors for cultural and racial bias in the *voir dire*. My father thinks that was a big mistake, and that the U.S. Court of Appeals will probably overturn any conviction because of it. Funny, dads almost sounded pleased as punch.

Bess (sincerely): He's a peach, pal.

George: Nancy, honey, you're already parlaying too much French for your own good. Hannah Gruen might have to get out the old rolling pin. *(stage whisper) Me wants to see!*

Nancy (rolling up her sleeves to recreate the day's drama): *So*, William Kunstler comes to court on National Moratorium Day wearing a black armband. The U.S. Attorney goes off on him: "Your honor, this is outrageous. This man is a mouthpiece. Any lawyer who comes into court, and acts in conjunction with that kind of conduct before a court, your honor, the Government protests his attitude, and would like to cite—to move the court to make note of his conduct before this court."

And then Mr. Kunstler responds: "To call me a mouthpiece, and your honor not to open his mouth and say that this is not to be done in your court, I think that violates the sanctity of this Court. That is a word your honor knows is contemptuous and contumacious."

Bess (gnawing on George's Snickers bar): Hunh?

Nancy: Then Judge Hoffman says: "Don't tell me what I know."

And Kunstler replies: "I'm wearing an armband in memoriam to the dead, your honor, I request that you do that. The word 'mouthpiece' is a contemptuous term." ("Unless applied to the Mensheviks," *declared Nancy inadvertently*.)

Hoffman says: "Do you want to admonish me?" Kunstler replies: "No, I want you to admonish him." Then Hoffman says: "The record may indicate you said that, and I disagree with you."

Kunstler rejoins: "I know, we disagree frequently."

"'*Not infrequently!*' is Hoffman's retaliation, which that buffoon must have considered quite the *coup de grace*: 'not infrequently!' Gosh! I used to respect Judge Hoffman, but now...Creepsville, U.S.A!" *(Nancy discreetly utilized the stylized spittoon.)*

Bess (stunned): Golly, I always thought *coup de grace* was a kind of *paté!*

Nancy: Today an FBI informant testified that he knew Abbie Hoffman by his big nose. *(giggles)* Mr. Kunstler just laughed, and said that's okay, "A nose is a nose is a nose." *D'accord!*

George (wearily): Anyways, let's go back to the hidden cabin at the ski dump, and skin us some minks. Then maybe you'll stop ignoring everybody, Nancy, namely *moi.*

Nancy (pensively): You know, I always thought I could just catch the bad guys and move on to the next slightly dangerous but quite trivial case. But now I recognize that there *are no* wholesome mysteries!

Our Town **Narrator:** *Oy gevalt!*

Trapper's Tale

The weather was clear that afternoon and Nancy's flight was smooth. She took a taxi home from the River Heights airport, and slipped quietly into the Drew home where she found a bustling Hannah Gruen taking a pie from the oven.

"Mighty fine victuals, honey. But if Bess ever saw that cherry pie—" Nancy began frothingly. Both women rolled their eyes until they were blue in the face.

"Tell me about the trip," Hannah Gruen said eagerly, placing Nancy on her lap.

Gingerly removing the seat of her pants, Nancy cried, "But first let me tell you about my day in court. You know I'm really starting to see our judicial system as prejudicial and racist. It's like daddy's the last man boinging with integrity."

"Uh oh," whispered secretive Hannah Gruen, "guess Nancy don't know nuttin' about them sacred turtles."

"Anyways, you'll recall that Black Panther leader Bobby Seale was originally supposed to be tried with the Chicago 7—it was the Chicago 8 then—until he was bound and gagged and his case was severed, so to speak. Today, I just happened to be sitting next to that nutsy actress, Jane Fondu, who leaned over and whispered confidentially, 'Wait till you hear what Bobby—*we* call him Bobby— was calling the judge before he was bound and gagged.' Then she quoted him:

"'You're lying. Dirty liar, I told them to defend themselves. You are a rotten racist pig, fascist liar, that's what you are. You're a rotten liar. You're a rotten liar. You are a fascist pig liar.'""

"'How outré!' I almost gasped," gasped Nancy. "But I stopped myself in time for Miss Fondu to reveal all."

"It seems that once Bobby had made it clear that he was going to continue interrupting the procedure," Miss Fondu expounded, "we all knew it was just a matter of time before the fascist insect judge had to act. There were rumors that they'd all be locked up in soundproof glass booths. But when they decided to bind and gag Bobby, they realized it couldn't be done that easily: at first it was a simple folding chair with handcuffs and a towel gag. Child's play for Bobby! Each time the chains got heavier, the gag and bindings more elaborate, yet each time, no matter what the muzzle, a faint voice demanded to be heard. A remarkable testimony to the human spirit, and one that we all knew, especially Bobby, would permanently turn the public against the fascist pigs."

"That *does* seem rather damning," the good Hannah Gruen gurgled gracefully.

"Indeed!" Nancy muttered, darkly. "Today, Mr. Kunstler piped up with: 'Your honor, is someone being removed from the courtroom? Again, another black person, I see.'"

"Land's sake," retorted Hannah Gruen.

Eager to enact all the parts, Nancy taped hapless Hannah's mouth decidedly shut.

> **Mr. Schulz** (government attorney): Say—this repeated comment about "another black person"—
>
> **Spectator:** You hate black people or something?
>
> **Mr. Schulz:** This constant repetition is not warranted, this attempt to make it appear that there is racism in this courtroom. It is they who are engendering and who are looking for racism.
>
> **Kunstler:** Your honor, it's only been black people ejected that I have seen. I have never seen a white person removed from this courtroom when I have turned around. And this makes about the eleventh black person that's been—

Hoffman: I don't know how from your position you can see what person has been ejected. I'm facing the door. I've never seen anybody ejected— or even dejected! I've seen people go out, I can't say they were ejected, and I don't think it is proper for a lawyer to refer to a person's race.... And I direct you now, I order you now, not to refer to the ejection of a black person again.

Kunstler: I will not, your honor, if black people are not constantly ejected from this court.

Hoffman: I order you not to, sir. That is my order.

Kunstler: I think that violated the constitutional rights, your honor, of these clients.

Hoffman: I think I am as familiar with the Constitution as you are, sir. I lived a long time and you are the first person who ever suggested that I have discriminated against a black man. Come to my chambers and I will show you on the wall what one of the great newspapers of the city said editorially about me in connection with a school segregation case.

Kunstler: Your honor, this is not a time for self-praise on either side of the lectern.

Hoffman: It isn't self-praise, sir. It is defense. I won't let a lawyer stand before the bar and charge me with being a bigot.

Kunstler: For God's sake, your honor, we are seeking a solution of a human problem here, not whether you feel good or bad or whether I feel good or bad.

Having reached her denouement, Nancy merrily ripped off Hannah Gruen's tape.

"Owww!" she growled, "what the fuck?!"

"*Who's* on trial, again?" bleated bodacious Bess: back from the ski dump, out of breath and clueless, with her cousin, the invert, George Fayne, Jr.

"Well, some very established leaders of the anti-war movement like Tom Hayden, and elder statesman, David Dellinger. But really it seems like Hoffman is on a huge vendetta against Abbie Hoffman and Jerry Rubin, because of their cocky Yippie antics!" Nancy nearly smirked. "They mock him every chance they get, and they're really funny about it!"

"Quel Dada, n'est-ce pas?!" Hannah adroitly rejoined, to Nancy's great surprise. "See I can do it too, Missie! Incidentally, I've read in the papers that Tom Hayden is Jane Fondu's main squeeze. Wasn't she *too* divine in *A Tall Story*!"

"Oh, wake up and smell the bananas, Hannah! You know, I've never *really* been skiing…" Nancy enunciated ominously, as she began waxing her skis.

"All I know, honey, is that you could never get yourself off that fershuggenah skateboard—"

"Anywhoo," Nancy interrupted, "Chuck Wilson told me I was going to enjoy jumping. He said: 'It's a great thrill and it might come in handy someday if you're schussing a mountain and suddenly come upon a sizable hummock with a big mogul in the middle.'"

"Honey, didn't George warn you about overdoing that French? And you know what the doctor said!"

"What doctor?!" As they were fastening on their snowshoes for the long hike back to camp, Nancy turned to Chuck. "By the way, do you know of any mink ranches around here?"

"There's one up on that ridge where the run for the ski dump starts," tooted the Old Trapper. "That ranch is owned by Melvin and Mitzi Gaynor. But it's strictly on the level—like a flight of stairs."

Make Mine Mink

When they arrived, there was no sign of Mitzi Gaynor *or* Rossana Brazzio, or whatever that glandular guy's name was. They did find the limp body of the *Our Town* Narrator, spread-eagled across a big, blowsy blond. The old gent protested that he was all right, and needed no coddling. But Nancy insisted that he take a room at the "hotel," and had the ski dump's house psychiatrist shoot him up with Viagra and Haldol.

"You *do* know that my creator, Thornton Wilder, is asexual. Well, he's as gay as they come, naturellement, but he simply *can't*…" nattered the natty Narrator, before catatonically collapsing.

While they were "talking," Nancy had walked to a window to gaze at the beautiful moonlit landscape. Suddenly her attention was caught by a glimmer of light along the ridge at the top of Big Chill. She turned toward the lake and two giant snow statues which marked the end of the ski jump.

Nancy's heart pounded at the sight of Mitzi Gaynor, whose stage name was Mrs. Channing, doing some superb wheelies. Though *how* she can carry them off in those hot pink shorts, Nancy practically panted. (What if she fell, and…*ooouf!*)

Later, the *Our Town* Narrator emerged from his virile stupor, swimmingly.

Our Town **Narrator:** Thank you Carolyn Keene, non-existent author of Nancy Drew books. But I have to interrupt here again. You see, I'm awfully interested in how big things begin. You know how it is: you're twenty-one or twenty-two and you make some decisions: then (s)wisssh! You're seventy: that white haired lady at your side has assiduously schussed your dirty underwear into totally tiny tatters.

Nancy (grandly): How well I know! The cottage cheese, Sunday drives in the Ford, the children's Adderall, the rheumatiz', the mid-management lay-offs, the meth addiction, the second honeymoon, the endless porn, the grabbing of jewelry off the semi-sentient relative's dying body, the low-down heebie-jeebies.…

Our Town **Narrator:** Anyways, George and Emily are going to show you their road to perdition, er, I mean tradition.

George: Can I carry your books home for you, Emily?

Emily (coolly): Why…uh.… Thank you. It isn't far.

George: Excuse me a minute, Emily—Say Bob, if I'm a little late, start the "practice" sessions without me. And give Herb some long hard ones, *if you get my drift.*

Emily (calling out): Goodbye, Miss Corcoran! Goodbye, Mr. Chips! *(puzzled)* Hmmmm…*the old in 'n out?!*

George: Emily, why are you mad at me? You've been treating me so funny lately.

Emily: Well, since you ask me, I might as well say it right out, George— you're a raging narcissist. Up to a year ago, I used to like you a lot. And I used to watch you as you did everything…at least I did till the dog ate my binoculars. And then you began spending all your time at *"base- ball"*… and you never stopped to speak to anybody, not even to your own family...and George, it's a fact, you've got awfully conceited and stuck up, all the girls say so.

George: I'm glad you said it, Emily. I guess it's hard for a fella not to have faults creep into his character.

Emily (wimping out): No, I can see it's not the truth at all. It's just that I'm a girl, and girls are naturally nervous. And suddenly I feel that it isn't important, anyway.

Our Town Narrator dons spectacles and assumes the role of Mr. Morgan, positioned between the audience and the counter of his soda fountain.

Our Town **Narrator:** Hello, George. Hello, Emily. What you'll have? Why Emily, have you bee—

George (groping the Narrator for an explanation): She...just got an awful scare...hardware-store wagon, major asshole....

Our Town **Narrator:** Well, you've got to look both ways before you cross yourself on Main Street these days.

Emily: Speaking of hanging on the cross, I'll have a strawberry phosphate, thank you Mr. Morgan.

George: No, no Emily. Have an ice cream soda with me.

Our Town **Narrator:** Well— (*He claps his hands as a signal*) Now we're ready to get on with the wedding.

But just as the second most reliable trellis was being dragged on stage again, Nancy appeared out of breath and déshabillé, yet swathed in young pink mink, looking suspiciously like a partially plastered Patty Hearst. The Narrator practically plotzed right there on the pleasing plaza.

(She answered the phone.)

"Miss Drew, this is Chief Warner," came a man's voice. "We have these three suspects in jail, but they're a hard-boiled lot and refuse to crack. They swear they never laid eyes nor hands nor bollocks on one another in their life."

"Eyes, schmyes," cried an irate Nancy. "Don't you know that the conspiracy laws relieve the prosecutor of the necessity of proving any actual wrongdoing by the defendants. Why, they don't even have to know each other to be convicted of conspiracy!" she screeched, slamming the phone down.

> *Our Town* **Narrator:** Why, that's true enough. As Clarence Darrow put it, if a boy steals candy, he has committed a misdemeanor. If two boys plan to steal candy, *but don't do it*, they are guilty of conspiracy, a felony.

Nancy got excited. "Why, that's just how they tried to hogtie Dr. Spock with the Reverend William Sloane Coffin, Jr., Michael Ferber and others as co-conspirators for encouraging young men to turn in or burn their draft cards during Vietnam—"

> **George:** Even though most of them had *never even met* before their so-called conspiracy trial, right hon?

> **Nancy:** Exactement!

"*French*, Nancy," fretted George.

"Because of this extraordinary feature, conspiracy has long been favored by prosecutors as a means to convict union organizers, radicals, political dissenters, opponents of government policies, and other troublesome individuals who could not otherwise be put behind bars," Nancy declaimed.

> *Our Town* **Narrator:** In America, conspiracy charges were first used in 1806 against labor in the infamous Philadelphia Cordwainers case, in which the court ruled that a strike (an agreement of journeymen shoemakers to "withhold their labor") with the object of increasing wages was a criminal conspiracy.

> **Nancy:** *Oui*, but in 1821, when a group of journeymen sought to turn the tables and convict the employers for combining to depress wages, the court held it was not criminal: "When the object to be attained is meritorious, combination is not a conspiracy."

> *Our Town* **Narrator:** Disgusting! So about this conspiracy to get George and Emily hitched: they *have* commingled, and their mothers have done the obligatory kvetching.

> **Emily's mother:** I don't know why on earth I should be crying. I suppose there's nothing to cry about. It came over me at breakfast this morning: there was Emily eating her or my toes as she'd done for seventeen years

and now she's going off to someone else's house, to eat *their* toes! I guess I just feel superannuated, and darn old.

Our Town **Narrator:** Duh!

Zero Hour

Disappointed not to have found any trace of the eavesdropper, the boys and girls returned to the ski dump and made plans to go to Longview Inn.

"I'm driving to the village with Aunt Eloise," announced Bess. "Anything to get away from this squalid ski dump," she added, picking her way through decrepit furniture, an old and once trusted trampoline, seven desultory pickles, and even several assorted, severed pinkies. "We'll meet you at the hotel for lunch."

Just as Nancy was about to cruise on over to the mink ranch, the phone rang. Oddly, it was a Miss Mitzi Gaynor, sounding mighty worried.

"Nancy, doll, could you meet me at the rec hall? I can't seem to get my skates off, and it's awfully important."

In the rec hall of the old cotton mill, Nancy practically tripped over a supine Mitzi as she was administering "first aid" to a colorful chorus boy who'd just passed out from over-excitement. Nancy immediately observed that pert Mitzi was skateless. (*Narcotique?* Nancy wordlessly wondered.)

"Nancy!" cried the skateless skater. "I wanted you to come here so I could explain how testimony at conspiracy trials works. If a character witness is on the stand, he is *only allowed to present hearsay evidence!*"

"Damn stupid and counter-intuitive," Nancy suggested suavely, refusing to be intimidated by Mitzi's big tits. "I know something about this already, Miss Mitzi. (I have heard it said that there are thirteen exceptions to this rule, but these do not concern us here.)"

"Tell me about it."

"Here's how it worked at Dr. Spock's trial, according to the estimable Jessica Mitford's account. For some unfathomable reason known only to judges and God, the ordinary rules of evidence are not only suspended but completely reversed when a *character witness* takes the stand at a conspiracy trial. Hearsay evidence, which means pretty much what it sounds like—you can't testify 'I heard him say...'— is not normally admissible in a court of law."

"Oh, *how* I know," murmured Mitzi Gaynor (but that's another story). A character witness may *only* give hearsay evidence and he must under no circumstances say anything about the defendant's character. He may only testify as to the defendant's general reputation in the community. He may not discuss his own opinion of the defendant."

"Yes, yes," Nancy eagerly cried. "In Judge Ford's court where they were trying to incarcerate Dr. Spock, and the Reverend William Sloane Coffin, Jr. of Yale University, among others, they called Dr. Dana Greeley, president of the American Unitarian-Universalist Association as a witness for Michael Ferber, one of the indicted men. Dr. Greeley was asked by Ferber's counsel about his reputation for veracity."

"'I would say that he would be acclaimed very highly,'" began Dr. Greeley, but the judge cut him off: "'No, no, just answer good, bad or indifferent, or whatnot.'"

"I know," cried Mitzi, "And Dr. Greeley responded indignantly with, 'Excellent Excellent! *not whatnot!*'"

At that, Nancy threw her arms around Mitzi, and declared: "I could really take a shine to you, honey, if only I knew how you got here."

As Mitzi squeezed tightly, Nancy recoiled like an overripe radish. What's happening to me? she pondered. I don't respect authority blindly anymore, and my loins are becoming unhinged. *(gasps)* Could *I* be the Mystery at the Ski Dump? *(pause) Nah*, silly Jilly!

Just then George and Bess pulled up in the red roadster, with a dead radio and a barely breathing rabbit. In the back seat, the *Our Town* Narrator was madly making out with both a slightly jejeune Emily and her fiancé, garrulous George G. G®untington. Meanwhile, George *Fayne* threw Nancy a smoldering look, like she could punch out Miss Mitzi's lights.

"So what about those minks?" queried Nancy, eager to divert attention away from her own embarrassing display of emotion, so heady yet so inexplicable. Besides, Nancy was hot to solve *The Mystery of the Ski Dump*, so she could go on to investigate *The Case of the Velveteen Rabbit*.

"*Yeah, what about those monks?*" George demanded pugnaciously.

"*Yum!*" bellowed a bloated Bess.

"The minks?!" Mitzi proclaimed dismissingly. "*Oh, that!*"

Jesse Mancilla

Con Alma

It was mid-autumn in 2014. It was early morning. I was out for a run. It was dark, but not in the manner of lightlessness. It was a blurred darkness, or a fragile darkness, like the darkness of closing your eyes against a bright light. I felt like a dream (or like I was in a dream) and like I was formless or that my limbs weren't mine. I ran down Washington St. until 4th Ave. and then I ran down 4th. There's a bus stop on the corner of 4th and Robinson next to a 7-11. The 7-11 glowed green and floated in the dark. There were people loitering next to the 7-11 or maybe they were waiting for the early bus to Downtown, but I guess that doesn't really matter because it was around that black time of morning when time is disjointed and you can do everything and nothing all at once. There were eyes all around me or the feeling of eyes all around me and then I tripped on a rock or a discarded shoe or my thoughts or the voice in my head. As I fell or maybe when I fell but before I could feel my body again, there was a voice like a hand in the dark and the voice said, "In America, we're born at the top of a mountain. Behind us is the past and ahead of us, out of arm's reach, extending beyond our thoughts and dreams, is a void."

I looked up and there was a man sitting at the bus stop with his eyes on me. He was old and white and he had a kind smile, open like an ocean and then I thought I saw his mouth move like he was talking in his sleep. "What'd you say?" I asked him (or thought I asked him) but the question was a lie because I knew what I thought he had said and he just shook his head. I picked myself up and started running again or tried to start running again, but there was burning in my right ankle and the voice in my head was deep in my head like a red-tailed hawk lingering almost imperceptible in a blue sky.

◆ ◆ ◆

My grandmother died of pancreatic cancer in July of 2013. She was 76 years old. It happened in Visalia, CA or Fresno, CA on a Saturday night or early Sunday morning, but I guess that doesn't really matter because it happened during that black time of day when every hour is indistinguishable from the next. I was in San Diego. I live in San Diego. My mother called me at around 8:00 a.m. on Sunday to tell me. I think her call woke me up, but I haven't been able to stay asleep past 7 a.m. since I was 12 or 13 years old so that aspect of this memory is probably false. I do know I was still in bed and if already awake, was probably staring at V's face or body as she slept. V. is my partner. V. sleeps almost fully nude on a regular basis and I often dwell on V's flesh with self-obsession as if the span of my life or latent personality traits were spread across her bare skin for my own understanding. I think about sex often. It's a selfish lust that always starts and ends with me, an almost all-consuming hot urge in the pit of my stomach. I'm sex-obsessed probably because I fear death.

I can't remember if my mother was sobbing. I think she wasn't and I like to remember it that way. I couldn't concentrate as she spoke. My head hurt as if I had been hitting my forehead against a wall or with a hammer (or someone else hitting my forehead with a hammer). I might have had a hangover or at least have had a cocktail or a glass of sangria the night before. I had gone to bed without brushing my teeth. My breath was rancid. I have wisdom teeth erupting from the bottom left and right of my mouth so I regularly wake up with bad breath, a sort of metallic rottenness characteristic to overnight bleeding from the gums, but it was especially bad that morning.

No one knew my grandmother had pancreatic cancer until she was dying or already dead. It's said that pancreatic cancer is one of the worst cancers a person can develop so there was never anything she could have done even if she had known. Sometimes I think I can feel the cancer growing inside me too. It was a day or a couple of days or a couple of weeks after she died that I was driving home from work and found myself near-idle on the southbound 163 highway between the 6th and University exit and the Washington St. exit that I started thinking about my grandmother's death and began to weep. I would like to think I wept in sorrow for her passing, but the more I think about it the more I'm convinced that I wept for myself out of self-pity. My sense of my own nothingness had never been so clear and pervasive, as if while sitting in the car, I wasn't waiting for traffic to clear so I could make it home, but instead was wait-

ing to simply move again so I could orient myself in the void of existence and
resettle in a delusion of going somewhere.

◆ ◆ ◆

I saw a video of a beheading on the internet. It was around 9:00 p.m. on a late
summer night in 2014 and V. had fallen asleep on the futon in the living room. I
was in the kitchen. I was supposed to be washing dishes or preparing snacks for
the following day (I hold to a fairly strict and clean diet and eat the same foods
almost every day; sometimes, people will give me an odd look when they learn
this about me, but I think that's only because they don't think about sickness
and death as much as I do). The video was hosted on a site called Naked Islam or
Islam UnMasked. The headline at the top of the home page read, "It's not Islam-
ophobia if they REALLY want to kill you." The person beheaded was identified
as an Afghan man. The video began with the man pinned to the ground at knife
point. The video had no sound and the image resolution was poor so there was a
certain irreality to it, opaque and imprecise like the memory of a dream. I hadn't
witnessed a beheading before. The executioner wasn't wearing gloves. His hands
were covered in blood.

Our apartment is immediately adjacent to and above the 163 highway and
the roaring of vehicles doesn't stop until about 2 a.m. I looked out from the
kitchen to the living room window and could only see headlights or the ghosts
of headlights (and tail lights) barreling north and south across the darkness.
My eyes were watering because the video of the beheading made me want to
vomit and I could only think about how fucking awful it is to be alive. Space-
time doesn't operate the way most people think it does and if anyone focuses
hard enough, they'll see that the linearity of their experience is only an illusion.
They'll discover that they've always been and will always be and that life and suffering are unending burdens that will persist until the universe itself disappears.

I stared at the window long enough to see that the apartment was reflected in
the glass. I could see myself, but my face was distorted or maybe gone altogether.
It's in moments like those that I can close my eyes and forget myself. V. stirred
on the futon and extended a bare leg out from under her blanket. I imagined her
skin on my lips and then I felt my breath again.

◆ ◆ ◆

It was early winter in 2015. I raised the mug to my mouth and stared into the blackness of the coffee. She had a look in her eyes that I couldn't take for more than a second at a time. It gave me the sensation of freefalling and I experience that enough in my nightmares to care to experience it in waking life.

"So?" she asked.

"I don't know," I said. "I don't know."

"You don't know where you're going?"

"I don't know who I am."

"Do you ever think about the future?"

"I don't know. I guess I don't," I said. Then I had the image of someone coming up behind me and shooting me in the head at contact range or maybe it was the thought of a wish that someone would shoot me just then.

"I love you," she said. "I really do, but this is so difficult."

I wanted to tell her that nothing is difficult and that that notion only exists for her because she's so wrapped up in herself and in the idea that life means something. I was a teenager (maybe 16 or 17) still living in Dinuba, CA when I realized that God doesn't exist. I think it was a little after that when I began to understand (in an intuitive, wordless manner because I was too anxious and horny to think clearly about anything) that a person's experience of reality (past, present, future) is simply a narrative they construct for themselves in an act of biological determinism. A person's life has to make sense to them so they sort their experiences into a digestible form with a beginning and an end, and thoughts of the future and any plans and goals only serve to further that purpose. I wanted to tell her that the way we perceive reality is false and that there is nowhere to go and nothing to do until we die.

"I hate it when you just stare at me," she said.

I didn't know what else to do and so I just breathed and tasted the air in the room (full of coffee and honey and syrup and bread and the sound of forks and gaping mouths full of small teeth) and just shrugged and apologized to her. I didn't know how to explain to her that I had stopped believing in narratives and so I didn't see the point in worrying so much over mine. Then I said, "I love you, too."

◆ ◆ ◆

There's a dream in my head that plays out like the end of a movie. I'm in Hillcrest standing on the rooftop of the Scripps Mercy Surgery Pavilion with my back to 5th Ave. Behind 5th Ave, floating like a dream, is the downtown skyline. I'm holding a gun to my temple. I'm staring at the camera, but the camera is not really a camera, it's a loved one, a lover, or the audience. I pull the trigger and all goes black. Then the credits roll.

◆ ◆ ◆

It was June of 2012. He stood there under the eaves of his porch holding a cigarette in the fingers of his right hand. It was nighttime and the porch light was off and he looked half-real in the darkness like he was only the reflection of a person. He raised the cigarette to his mouth and inhaled. "Fuck," he said.

"What?" I asked.

"Nothing. Just, fuck."

I felt flat in the darkness and like I was at the edge of an abyss. I had forgotten that nights in Dinuba grew heavier and more suffocative with every hour.

"Is the smoke bothering you?" he asked.

I told him it was bothering me a little, but that what was bothering me more was the feeling that the night was growing larger, that it was swelling like a thick balloon and would smother me until it burst (if it ever burst).

"I know what you mean," he said, "I fucking hate this town."

"There's something to hate anywhere," I said. "In San Diego, the nights make you feel like you're disappearing. It gets dark and you start feeling like a dream, like your body is made of light or sound and after a couple of hours you feel like your body isn't yours or like you're outside of your body. You feel like you're disappearing."

"Shit," he said and laughed. "We're fucked anywhere we go." He inhaled from his cigarette and closed his eyes against the dark. "I'm going to tell you something," he said, "and you better swear you're not going to tell fucking anyone." He cleared his throat and spit out onto his lawn. "No one can know this."

"I won't," I said.

"I'm dead serious," he said. He dropped the cigarette on the floor of his porch and removed his glasses. He stepped on the cigarette and cleaned his glasses with this shirt. "I'm really fucked," he said. "I'm so fucked."

"Ok, what is it?" I asked.

He pulled a cigarette from behind his ear and lit it with a small, blue plastic lighter. The cigarette burned in his fingers and he had a look in his eyes like he could see through everything and that all he saw was a void or himself in a void. "I killed someone," he said. He paused and inhaled from his cigarette. He coughed and spit out onto his lawn. "It was 2 months ago. It was this guy I met when I was still going to school in Reedley. We got along well and so I invited him over here a couple of times and smoked him out, you know, just hanging out and watching shit on TV." He sighed. "It was all good until I noticed that some money and some CDs were missing. I wanted to give this fool the benefit of the doubt, but this was shit that only he knew about so I tried to get a hold of him, but he wouldn't answer his fucking phone and everyone who knew him told me they hadn't seen him in a while and that I was the person he hung out with the most." He laughed and inhaled again. "I tried to let it go, but I couldn't and then one morning a few weeks later, I'd really just fucking had it, you know, because I got into an argument with my mother over money and so I was so fucking pissed and there was no way I could stay in the house." Then he turned and looked at me for the first time and shook his head. "I'm not even sure what it was, "he said, "but everything became a bit hazy then, like my head was in my chest and I couldn't see clearly out from between my ribs and then I just walked into my room and grabbed the gun I had bought from my dealer and just rode my bicycle to Reedley faster than I ever had before and then just fucking walked around hoping that I'd run into the fucker. And guess what?" he said, turning to me again with that look in his eyes like he was staring into a void.

"What?"

"There he was at the fucking Main Street Café. He was sitting at a table there with his back to the front window. He was with a woman and they were sitting there talking and eating and I'd never felt as calm as I did then. It was like everything I had been holding inside left my body and like my feet weren't touching the ground and so just I just floated in and pulled out my gun and floated right up to him like a ghost and shot him in the head. The gunshot was so loud that it made everything go black and then suddenly I found myself running and running, but I felt like I was fucking flying or like my body wasn't mine, like I was watching it all from a safe distance and then I jumped back onto my bicycle and rode back to Dinuba." He inhaled from his cigarette. "I haven't heard anything about it since. It's like it never happened, like I fucking imagined it, but I know what I did and I don't know why it hasn't come back to me yet."

I looked at him and shook my head. The night had become so heavy that I couldn't speak.

"I'm fucked," he said, "I'm fucked and I'm scared."

I looked up and I had the feeling of freefalling, like time and sound had stopped and I was falling to the ocean and I didn't know what I was or when I would stop or start.

Sonia Gutiérrez
Big Bad Wolves

I remember no one wanted to talk about it. Nobody could believe this happened in our town, but it did. These boys let themselves in on you. No one told them that it wasn't right to shove a remote control between your legs. Pobre huerita with crystal blue eyes and soft blonde hair. No one heard you whimper in that room, where boys turned into big bad wolves circling in on you, clawing at you with their fingernails, and spiting you with words.

Did they put something in your drink? Why did these boys put a broom where babies are born? Did they think their mothers and sisters would never find out? When you woke up, did you remember their ugly faces? Did you need a need a bucket of ice to sit on for the bleeding and pain to stop? When you went home, did your Momma and Poppa hold you in their arms as your tears wet their red faces, or did they push you away? And when you looked at yourself in the mirror, did you want to clean the smudgy reflection with hollow eyes staring back and want to run and hide in a forest under a cypress tree? Did *anyone* at your new school find out?

Leilani Riingen Gobaleza
Every Day Vanilla

I once heard that happiness was both a hair and a world away for Alcatraz Federal Penitentiary inmates. The reminder of it—the echoes of celebration, ladies laughing, bottles popping, and water lapping—was part of the punishment. Some men died in their efforts to taste it again. I often felt that way in San Diego though it was never clear to me what unforgivable crime I had committed to be confined to such a place—sunny on the outside, lacking on the inside. It was the perfect place for anyone who liked vanilla. Every day.

My grandparents, respectfully named Honor and Mercy, left behind 8 hectares of farmland in the Philippines to retire in America's finest city and as the immigrant story goes, to provide their family with better opportunities. They hadn't anticipated their granddaughter hating vanilla ice cream, but they should've known better. When raising a child American, ungratefulness is expected. A delayed sense of gratitude at best.

At 2:27 p.m. on a Sunday, I clocked in for a 2:00 p.m. shift. Late again.

"Where'd you park? Did you run here?" my co-worker asked. Her newly-dyed hair was done up in one of the store rubber bands.

"Yes. On State and G," I groaned. "Sorry I'm late." Hands shaky from the adrenaline, I grabbed an apron from the crate in the backroom and tied it around my waist until it hit my bone.

The afternoon moved slowly. Tourists and locals popped in, their jaws dropping at the variety of fudge and caramel apples we offered, and told me how lucky I was to work in heaven. I thought to myself that if this was heaven, I need not repent. Standing behind the counter, I felt as though I was watching the same commercial again and again. Beautiful white people with beautiful white teeth. I added one of my own dollars to the empty tip jar, packed the espresso, and waited for some sort of magic to happen. Magic. *Happen.* I hoped hard.

"Are you from Thailand?" a tall man asked, over enunciating each word like I'd never heard them before. He leaned in trying to gauge whether or not I could understand. Now, this man had a pink face, a wallet that poked out from the front pocket of his cargo shorts, and a wife well-dressed in comparison. He was a lobster and she an apricot—an odd pairing though alarmingly common. It was so common in fact I had learned to stop reacting.

"No," I managed despite my anger. I visualized the espresso relaxing my jaw and putting the monster to sleep. "I'm from here."

"Oh, I gotcha. Where's about? Me and my wife here are from La Jolla. Born and bred," he said proudly. He pressed an index finger onto the glass case and left a print. "Oh, look honey. Chocolate peanut butter. That's my jam. $5.90? Ha! The hell kind of tourist trap is this?" His watch glistened. I remembered seeing one of those in a department store, never touched one though. The ones who complained about the prices out loud were usually the ones who could afford it.

"I'm more of a chocolate walnut, but whatever you want," his wife responded.

"What about a peanut butter cup?" the man suggested.

"*You* can get what *you* want," she sighed. "And *I'll* get what *I* want."

"Southeast," I said.

"Oh, that's nice," she said with her eyes scanning the top part of the case. "I've passed through there. Where do you go to school?"

"I graduated," I said.

"You thinkin' bout going to State?" the man asked.

"I graduated from college," I replied. He raised an eyebrow.

"Good for you," his wife intervened. "Where'd you go, honey?"

"Berkeley," I hesitated. The lobster raised the same eyebrow once again. The hairs were long and coarse. I thought I'd enjoy plucking each one out one at a time.

Education, my mother often told me, was the single most important thing in life. I was secretly inspired by these words. I couldn't openly show her how much I loved school and how much I loved reading, because it was so much more rewarding to believe that I had made a commitment to learning on my own accord. When I received my college acceptance letters, it was the first time I felt like a real person. Books gave me that experience, but student debt took it away. In fact, I am still paying for that short-lived freedom today. Those four years were everything and then, they were nothing. As though no time had passed, I was serving coffee and candy to folks just as I did when I was seventeen. Even the musicians outside were the same.

When I first returned to San Diego, I wasn't thinking about jobs or success. All I knew was that I spoke a new academic language that nobody around me understood. So, I pretended to unlearn it. To trade in my broken language for an academic one was to lose the color my family and community had loved into me during my earlier years.

"Some Berkeley graduate," the lobster mocked.

Fucking asshole, said every part of my body except for my mouth. Growing up the way I did on the Internet and in classes where kids flipped tables and threw their fists up, half of my thoughts were angry ones. Violent ones. Lucky for the lobster, I also grew up watching *Family Guy* and *Malcolm in the Middle* which meant the other half of me was humor. So, I let him humor me. *I could take you*, my thoughts continued, *but for now I'm going to play a game of compassion*. I often tricked myself into positivity.

As if she could peer into my internal struggle, his wife spoke sternly, "Mark, why don't you go find Molly? I think she went to the Magic Shop." It was clear that her husband had offended others before and that she, with or without his knowing, had saved them. Her beauty was made clearer to me just then—her hair smooth, her eyes soft, her brain working.

"It closed down a few years back," I said.

"Great," grunted the man as though it were my fault.

"Maybe a chocolate peanut butter would cheer you up," I said.

"Oh, you're something," he laughed. After a sigh, he shrugged. "Sure, why not? This big one up front and whatever you want." He slipped his wife a few bills and walked out.

After he left, I forgot how much I disliked him. His wife continued to browse. In the end, she picked up over fifty dollars worth of chocolate. The way she overspent led me to think that she did so to apologize for her husband. I wish I could've said that that wasn't enough, but I had goals. Numbers to meet. Working a service job, you let your emotions turn to puddles—puddles that only existed behind the counters where customers couldn't see, puddles you cleaned up yourself. Fifty dollars was enough that day.

A line formed behind the lady. I acknowledged the crowd but continued to gift-wrap her boxes with cellophane and wide pink satin ribbon before double-bagging them. We had the cheap bags. The woman dropped a five into the tip jar and thanked me. I powered through the line of customers with ease. Money had that effect on me.

4:17 PM. I heard a lady outside say she had bought authentic Mexican candy from a shop towards the center of the village. I wondered if this was the furthest south she'd ever gone. The store phone rang.

6:10 PM. The shop slowed down like it usually did and my co-worker left for the day.

10:15 PM. I locked the door and had everything done—espresso machine cleaned, cases restocked, money counted with two cents over—in a quarter of the time it took me six years prior. I smiled, felt somewhat proud, but remembered that no one in the professional world cared about how quickly you wiped counters at your part-time job.

10:24 PM. "Mom, who's home now?" I said over speakerphone as I drove towards the 94. I had made forty-seven dollars in tips and hit all the green lights. Petty things like that made me feel all right.

"It's just me, your aunties, your uncle, your Kuya, your cousin and his girlfriend, you know, your cousin, and Magic. Gelo went out with this friends maybe ten minutes ago. Auntie Raquel is working still." She said "just" like the number was small. Thinking back on it, missing one person meant the whole was incomplete. So, she was right in choosing her words. I was wrong. It usually happens that way.

My father left when I was younger, so I was raised by my mother, three aunts—two divorced and the other never married, easily identifiable by her smile of pure joy from having lived a life of complete independence, and my uncle, a retired pastor. For as long as I could remember, our four-bedroom house was always full but never too full to welcome other relatives. Some lodged with us for years before finding a place of their own. My uncle said that this sense of family and community so natural to them in the Philippines didn't really exist in the states. Even though I never understood the weight of what he meant, I tried my best to be a good family member. I tried as hard as I could despite my selfishness, which as you know, is the most common disease for people in their 20s.

"Do you want any food?" I asked.

"Oh, yes. I cooked *sinigang*, but your brothers didn't eat yet…."

"I can buy them something," I offered because I knew she didn't like to ask directly. "Only if you heat up some soup for me."

I exited Palm and drove to the neighborhood Mexican restaurant, the one with bars like a jail, and ordered a couple trays of carne asada fries. Thirteen dollars and another two for tip.

10:59 PM. I rang the doorbell. Didn't have a key because someone was always home. I gave myself thirty minutes to get ready. Magic approached me briefly before showing off an old toy, a purple unicorn he'd reconnected with. I greeted my mother, handed her the food, and summarized work in one breath before following the scent of tamarind into the dining room. There I discovered a hearty bowl of *sinigang na hapon*—a sour soup with plenty of spinach, green beans, and plump shrimp served with rice. A dozen spoonfuls later, I glanced at the clock. Twenty-six minutes left.

My mother took the empty bowl from my hands and removed my hair tie. There was a dent in the middle. She reached around to relieve me of my purse which I had forgotten to take off. I hopped into the shower—the only place I had any time to myself—and scrubbed my body hard under the hot water.

Stepping out, I quickly dressed myself like a little slut. I curled my hair, drew on cat eyes, and spritzed myself with something cheap. I learned a lot from the magazines I read at the drugstore and I wasn't going to let all that knowledge go to waste. I made my way to the living room with caution.

"Where are you going?" my mother said standing up from the couch, her pink blanket falling onto the living room tile. "And like *that*. Ay, Lani." I wasn't even standing in proper lighting yet.

"Lani," my uncle said emerging from his room. I had a propensity to rush through things, conversations especially, and the slow pace of his words stressed me out. "Have you read this article?"

My uncle was a younger version of Albert Einstein though much browner from having lived in Hawaii. After retiring, he kept busy at a work desk he built in our backyard where we used to keep our recyclables. He made miscellaneous goods like wooden necklaces and pen holders, but spent the bulk of his time reading and writing. One year, he sent a letter to Coca Cola expressing his love for Diet Coke—everyone in the family shared this addiction and hoarded cans under their beds, keeping tabs on the count—but his concern for their continued use of aspartame. They replied with a generic letter.

"No, I haven't," I said. "I'll read it tom—"

"Oh, Lani," Auntie Mimi said from across the hall. It was warm out but she was dressed in a red sweatsuit and pure joy, as aforementioned. "How was work?"

"Lani, it's too late. You can't go out. At *this* time?" my mother pouted as she pet a very sleepy Magic.

"It was okay, nothing special," I said to my aunt before turning to my mother. The espresso was still working. "Mom, I'm going out with Jaimee and some other friends. I'm not a bad kid and I've never been one. My friends are equally good rule followers, so you really don't have to worry."

"Where?" she said touching her heart like I had broken it. Like any good mother, she tended to die of worry. The mention of Jaimee, my best friend, seemed to calm her down a bit though.

"A bar, you know, the same one I always go to."

"Ayy, Lani. No kissing, kissing. Fucking, fucking. You're gonna get pregnant and I *don't* babysit," she said raising her voice. My mother was never actually angry when she yelled. She was theatrical.

"It's the gay one, Mom," I heard my older brother say from the hallway.

"Oh, Lani," Auntie Cris called from her room, an illegally renovated space where our backyard used to be. "I borrowed your shoes today. You weren't home, so I couldn't ask you. Oh, you look sexy, sexy!" She smacked my bottom. There are some things that your relatives do and don't realize are inappropriate. Or maybe they just don't really care.

"Thanks, Auntie Cris. Work was fine. Mom, you're crazy," I shouted. I was theatrical, too.

"Oh, ladies night. *Lesbianas*," Auntie Mimi giggled.

"Mom!" my Kuya yelled with the refrigerator light reflecting off his face. "Did someone drink my Coke?"

11:27 PM. I heard a door slam.

"Your cousin and his girlfriend are fighting again," Auntie Cris whispered. "But fighting is part of relationships. All relationships have fighting. You know, it is part of the health of the relationship—"

I nodded and began walking away hoping to cut her lecture short.

"You look cold," my mother said. "You don't have a jacket? Bring a jacket, *anak ko*. Or else someone will try to pick you up at a corner. They'll ask 'How much?'"

I thought about arguing but grabbed a jacket instead. It was faster.

"Oh, hey Lani," my cousin said on his way to the bathroom. "Going out?"

"Yeah," I said.

"Have fun," he smiled. He had a calmness about him that was so different from the tantrum toddler I grew up with. I was the opposite—a quiet kid turned lunatic adult.

Back in the living room, I kissed my mother on the cheek. "Love you, Mom, but you can't keep calling me a whore."

"Love you, too, *basang ko*. I never said that. Find me a boyfriend. A rich one."

"Mom," I said stepping out.

"Oh, sorry. Ladies night, *pala*. I mean a girlfriend," she laughed. My family often said offensive things with a laugh as if doing so would absorb the sting. It was dark, but I could feel her waving through the screen door.

I started the car and leaned back feeling my body ache from the day's work. The clock showed 11:32 p.m. I turned up the volume to Pachelbel and switched it to The Con just before picking up Jaimee. I told her about my family and she laughed. I realized I had talked too much by the time we got to University Heights, but she was always nice and never complained. If you didn't know her, you would think otherwise. She was often expressionless, sometimes intimidating, but that's because she never gave away anything so easily. I learned a lot from growing up with her, how to stop being such a pushover for instance, so I made it a point to always keep her close.

12:01 AM. Half a bottle of Jameson between the two of us was more than enough.

12:08 AM. The bar was busy with gays and their allies. A few girls were being escorted out by the security guards, something I hadn't seen happen in a few weeks. Jaimee spotted someone I might like and nudged me. She was drinking something clear, I assumed it was vodka, and had on a vest. We flirted from across the bar but turned our attention back to the company we came with.

Two gay boys from high school led us to the outdoor area where there were Christmas lights. We accidentally ran into a girl and decided to chat with her for some time. We talked about our jobs over a Marlboro Gold. She told us she worked at Fashion Valley, a fact alone that explained it all. Jaimee and I had both worked there before. It was the only mall worth going to in San Diego, but with its status came the fussiest, most unbelievable customers—you wondered where they even came from—and they usually came from up north and were probably neighbors with the lobster and the apricot.

We migrated over to a bar manned by a freckled bartender who smiled once a year. A few months earlier, she had pushed my cocktails aside and introduced me to whiskey.

"Don't drive home drunk," she yelled after we did a round of shots. That's the only kind of yelling you should do at bars. I gave her a firm nod.

The boys started a small dance circle south of the actual dance floor. We swayed our hips left and right to bad music. We learned how to dance from our mothers—strong women with stories to tell—and from the inappropriate middle school dances we had out in the lunch court. I didn't miss the caution tape.

12:30 AM. I e-mailed the girl I missed. Amy. I told her I missed her.

12:40 AM. A blonde girl came my way. Katherine was her name, but she went by Kat. The conversation slipped into hair, race, sex, and the enormous *daibutsu* in Kamakura after discovering we both had traveled there as undergraduates. Talking about Japan only reminded me of Amy, because that's where we met on a study-abroad program. I didn't mention this to Kat. The more I listened to her, the more I realized how clever she was. Clever was the most attractive thing a person could be in my opinion. And yet, it was no use against a heart already decided. I had my heart decided on Amy for years. Kat said something. What, I asked. She repeated herself. What, I said again. I can't remember what she said exactly, but I think she said she was from Oregon. We began talking about me.

"So, you don't speak the Filipino language?"

"No, not really," I said. I wondered if she knew that there were different dialects.

"What about culture?"

"Culture?" I repeated back. It wasn't that San Diego didn't have culture. It wasn't that I didn't have any either. It was just difficult to explain to someone who wasn't already part of it. The in-betweens, the pain, the emptiness, the richness. I could tell you that we break plates and slam doors, but I couldn't tell you why. I could tell you that we sing and dance, but I couldn't tell you why. If you weren't doing the breaking and the slamming and the singing and the dancing with us, then you wouldn't understand it.

12:51 AM. On the way to the restroom, the woman in the vest approached me. Her hair was jet black and styled with clay. I asked her what her story was. She told me that she was thirty-something, French, and had just finished up a gig with the circus. Wasn't in it, she said, just an usher. I told her it wouldn't have bothered me if she were. We danced. We kissed. I looked over to Kat. She was talking to someone new and I felt okay standing where I was.

Now, the Frenchwoman was interesting. Interesting was one of the most attractive things a person could be in my opinion—but being interesting was no match against a heart already decided.

1:12 AM. We kissed again. I imagined macarons—a rainbow of them, really—because that's all I could really think about when I thought about France. I was in awe of how little I knew about such a famous country. I didn't even know the things I had learned about it. I forgot everything I learned.

1:14 AM. Amy said she missed me, too.

1:20 AM. My friends and I sobered up at a Thai place in Hillcrest. Everyone was laughing hard at something. I felt just then that the harder you laughed, the more pain you kept inside.

2:32 AM. Nine missed calls. Eight from my mother and one from a boy I called by accident. He probably thought I wanted it.

The next morning, I woke up with no hangover and forty-dollars in my pocket. I still don't know where I got the extra money from.

During the week, I worked at my second part-time job at a middle school down south. It was bizarre, it always was, but the kids made me laugh long after I went home for the day. Friday came. I gave my Friday nights to the friends who gave me their Sundays. I liked the glamour of downtown and I liked that people made an effort, but I didn't like being there. Everyone acted the same. Cold, distant, hungry. Girls forgot how to be friends there. No one said excuse me unless they wanted something from you, and by something I mean that *something something*, and parking cost a pretty penny.

"Ey girl," a boy walked up to me. He must've bathed in cologne before making his debut on 6th. I ignored him, but he blocked my path.

"I said 'hello' and you're just gonna do me like *that*?"

I found an open space to my left and walked on.

"Girl, I know you freaky. Tryna' front like you ain't."

"If my mother were here, she would castrate you," I leveled with him.

"Ooh, girl. You are *crazy*," he said holding both hands up before walking away. "Crazy."

The rest of the night, I danced my unwanted feelings out in a crowd of friends and let my thoughts drift between two ex-lovers: one with long legs and a massive heart and Amy, who was never really mine.

8:30 AM. Sunday came again. I woke to the familiar sounds of my Auntie Mimi watering the garden just outside my bedroom. We had a small backyard but she managed to do a lot with the space. When I was younger, she would let me pick the *ampalaya* when the time came. From a distance, I heard the elders talking about how the bread they bought wasn't as fresh as it usually was. They'd go earlier to get the first batch next week, they said.

After having a bowl of fried rice and eggs, which my mother cooked until the edges curled and crisped, I went to church. I sat in the balcony but I didn't pray to God. I talked to my grandparents. I asked my grandmother if she still chewed double mint gum and my grandfather if he still liked *mamon*. For a second, I heard laughing.

I asked them to make me a better person and to remind me to want to be one.

I asked them to help me take care of my parents—even my father—when they grew older, because I was starting to feel the harsh realities of studying a major I liked rather than one that promised a future.

Lastly, I admitted that I wasn't sure what I was living for but promised I would live until I found whatever it was and hold it up to the heavens—not the candy store heaven but a place I imagine I'd find them.

2:01 PM. I was almost on time for work.

2:04 PM. My first customer walked in and asked for a vanilla latte. Sugar-free. I looked to my right and saw a crowd smiling under the sun, holding ice cream cones, and applauding a Sinatra impersonator who was actually quite good. I could never feel the sun like they did. I saw it from a window. The customer leaned over the counter to make sure I pumped in sugar-free. I understood. Maybe she had diabetes.

2:05 PM. I packed the espresso.

Michael Desrochers

Another Day in Paradise

(In Memoriam David Velasco)

Another day in paradise.
Apple trees forbidden
here. Pliant palms
welcome Pacific breezes.
Rainbowed umbrellas—
volleyballs and kites aloft—
merry midday sun.
Butterflies chase butterflies;
dolphins ply aqua'd aerobics;
pelicans flash their peace sign.
Exciting childish shrieks,
gentle waves lap the shore.
Graceful school of anchovies
slithers the hidden current
that late yesterday lured
unschooled *nadador*,
took him down,
banished his fallen body
two miles north, beyond
brackish lagoon boundary,
the other side of paradise.

OB Sunset | *Kelly Mayhew*

Sandra Alcosser's books of poetry include *A Fish to Feed All Hunger* and *Except by Nature*, which have been selected for the National Poetry Series, the Academy of American Poets James Laughlin Award, the Larry Levis Award, the Associated Writing Programs Award in Poetry, and the William Stafford Award from Pacific Northwest Booksellers. She became National Endowment for the Arts' first Conservation Poet for the Wildlife Conservation Society and Poets House, New York, as well as Montana's first poet laureate and recipient of the Merriam Award for Distinguished Contribution to Montana Literature. She founded and directs SDSU's MFA each fall and serves on the graduate faculty of Pacific University. She received two individual artist fellowships from NEA, and her poems have appeared in *The New York Times*, *The New Yorker*, *The Paris Review*, *Poetry* and the *Pushcart Prize Anthology*.

Marie Alfonsi received her Master of Arts in Comparative Literature at SDSU. She currently resides in North Park and teaches at San Diego Mesa College.

Adrián Arancibia is an author and critic based in San Diego, California. He is a founder of the seminal Chicano/Latino performance poetry collective Taco Shop Poets. Born in Iquique, Chile (1971), Arancibia is the co-editor of the *Taco Shop Poets Anthology: Chorizo Tonguefire*. He has authored the collections of poetry titled *Atacama Poems* and *The Keeper/El guardador* and will release another collection of poetry in 2015. A Literature PhD, he currently works as a professor of English at Miramar Community College.

Born in 1952 in Santa Fe of Chicano and Apache descent, **Jimmy Santiago Baca** was abandoned by his parents and at 13 ran away from the orphanage where his grandmother had placed him. He was convicted on drug charges in 1973 and spent five years in prison. There he learned to read and began writing poetry. His semiautobiographical novel in verse, *Martin and Meditations on the South Valley* (1987), received the 1988 Before Columbus Foundation's American Book Award in 1989. In addition to over a dozen books of poetry, he has published memoirs, essays, stories, and a screenplay, *Bound by Honor* (1993), which was made into a feature-length film directed by Taylor Hackford. Baca's other poetry titles include *Healing Earthquakes* (2001), *C-Train & 13 Mexicans* (2002), *Winter Poems Along the Rio Grande* (2004), and *Spring Poems Along the Rio Grande* (2007). In addition to the American Book Award, Baca has received a Pushcart Prize and the Hispanic Heritage Award for Literature. His memoir, *A Place to Stand* (2001), garnered the International Prize. Baca has conducted writing workshops in prisons, libraries, and universities across the country for more than 30 years. In 2004 he launched Cedar Tree, a literary nonprofit designed to provide writing workshops, training, and outreach programs for at-risk youth, prisoners and ex-prisoners, and disadvantaged communities. Baca holds a BA in English and an honorary PhD in literature from the University of New Mexico.

Chris Baron earned his MFA in poetry in 1998 and now enjoys working as a professor at San Diego City College, where he is director of the Writing Center. Chris's fiction, nonfiction and poetry have been published in numerous magazines, journals, and anthologies. His first book, *Under the Broom Tree*, which appears in *Lantern Tree: Four Books of Poems* was released 2012. It won the San Diego Book Award for Best Poetry Anthology. www.chris-baron.com.

Josh Baxt is a freelance science writer based in La Mesa, California. He only rarely complains about the weather.

Brent E. Beltrán was born and raised in San Diego and lives with his family in Barrio Logan. He is on the San Diego Free Press Editorial Board, writes the column "Desde la Logan," and is the former co-owner, publisher and editor of Calaca Press.

Raymond R. Beltrán is from San Diego, California. He graduated from San Diego State University with a BA in English and
has been a contributor to *La Prensa San Diego* and a member of
the former Red CalacArts Collective. "From Imperial, Up Euclid"
was included in a self-published chapbook *From Imperial, Up
Euclid and Other Poems* with the help of Calaca Press in 2002.
The audio version of this poem was produced by Brent E. Beltrán
in 2004.

Michael Billingsly is a 52-year-old English major at San Diego
City College. He was raised in Southeast San Diego.

Sydney Brown is a native of El Cajon and teaches composition,
creative nonfiction, and literature at Grossmont College. In addi-
tion to her teaching responsibilities, she co-coordinates the Creative Writing Program and directs the college's annual Literary
Arts Festival. Her writing has appeared in *Sunshine/Noir: Writing
from San Diego and Tijuana*, *Inside English*, *Red*, *two girls review*,
The Southern Anthology, *Zaum: The Literary Review of Sonoma
State*, *Angelflesh*, *San Diego Writer's Monthly*, *Drunken Boat*,
How2: Contemporary Innovative Writing Practices by Women, *The
Fat City Review*, *Muck and Muse*, *Hunger and Thirst*, and *Mamas
and Papas*.

Justine Bryanna spent her adolescence on the streets of San
Diego, but it didn't stop her from starting her own business,
becoming an activist, and going to college. She has been working
with Photocharity for the past ten years to open a new homeless
youth shelter, and is also working on an autobiography detailing
the life lessons a teenage girl learns sleeping on park benches.

Francisco J. Bustos is a bilingual poet and musician who grew
up in Tijuana and San Ysidro. He now lives in San Diego and is a
professor of English Composition at Southwestern Community
College (Chula Vista, CA) where he is a coordinator for the
Southwestern College Guest Writer Series. He also forms part of
the poetry/music group Frontera Drum Fusion where he plays
guitar, bass, indigenous percussions, digital music and performs
bilingual poetry in English and Spanish, with some Spanglish,
and Ingleñol.

Nancy Cary writes creative nonfiction and fiction, often set in San Diego and imaginary worlds she lives in. For the past couple of years she has been writing and performing for the storytelling community of So Say We All.

Elizabeth Cazessús is a poet, teacher and cultural journalist, born in Tijuana, Mexico (1961). She has nine books of poetry, including: *Ritual and Song, Twenty Notes Before Sleeping, Woman of Salt, House of Dream, Reasons of an Infidel Lady, No Lie This Paradise, Enediana*, and *Daughters of Wrath*. Since 1985 she has been actively engaged in cultural journalism for regional newspapers. As a performer, she is the creator of "poetic rituals" that fuse indigenous traditions of northern Mexico with performance art and music. Her short poems have been sung by soprano Lourdes Ambriz and included in the *Cancionero Bajacaliforniano*, a compilation of poems suited to be recorded as opera. Along with Gerardo Navarro, multidisciplinary artist, she made the production of two poeticas video, "Reasons of Lady infidel," 2009, and "Enediana," 2011.

Marilyn Chin was born in Hong Kong and raised in Portland, Oregon. Her books have become Asian American classics and are taught in classrooms internationally. Marilyn Chin's books of poems include *Hard Love Province* (W.W. Norton, 2014), *Rhapsody in Plain Yellow, Dwarf Bamboo*, and *The Phoenix Gone, The Terrace Empty*. Her book of fiction is called *Revenge of the Mooncake Vixen*. She has won numerous awards, including the United Artist Foundation Fellowship, the Radcliffe Institute Fellowship at Harvard, the Rockefeller Foundation Fellowship at Bellagio, two NEAs, the Stegner Fellowship, the PEN/Josephine Miles Award, five Pushcart Prizes, a Fulbright Fellowship to Taiwan, residencies at Yaddo, the MacDowell Colony, the Lannan and Djerassi Foundations.... She is featured in a variety of anthologies, including *The Norton Anthology of Literature by Women* and *The Norton Anthology of Modern and Contemporary Poetry, The Penguin Anthology of 20th Century Poetry*, and *The Best American Poetry*.... She was featured in Bill Moyers' PBS series *The Language of Life*, and *Poetry Everywhere*, introduced by Garrison Keillor. She has read and taught workshops all over the world. Recently, she was guest poet at universities in Beijing, Singapore, Hong Kong, Manchester, Sydney and Berlin and elsewhere. In addition to writing poetry and fiction, she has translated poems by the modern Chinese poet Ai Qing and co-translated poems by the Japanese poet Gozo Yoshimasu. She presently lives in San Diego and teaches in the MFA program at City University, Hong Kong.

Jeeni Criscenzo has been a mom, a technical illustrator, graphic designer, serial entrepreneur, database designer, website developer, author of a published historical novel, web application developer, traveling political blogger, congressional candidate, cancer survivor, peace and justice activist, homeless advocate, non-profit executive director and community organizer. But before all of this, she was that kid nobody could figure out who always had her nose in a book or was writing poetry and continues to this day to write and perform her poetry, yet still can't figure out why that old lady in the mirror is looking at her.

Jhonnatan Curiel (Tijuana, México, 1986) is a poet, writer and researcher of social studies. He has published seven poetry books in Mexico. The most recent one is *Prisma* (Observatorio Editorial Tijuana, 2014). Also, he was part of Colectivo Intransigente, an artistic collective who promoted poetic events during 2010 & 2012. Blog: www.jhonnatancuriel.blogspot.com.

Anna Daniels is currently an editor and writer at the *San Diego Free Press*. She grew up in a western Pennsylvania mill town and lived in Nags Head, NC and Key West, FL before settling into the inner city community of City Heights with her husband and a cat colony.

Ella deCastro Baron is a second-generation Filipina American born in Oakland and raised in Vallejo, California. She is a full-time wife and mother of three children, a part-time English and Creative Writing instructor at San Diego City College and Brandman University, and an "other"-times writer published in *Fiction International, Sunshine Noir, Lavanderia, Mamas and Papas, CityWorks Literary Journal* as well as co-editor of the anthology *Hunger and Thirst.* Ella's first book, *Itchy, Brown Girl Seeks Employment,* published by CityWorks Press in 2009, was a finalist for the San Diego Book Awards.

Michael Desrochers has taught history at both the high school and university levels. A resident of Los Angeles, he often spends time bodysurfing in Carlsbad, where he chanced to witness the tragic death of David Velasco, a resident of Vista, this past summer.

Kevin Dublin is an editor at Etched Press and writing consultant. He enjoys working with young writers, shooting video adaptations of poetry, and poetry busking. San Diego is where he came for an MFA, but where he stays because it has fantastic people like you.

Susan Duerksen is Senior Communications Advisor at the Center on Policy Initiatives, a nonprofit research and advocacy institute based in San Diego. Her previous careers include newspaper journalism and public health research.

Mel Freilicher has published fiction, non-fiction and book reviews in numerous art and literary periodicals and chapbooks, and has two books out from San Diego City Works Press, *The Unmaking of Americans: 7 Lives* and *The Encyclopedia of Rebels*. He's been teaching creative writing in UCSD's Literature Department's writing program for several decades.

Diane Gage has been making art and poetry in San Diego since the 1970s, at which time she helped to produce a poetry journal called *Antenna*. She has published in print, online, on art gallery walls, and was recently interviewed at http://bluevortextpublishers.wordpress.com/interview.

Richard Gleaves is a writer and artist based in San Diego. He received a degree in computer science from UC San Diego, and a Masters in Educational Technology from San Diego State. His recent projects include an anonymous contribution to Olfactory Memoirs, and a performance at the Balboa Park Carousel which involved pre-empting the regular carousel soundtrack with a 30-minute song cycle of American ritual music.

Leilani Riingen Gobaleza is a freelance writer and English instructor in Chiba, Japan. Her work has appeared in projects such as Savvy Tokyo and Homodachi, and she is currently finishing up her first novel.

Frank Gormlie has been involved in the movement for democratic planning in Ocean Beach since the early 1970s, was Chair of the Ocean Beach Planning Board, and sat on the Board for another two years. He founded the original *OB People's Rag* in 1970, published the alternative magazine for San Diego *The Whole Damn Pie Shop* during the first half of the 1980s, and along with Patty Jones began publishing the current online *OB Rag* in 2007. Today he is a semi-retired lawyer, a citizen journalist, the editor of the *OB Rag* and sits on the editorial board of its online media partner, the *San Diego Free Press.*

Sonia Gutiérrez is the author of *Spider Woman / La Mujer Araña.* La Bloga's On-line Floricanto is home to her Poets Responding to SB 1070 poems, including those appearing in "Best Poems 2011" and "Best Poems 2012."

Jill G. Hall is inspired to write about nature's awe, love gone good and bad as well as life's ironies. Her first novel, *The Black Velvet Coat*, will be released Fall 2015 by She Write Press. www.jillghall.com.

Justin Hudnall received his BFA from Tisch School of the Arts at NYU and currently serves as the Executive Director of So Say We All, a San Diego-based literary and performing arts non-profit. In a prior career, he served with the United Nations in South Sudan as an emergency response officer. He is a recipient of the San Diego Foundation's Creative Catalyst Fellowship and Rising Arts Leader award, an alumni of the Vermont Studio Center, and a proud native of San Diego's east county.

Una Nichols Hynum's most recent book is *At the Foot of the Staircase*, which is self-published. In the Trauma unit at the hospital the doctor quoted a line of her poetry and she was shocked. He said, "I Googled you."

Marianne S. Johnson is a practicing attorney in San Diego. Her poetry is published in several journals including *Calyx, Sport Literate, Slant*, and *New Millennium Writings*, and in City Works Press's anthologies *Lavanderia* and *Mamas and Papas*. Her chapbook, *Tender Collisions*, is forthcoming from Aldrich Press in 2015. "Courthouse Portrait" was originally published in *The Far East Project: Everything Just As It Is.*

Nancy Farness Johnson is a graduate of SDSU where she received a BA in English Literature, an MS in Secondary Education, and a career as a high school English teacher from which she could retire. And so she did. Her published work includes her blog, SlightlySquinting.com, and *Sunshine Noir II*. Her unpublished work includes her husband, children, and grandchildren, and her first book, *The Witnessing.*

Tamara Johnson is the author of *Not Far From Normal* (City Works Press, 2014).

Andy Koopmans is a writer, artist, and sit-down comedian living in Seattle. He inhales.

Steve Kowit was raised among the savage war-like tribes of North America but was able to learn their language and manner of dress quickly enough to pass as one of their own. He pledges his allegiance to a much larger and much different nation.

With an MA in English Literature, an MS in Molecular Biology, and an in-process MFA in Creative Writing, **Breeann Kyte** is officially a master of all trades and doctor of none. Firmly grounded in both science and literature, she works in both fields, facilitating collaborations between scientists, writers, and artists. You can see more of Breeann's work at www.sciencereasoncalifornia.com.

David Lemmo, born in San Diego California, was an antiquarian bookseller for thirty years. In 2009 he created the Museum of Modern Mythology and Pop Culture, and two years later helped found a new chapter of the (Edgar Rice) Burroughs Bibliophiles, which is dedicated to the life and works of the "grandfather of American science fiction."

Sylvia Levinson has witnessed the growth, development and changes, both positive and negative, in San Diego, since she moved here in 1974. Her work has been published in many volumes of *City Works*, beginning in 1997, as well as *Mamas and Papas, Hunger and Thirst, Serving House Journal, San Diego Writers Ink, Magee Park*, and others.

Mario Lewis owns the Imperial Barber Shop in Encanto and is also a founder of 100 Strong.

Juanita Lopez was born and raised in Barrio Logan. Currently she is a student at San Diego City College where she is finishing her AA in English and Chicana/o Studies.

Jesse Mancilla is a second-generation Latino writer and a native of Dinuba, CA who currently lives in San Diego, CA. He graduated from the University of California, San Diego in 2011 with a BA in Literature and Writing.

Stephen-Paul Martin has published many books of fiction, non-fiction, and poetry. His most recent short story collections are *Changing the Subject* (Ellipsis Press, 2010) and *The Possibility of Music* (FC 2, 2007). He teaches fiction in San Diego State's MFA program.

Jim Moreno (jimpoet.com) is the author of *Dancing in Dissent: Poetry for Activism* (Dolphin Calling Press, 2007). Moreno's show of poetry and social justice interviews, *The San Diego Poetry Cafe*, will be aired on KNSJ, 89.1 FM in 2015.

Kinsee Morlan has been covering culture in San Diego and Tijuana for a decade as the Arts Editor for *San Diego CityBeat*. She's a proud new mother of two, a podcast nut and a wannabe homesteader living in the urban-suburban 'hood, Lemon Grove.

Mychal Matsemela-Ali Odom is a history doctoral candidate and adjunct professor in Black Studies. His interests are in Black social movements and hip-hop culture.

Katrin Pesch is a filmmaker and writer based in San Diego. Her current film and book project uses objects and stories circulating around the Bancroft Ranch House Museum in Spring Valley, California to explore material encounters of persons, animals, places, and things.

Doug Porter writes a five-day-a-week column on politics for the *San Diego Free Press*. He won awards for "Daily Reporting and Writing: Opinion/Editorial" from the Society of Professional Journalists in 2013 and 2014.

Sarah Saez is the Program Director of the United Taxi Workers of San Diego, a multi-ethnic organization that fights for justice, rights, and dignity for taxi drivers and their community.

Arthur Salm is a former book review editor, columnist, and feature writer for the *San Diego Union-Tribune*. His middle-grade novel *Anyway** was published by Simon & Schuster in 2012.

Perry Vasquez shambles between three mistaken identities as disappearing border artist; born-again shaman; and Appala-Chicano history painter. Learn more about his work at www.perryvasquez.com.

DeJe Watson writes, teaches and produces in southern California. To say "writing is in her blood" is no stretch for this 6th generation descendant of Lorenzo Dow Blackson, one of the first African Americans to publish a novel in 1867. Most recently she produced *Be Out of Heaven by Sundown Nigga*, a poetic tribute to Wanda Coleman at the World Stage Performance Gallery in Los Angeles, CA (2014). Watson also edited *Lavandería: A Mixed Load of Women, Wash and Word*, which won a San Diego best anthology book award (2009). In 2012 she published "I Am a Cowgirl in the Boat of RA" in the *Los Angeles Review*'s tribute edition to Ishmael Reed. She is currently producing an anthology and film for the city of Inglewood's public arts project (forthcoming 2015).

Megan Webster's work has appeared in numerous publications, including *Sunshine/Noir 1*, *Connecticut Review* and *POIESIS: A Journal of the Arts & Communication*; her third chapbook, *Bipolar Express* (Finishing Line Press), was awarded the 2004 San Diego Book Award for Best Unpublished Poetry Chapbook. A former community college ESL teacher, she is a freelance editor specializing in manuscripts by foreign-born American authors, and a translator of prose and poetry from Spanish to English.

Michael Cheno Wickert has lived in various places throughout San Diego, and now lives in Chula Vista with his wife and children. He has worked in the building trades, as an elementary school teacher, and is currently a professor of English and Education at Southwestern College.

Mary Williams is a writer, editor, and aspiring transcriptionist living in San Marcos with her husband, Kirk. She continues to peck away at her memoir, *All the Lurking Mothers of God*.

Gary Winters authored *The Deer Dancer*, a multicultural coming-of-age novel that won four awards. His poetry has won international awards, and was published in an award-winning literary journal in Ireland.

EDITORS

Jim Miller is the author of the novels *Flash* (AK Press, 2010) and *Drift* (University of Oklahoma Press, 2007). He is also co-author of a history of San Diego, *Under the Perfect Sun: The San Diego Tourists Never See* (with Mike Davis and Kelly Mayhew on The New Press, 2003) and a cultural studies book on working-class sports fandom, *Better to Reign in Hell: Inside the Raiders Fan Empire* (with Kelly Mayhew on The New Press, 2005). Miller is also the editor of *Sunshine/Noir: Writing from San Diego and Tijuana* (City Works Press, 2005) and *Democracy in Education; Education for Democracy: An Oral History of the American Federation of Teachers, Local 1931* (AFT, 2007). He has published poetry, fiction, and non-fiction in a wide range of journals and other publications, and has a weekly column in the *San Diego Free Press* and the *OB Rag*.

Kelly Mayhew is the co-editor with Alys Masek of *Mamas and Papas: On the Sublime and Heartbreaking Art of Parenting* (City Works Press, 2010). She is co-author with Jim Miller of *Better to Reign in Hell: Inside the Raiders Fan Empire* (The New Press, 2005) and co-author with Jim Miller and Mike Davis of *Under the Perfect Sun: The San Diego Tourists Never See* (The New Press, 2003). She is also the coeditor with Paula Rothenberg of the 9th edition of *Race, Class, and Gender in the United States* (Worth). Mayhew is a founding member of San Diego City Works Press, for which she serves as Managing Editor.